The Christian Guide To The Enneagram; Why We Think And Act The Way We Do

Randall Lee Tucker

A detailed study of personality typing from a Christian perspective

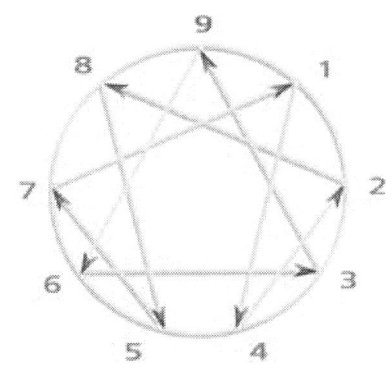

This book is for information purposes only and is not intended to diagnose, treat or cure any illness. The author assumes no responsibility for any use of the information which the reader may choose to apply. The application of the information is solely the choice and responsibility of the reader. Sections on counseling are meant as information for licensed counselors and not as a substitute for therapy. Randall Lee Tucker and createconnectcommit.com assume no responsibility for the use of the information in this book. Create, Connect, Commit is the intellectual property of the author. Copyright 2010 All Rights Reserved

Contents

Introduction - 6

Personality Typing - 30

The Enneagram - 54

Personality Typing, Christianity and The Enneagram – 66

How The Enneagram Works - 75

Type One - 94

Counseling Ones - 113

Type Two - 123

Counseling Twos - 143

Type Three - 151

Counseling Threes - 168

Type Four - 179

Counseling Fours - 193

Type Five - 206

Counseling Fives - 219

Type Six - 227

Counseling Sixes - 245

Type Seven - 256

Counseling Sevens - 268

Type Eight - 276

Counseling Eights - 289

Type Nine - 296

Counseling Nines - 310

The Enneagram of Change - 317

Kaizen - 319

The 6 Stages of Change - 323

Concept One; Create

Preconceived Notions - 330

Windows to the World - 337

Why Can't People Change? - 353

Mental Frames - 359

Create New Boundaries - 369

Create a New Self Image - 389

Concept Two; Connect

Connect With What You Want - 393

Connect With Other People - 417

Connect With God - 421

Concept Three; Commit

Commit to Change -423

Commit to Progress - 426

Introduction

When it comes to psychology there are two schools of thought among orthodox Christians. At one end of the spectrum are those who believe all we need to do to heal our inner hurts, fears, depression and painful past experiences is to appropriate the fact that Christ died for our sins and has risen from the grave to live His life in us. At the other end of the spectrum are those who believe the only way to deal with such issues is through years of therapy, inner healing, healing of the memories, visualization and other endless methods. The truth lies somewhere in between. Jesus paid the ultimate price to heal our inner hurts and He has given us tools such as the Enneagram, Christian Counseling, and Create, Connect, Commit to aid in our recovery.

Isaiah 53:5 "But he was wounded for our transgressions, he was **bruised** for our iniquities: the chastisement of our peace was upon him; and with his stripes we are healed."

Wounds are on the outside of the body. Bruises are on the inside, blood trapped beneath the skin. Transgressions are outward acts; committing sin by willfully transgressing the law. Iniquities are often on the inside. Iniquity refers to immorality, but I believe there is a deeper meaning in this verse. The word translated as iniquity is the Hebrew word: עָוֹן
Transliteration: Avon or Avon
Phonetic Spelling: (aw-vone')
Short Definition: fault. The basic definition of "avon" (the word translated as "iniquities") is fault.

Jesus shed His blood on the outside of His body and on the inside of His body. The chastisement *of our peace* was upon Him and with His stripes *we are healed.* By His bruising, our *faults* are healed.

The shedding of Jesus Holy blood was no accident. We appropriate the fact that Jesus was bruised for our faults and by His stripes we are healed through affirmation and prayer. But we still have an obligation to use the tools He has given us to overcome our faults. The bible unapologetically teaches both God's sovereignty and man's responsibility. God told Noah HOW to build the ark; He didn't build it for him. We need both; prayer and action.

Personality Typing

I developed Create Connect Commit to overcome depression, the fear of failure, low self esteem, addiction, co-dependency, and many other psychological problems that have a common root; the inability to change. CCC will create enduring change in the lives of those who practice it. It is a scientifically based complete process that will enable you to Change Anything.

Personality Typing is at the heart of CCC. This book details the most accurate and useful system of personality typing; **The Enneagram**. Links are provided to help you take a personality test and determine your type. Tests are accessible at <http://www.enneagraminstitute.com/> . There are free sampler tests, the complete test is $10 and the results include detailed analysis of your type, subtype and instinctual variants.

You can determine your type or your counselee's type without spending the money for these resources. Take the free tests. When taking the test, choose the answer that best describes how you have been most of your life. They are forced choice questions. Do you like apples or oranges? If you like both, you will have to choose the one you like best. If you have preferred apples most of your life, but recently decided you like oranges better, your answer should be apples.

Take one of the free tests and then read your type description in this book. If the information is not shockingly accurate, you have mistyped. Take another test and try again until you find the type description that unquestionably fits you. There should be no doubt that you are reading about yourself when you are correctly typed. You can take a free test at this sight.

http://similarminds.com/personality_tests.html

Take the Enneagram –Jung Test. This will give you your MBTI type and a breakdown of which Enneagram traits are strongest in you. You can match your MBTI type to your Enneagram type by reading the section on the 16 personality types. Another way to determine your type is by examining your childhood relationship with your parent figures.

Childhood Origins

As children, **Ones** identified negatively with their father figure. They learned to avoid criticism and condemnation by attempting to be perfect. They aim for perfection and try to please everyone by being blameless and doing for them.

As children **Twos** had ambivalent relationships to their fathers, or father figures. **Ambivalence** is a state of having simultaneous, conflicting feelings toward a person or thing. Stated another way, ambivalence is the experience of having thoughts and emotions of both positive and negative valence toward someone or something. A common example of ambivalence is the feeling of both love and hate for a person. Twos have superego problems which result from their ambivalent orientation to their father figures. This helps explain the fact that the self esteem of a Two is conditional. They do not love themselves unconditionally, nor do they lack self esteem. Their self esteem is conditional upon the perception that they are absolutely good.

As children, **Threes** identified with their mother figure. Their mothers lavished attention on them and they come to expect this from every relationship. They expect the world to admire them unconditionally, just as their mothers did.

As children, **Fours** didn't identify with either parent. They probably had unhappy or isolated childhoods due to illness, divorce, their parents relationship or personality conflicts. Without role models they turned inward and constructed their identities from their feelings and imaginations. They felt alone in life.

Fives had ambivalent relationships with both parents. Their parents were not dependable sources of love and reassurance. They may have been nurtured erratically or had parents who were emotionally disturbed, caught in a loveless marriage, divorced, alcoholic or who had some other dysfunction. They became ambivalent toward their parents and toward the world.

Sixes identify positively with a father figure. As children, they wanted the security of being approved by their father figure and felt anxious if they didn't receive it. As they grew up, this need of approval from a father figure shifted; to other individuals, a teacher, a mentor, a supervisor, a boss or a spouse. It also shifted to more abstract father figures; civil authorities or belief systems from which they could obtain security.

As children, **Sevens** had a negative orientation to their mother figures. They feel frustrated by their mothers, who did not make them feel secure. Deprivation, unfortunate circumstances, a long illness, being orphaned or some other experience may have shaken their expectation that the good things of life would be given to them. The fear of deprivation becomes their fundamental motivation. Possessing all they think will make them happy becomes a substitute for their mother's love.

As children, **Eights** became ambivalent to their mother figures. They had to assert themselves aggressively to get their mothers to respond to their needs. Dominating their mothers created the belief that they, though mere children, were stronger than an adult. They learned that asserting themselves was the way to get what they wanted. They got comfortable dominating others without fear of retribution or guilt.

As children **Nines** identified with both parents. They didn't need to distinguish themselves from their parents because their emotional needs were thoroughly satisfied by positive identification with both parents. They enjoyed having all their eggs in one basket and usually had their way. Easy going, obedient and happy, they generally required only minimal discipline. They had happy, stable childhoods during their developmental years when their personalities were formed. Either the "perfect child" or in trouble for following the group.

Everyone's personality type is a result of having had a primary orientation to his/her mother, father, or equally to both. 3 choices. The orientation was positive, negative or ambivalent. These 9 possible combinations form the 9 types of the Enneagram.

Create, Connect, Commit

I descended into a depth of depression few recover from. You can read my story in **"Change Anything" available at**

createconnectcommit.com

Depression and insomnia took over my life. At one point I thought that I would not be able to function and hold a job. I considered suicide. Yet, somehow I recovered, started from scratch and built a new life and a new career. I developed CCC and incorporated personality typing into the process. Learning about the personality types of my ex-wife and myself revealed the co-dependent relationship we had lived in for a quarter of a century. Reading the Type Six description was like reading the notes from years of psychotherapy and analysis. It was accurate to the point of being eerie.

Discovering your personality type is the first step in the CCC process. The self discovery that results will open your eyes to the underlying fears that have held you back, robbed you of your dreams, and prevented you from becoming the person you were created to be. You'll understand what motivates you, your strengths and weaknesses and other crucial information about yourself. You'll be given a model to grow toward (integration) and a model to avoid (disintegration). You'll then apply this knowledge about yourself in the CCC process to create enduring change in your life. You'll not only learn how to change, but also how to make those changes permanent. You'll learn how to prevent stagnation and regression and set goals to stay motivated and make continuous progress.

Create, Connect, Commit To God

The first thing you should ask yourself is "Am I a New Creation?"

2 Corinthians 5:17

<u>New International Version (©1984)</u>
"Therefore, if anyone is in Christ, he is a *new creation*; the old has gone, the new has come."

Galatians 5:17

New Living Translation (©2007)
"It doesn't matter whether we have been circumcised or not. What counts is whether we have been transformed into a *new creation*."

Colossians 3:11

Weymouth New Testament
"In that *new creation* there is neither Greek nor Jew, circumcision nor uncircumcision, barbarian, Scythian, slave nor free man, but Christ is everything and is in all of us".

Concept One; Create

In order for this conversion to take place the Holy Spirit must change the way you think. A shift in your mental frame must take place.

1 Corinthians 2:14.

English Standard Version (©2001)
"The natural person does not accept the things of the Spirit of God, for they are folly to him, and he is not able to understand them because they are *spiritually discerned."*

In our natural or *carnal* states, we cannot accept the things of the Spirit of God because they are spiritually discerned.

1 Corinthians 1:21

New Living Translation (©2007)
"Since God in his wisdom saw to it that the world would never know him *through human wisdom*, he has used our *foolish preaching* to save those who believe."

There is no path to God through human wisdom. We were saved through the *foolishness* (to the carnally minded natural person) of what was preached (God's word) to save those who believe (those who are *spiritual*);

1 Corinthians 2:14

GOD'S WORD® Translation (©1995)
"A person who isn't *spiritual* doesn't accept the teachings of God's Spirit. He thinks they're nonsense. He can't understand them because a person must be *spiritual* to evaluate them."

When we become a new creation in Christ a shift in our mental frames takes place and we move from being carnally minded to being *spiritual*. This is the work of the Holy Spirit. We begin to understand the things of God which may have once seemed foolish to us and we are transformed by the renewing of our minds.

1 Corinthians 1:27

New International Version (©1984)
But God chose the foolish things of the world to shame the wise; God chose the weak things of the world to shame the strong.

1 Corinthians 1:18

New International Version (©1984)
For the message of the cross is foolishness to those who are perishing, but to us who are being saved it is the power of God.

Romans 12:2

New International Version (©1984)
"Do not conform any longer to the pattern of this world, but *be transformed*

by the renewing of your mind. Then you will be able to test and approve what God's will is--his good, pleasing and perfect will."

New Living Translation (©2007)
"Don't copy the behavior and customs of this world, *but let God transform you into a new person by changing the way you think.* Then you will learn to know God's will for you, which is good and pleasing and perfect."

This shift in your mental frames must take place if you hope to become a new creation. Without this change in your belief system, you will remain carnally minded and drift back into your old way of thinking, acting and feeling. You will become a carnal Christian, living a spiritually defeated live

. Without programs and training geared specifically for their needs, new converts become a statistic, another one of the 2.7 million church members who fall into inactivity. **New converts must be taught the fundamentals of the faith** and they desperately need **CCC to God** to teach them how to change and to make those changes permanent. Create, Connect, Commit to God is available at **createconnectcommit.com**

Carnal Christianity is not a phenomenon relegated only to new converts. Long time believers can become stagnant and fall away or half heartedly go through the motions of attending church. They must change the way they think, continuously renewing their minds with the word of God or they too could become a statistic. Programs and training geared specifically toward the needs of long term converts are crucial to keep them active in church and spiritually renewed. Many believers grow tired of the repetitive nature of church services and Sunday school. They need fresh, inspirational yet biblically sound preaching and teaching to keep them motivated. They need to be challenged to set goals for outreach, church attendance, Bible study, and the amount of time set aside for meditation and prayer. They need **CCC to God** to break out of their routines, awaken spiritually and set new goals to stay motivated and determined to become the best Christians they can be and the best people they can be. **CCC to God** inspires both spiritual and personal growth.

While it is the Holy Spirit who transforms the believer, renews his/her mind and changes his/her way of thinking there are actions we can take as believers to shift our mental frames.

Create

Psalms 51:10

<u>New International Version (©1984)</u>

"Create in me a pure heart, O God, and renew a steadfast spirit within me."

Concept One; **Create** teaches us how our underlying fears and preconceived notions limit our perception and trap us into negative cycles of behavior. As part of the **Create** process you'll discover your personality type, and learn how your underlying fears and motivations have held you back and helped to create your preconceived notions. You'll learn your strengths and weaknesses and what areas you need to focus on to become the best person you can be. You'll learn to examine your beliefs through the lens of scripture, logical thinking and truth. You'll learn to challenge the flawed premises which your preconceived notions have helped create. You'll learn to create a new belief system based on truth, positive thinking and God's word. You'll learn to create a new self image, and step into that image as a new creation in Christ.

Concept Two; Connect

To effect lasting change in our lives, we must connect with other people. Programs that are successful in bringing about change all use the power of socialization; Weight Watchers, 12 Steps, AA, and various religious organizations all utilize the power of connecting. We are more likely to do something if we know that other people are doing it too. We must have a support group, even if it is a makeshift one, to help us through our struggles, share our battles, socialize and build support for the positive steps we are taking.

Connecting is the key to maintaining healthy relationships, feeling well deserved and being part of someone's life. For most individuals with a healthy social support network, major stressors in life can be more easily managed. A proper support network consists of a reinforcing family, friends and fellow Christians who can help you to work through any major problems, such as the death of a family member, loss of a job, major injury, or any of a number of other stressors. Connecting is especially important for the new convert, who is looking to create new habits and adapt to the Christian lifestyle (become a new creation). We must connect first with God, then with other Christians.

Hebrews 10:25

New Living Translation (©2007)
"And let us not neglect our *meeting together*, as some people do, but encourage one another, especially now that the day of his return is drawing near."

Hebrews 3:13

"But *encourage one another* day after day, as long as it is still called "Today," so that none of you will be hardened by the deceitfulness of sin." (NASB ©1995)

1 John 1:3

New Living Translation (©2007)
"We proclaim to you what we ourselves have actually seen and heard so that you may *have fellowship with us*. And our fellowship is with the Father and with his Son, Jesus Christ."

James 5:16

New Living Translation (©2007)
"Confess your sins to *each other* and *pray for each other* so that you may be healed. The earnest prayer of a righteous person has great power and produces wonderful results."

The Body of Christ (the Church) is to be connected. Each believer serves a purpose, and the body should work together as one unit. Everyone plays a part;

New Living Translation (©2007)
1Cr 12:14 - 27 Yes, the body has many different parts, not just one part.
 If the foot says, "I am not a part of the body because I am not a hand," that does not make it any less a part of the body.
 And if the ear says, "I am not part of the body because I am only an ear and not an eye," would that make it any less a part of the body?
 Suppose the whole body were an eye--then how would you hear? Or if your whole body were just one big ear, how could you smell anything?
 But God made our bodies with many parts, and he has put each part just where he wants it.
 What a strange thing a body would be if it had only one part!
 Yes, there are many parts, but only one body.
 The eye can never say to the hand, "I don't need you." The head can't say to the feet, "I don't need you."
 In fact, some of the parts that seem weakest and least important are really the most necessary.
 And the parts we regard as less honorable are those we clothe with the greatest care. So we carefully protect from the eyes of others those parts that should not be seen,
 while other parts do not require this special care. So God has put the body together in such a way that extra honor and care are given to those parts that have less dignity.
 This makes for harmony among the members, so that all the members care

for each other equally.

If one part suffers, all the parts suffer with it, and if one part is honored, all the parts are glad.

Now all of you together are Christ's body, and each one of you is a separate and necessary part of it.

Connect With What You Want

Christians must also connect with what they want. Why are Christians rarely if ever taught to set goals? We should set goals to improve church attendance, outreach and service. We should set goals for the amount of time we spend in prayer and Bible study; setting a goal to read the entire Bible in a year for example. We should set goals to improve our spiritual walk, change negative thinking and negative behavior and eliminate sin from our lives. How many converts fall away because they simply cannot give up the sinful lifestyle they came to the church to escape? They must learn to change in steps. Setting goals is the key to this process.

Christians should also set goals for other areas of their lives. Nowhere in the Bible does it call on Christians to be unsuccessful. Happy, successful people are more likely to stay committed to God and faithful to their churches.

Happy, successful people are also more likely to attract other people to Christ. People are naturally attracted to them. ***Setting goals is crucial to success.*** We must set goals for our careers, education, health and fitness, weight control, eliminating bad habits, spending more time with our family, etc. The list is endless. We should have goals for every area of our lives. Setting goals is a critical part of **Create, Connect, Commit to God.**

This doesn't mean we won't have problems. Accepting that life is filled with difficulty and adversity and that there are things which we cannot control are both elements of the **Create, Connect, Commit** philosophy.

Getting saved and becoming a new creation are sweeping, dramatic lifestyle changes. **Create, Connect, Commit** teaches that change must take place in two ways. We need big changes to motivate us; small changes don't foster the encouragement that big changes create. However, we must break these big changes down, making them ever smaller, 5 years, yearly, monthly, weekly, daily is the way we break down our goals. We make small changes which we can manage, and we celebrate small victories along the way to keep us motivated, until we see progress. Progress is the greatest motivator of all; it encourages us to stay on the path until we reach our goals. **Thought, Action, Habit** is the way the process works. Making small but constant changes is one of the key principles of the **Create, Connect, Commit** philosophy.

Continuous Improvement Process (CIP or CI) is an ongoing effort to improve products, services or processes employed by Japanese businesses. These efforts can seek "incremental" improvement over time or "breakthrough" improvement all at once. **Create, Connect, Commit** incorporates the philosophy of **CIP**. We must continually improve, becoming the best we can be and the best Christians we can be. We must make small incremental improvements daily, but also have breakthrough moments, such as when we are saved, filled with the Spirit or rededicate ourselves to God.

Plan – Do – Study- Act

Plan – Do- Study – Act is the cycle the individual and the church must enact to create enduring change and foster commitment. **Thought, Action, Habit** is the process by which change occurs in the individual. **Plan-Do-Study-Act** is the process by which we not only change, we evaluate our progress (**study**) and make necessary adjustments and improvements **(act)**.

In the **Thought** stage, we shift our mental frames and set realistic goals (**Plan**). In the **Action** stage, we put our plan into action and repeat it until it becomes a **Habit (Do).** Next we must measure the results of our actions **(Study)**. For the church, this means taking surveys and analyzing attendance records. Surveys should be taken to evaluate member and visitor satisfaction, and to determine if members feel they are learning and growing. Suggestions for improvements must be taken seriously and everyone must feel that they have a voice and a sense of ownership. **CIP** involves everyone from the Pastor to the janitor. Each individual has his/her own area of expertise and must be actively involved to make the church function and grow. Attendance should be improving in secondary church functions i.e. Sunday and Wednesday night services, Sunday school, Growth Groups, volunteering and extracurricular activities. It is in these areas (not Sunday morning attendance) that commitment is measured.

The surveys and suggestions must be evaluated and action must be taken based on the results (**Act).** This process of continuous improvement must be enacted if the church is to grow to a deeper level. CIP will prevent stagnation, boredom and falling away. It will lead to higher retention rates and increased commitment. The sense of ownership it fosters is the key to making members feel **connected.**

Likewise, the individual must examine his own progress, evaluate and make improvements. **Plan-Do-Study-Act** must be enacted in study groups, Growth Groups and Sunday school not only to evaluate the programs, but to evaluate member progress. The groups should have members set goals for 5 years out, yearly, monthly, weekly and daily goals. Every few months members should evaluate their progress and make necessary adjustments. **Thought, Action, Habit** should be incorporated at every level of the church. Believers should set goals for both personal and spiritual growth. You need to set goals in every area of your life. This will be covered in more detail in later chapters.

Christians should set goals for increased time in church attendance, volunteering, prayer, study and reflection. They should set goals and evaluate progress not because they have to, but because they want to. As a New Creation in Christ, they will want to spend more time in these areas and should let The Holy Spirit guide them in the goals they set. Care must be taken to not make believers feel that they are under pressure to measure up or meet some type of performance standard. This is the opposite of what CCC to God hopes to achieve. Trusting God and learning the fundamentals of the faith should be their primary concern and they should never be made to feel that they MUST do anything

Concept Three; Commit

Luke 9:62

<u>New Living Translation (©2007)</u>
But Jesus told him, "Anyone who puts a hand to the plow and then looks back is not fit for the Kingdom of God."

None of us want to go back where we've been. As Christians, we've made changes in our lifestyles and lived according to Biblical principles. Even lifelong Christians have grown in their spiritual walks, and do not wish to regress. We must always look forward, not back. We must constantly challenge ourselves to grow in our spiritual walks, setting goals, reading books, attending church, Sunday school, Growth Groups and spending more time in Bible study and prayer. We must constantly be renewed, otherwise we can grow stagnant; bored with the routine of church and Sunday school, going through the motions but not feeling connected. **Psalms 51:10** *"Create in me a pure heart, O God, and renew a steadfast spirit within me"* is the dedication prayer of **CCC to God.** Once we become a new creation, we must constantly be renewed, creating a steadfast spirit which never regresses and returns to our old ways. As a new creation, we must constantly study, learn, pray earnestly and set new goals for both our personal and spiritual development. We must avoid complacency and stagnation. Getting comfortable with where we are causes growth to cease and regression to set in.

Romans 8:29

<u>New International Version (©1984)</u>
"For those God foreknew he also predestined to be ***conformed to the likeness of his Son***, that he might be the firstborn among many brothers."

2 Corinthians 4:16

<u>New International Version</u> (©1984)
Therefore we do not lose heart. Though outwardly we are wasting away, yet inwardly we are ***being renewed day by day.***

  Regression is a psychological defense mechanism leading to the temporary reversion of the ego to an earlier stage of development rather than handling unacceptable impulses in a more adult way. The defense mechanism of regression, in psychoanalytic theory, occurs when thoughts are temporarily pushed back out of our consciousness and into our subconscious. We are troubled by temptation, unpleasant thoughts or we do something wrong, then we choose not to think about it. We push these feelings back into our subconscious mind and never deal with them. This can actually result in reverting back to the type of behavior we eliminated in the first place. These regressed feelings can resurface, causing frustration, anger and disappointment. These feelings can cause us to revert to an old behavior.

  We must learn to deal with unacceptable impulses in a mature way. We should seek to understand where these feelings come from, why we have them, and accept that we will never be perfect. We should confess our sins and move on, not deny that unacceptable impulses exist. Failure to do so leads to frustration. Setting the bar at perfection increases this frustration and is one of the causes of regression. We should seek to be the best we can be in our fallen (yet redeemed) states, but not impose standards on ourselves which we can never hope to achieve.

While we should all as Christians set standards (goals) for our behavior and constantly strive to improve, we must understand that we are only human and perfection is unattainable. We are to be conformed to the likeness of Christ, but this is the work of the Holy Spirit; not the result of our own imperfect attempts at self improvement. **God requires obedience** (you have obeyed Him and been cleansed by the blood of Jesus Christ). He supplies you with grace and peace.

1 Peter 1:2

<u>New Living Translation</u> (©2007)
"God the Father knew you and chose you long ago, and his Spirit has made you holy. As a result, *you have obeyed him and have been cleansed by the blood of Jesus Christ.* May God give you more and more grace and peace."

Still, we must do our best to be obedient and know that there is nothing wrong with improving oneself. We must take action to change, be obedient and not resist or hinder the Holy Spirit. We will learn that change begins in the mind, but must be followed with ACTION. *Thought, Action, Habit* **is how the process of change occurs. If one of the elements is missing, change does not take place, the new convert falls away or the dedicated follower of Christ becomes stagnant and disillusioned with church.** *Create, Connect, Commit to God* **calls on us to become a new creation, change our way of thinking, accept what we cannot change and then to** *put action behind our faith and change everything that is within our power to change.*

The goal of **Create, Connect, Commit to God** is to have Christians become wholly committed to their faith and to become the best they can possibly be. It seeks to create meaningful, purpose filled, successful lives for those who follow the steps and live the commitment. If you've grown weary in your spiritual walk, bored with the routine of church or you can't identify the problem but you know something is missing **CCC is** what you're missing. It's the answer to your prayers and the path to a closer relationship with God. You need to be renewed and put **CCC into** action. Action is a key element of the **Create, Connect, Commit** philosophy. God also requires us to put action behind our faith. **Faith without works is dead**.

James 2:18 NLT- Now someone may argue, "Some people have faith; others have good deeds." But I say, "How can you show me your faith if you don't have good deeds? I will show you my faith by my good deeds." ...For just as the body without the spirit is dead, so also *faith without works is dead*. **James 2:26 NASB**

Unrealistic Goals

Setting our standards at unattainable levels will lead to frustration, disillusionment and in some cases falling away. Having unattainable standards can increase a person's sense of anger, frustration or helplessness. It can lead to regression and even result in depression. Perfection is an unrealistic goal. Such unrealistic approaches to goal setting have been characterized as Conditional Goal Setting (CGS). Some individuals make the achievement of only one or two specific goals a prerequisite for personal happiness. Findings suggest that CGS is significantly related to depression. Make sure your goals are realistic and your standards attainable; don't set yourself up for future failure, regression, depression and lack of commitment.

A person may revert to an old behavior to ventilate feelings of frustration and disappointment in themselves. This is another way in which we lose both new converts and dedicated followers. Frustration over small failure, temptation or thoughts they feel they shouldn't have is pushed back into the subconscious. Being unable to conform to unattainable standards causes frustration, anger, feelings of unworthiness, and even causes some people to give up. They decide that they can't live up to the expectations which they feel Christianity imposes on them, so they quit and return to their old lifestyles. They "don't want to be hypocrites" so they stop attending church, failing to realize it's their own expectations they can't meet, not those of God. Avoid this trap. Confess your sins and move on.

Psalm 103:12

<u>New Living Translation (©2007)</u>
"He has removed our sins as far from us as the east is from the west."

Regression is also defined as a relapse to a less perfect or developed state. The new creation starts to think, act and feel more like the natural, carnal minded person. Regression is what you want to avoid. You don't want to go back where you've already been. You must constantly set new, realistic goals and strive for attainable standards in your spiritual walk. Once a goal is reached, a new goal must immediately be set. This is the only way to stay motivated and prevent regression. Continuous improvement is your goal. If you reach a stage where you can't think of any new goals to set for your spiritual life; great! Congratulations, you are doing exceptionally well! What about goals for reading books, earning a degree, teaching a study group, breaking a bad habit, finding a new way to help your Pastor or a new method of raising money? How are your communication skills? Set a goal to get over your shyness or be more outgoing. What area of the church are you serving in? Is there anything about it that can be improved? How are your relationships and your family life? Set goals to better manage your time. There is always room for improvement somewhere. You'll learn to set goals and to prioritize in Concept Two; **Connect With What You Want.**

Be creative, there is always something you can improve upon. There must be areas in your personal life in which you can make improvements, set goals for these. You must always have a new project to be excited about, a new goal to reach, or a new standard to strive toward. Setting higher standards will help you to stay motivated and avoid stagnation and regression. Continuous improvement in our spiritual lives, relationships, personal lives, health, diets, exercise routines, careers and every individual area of our lives is our goal. We are aiming for both spiritual and personal growth.

Create, Connect, Commit is a complete process and focuses on every area of our lives, not just one. Our goal is to become the best we can be in every way possible. Happy, well rounded, successful Christians will attract more people to our faith than stagnant, dissatisfied church goers. Wouldn't you rather go to a church filled with enthusiastic, committed Christians who are excited about their faith? Implementing **Create, Connect, Commit to God** in your church will surround you with believers who are a new creation, connected to God and their fellow Christians and committed to serving God faithfully and reaching the goals and standards they have set for themselves. We'll learn in Concept Two; **Connect** how the people we surround ourselves with influence us. Their mental frames become our mental frames. Their belief systems become our belief systems. You have a vested interest in seeing that your fellow church members become the best they can be.

Concept Three; **Commit** teaches us to use goal setting as a method of continuous improvement as we commit to progress. We must never accept the status quo, sit back and get comfortable. Progress is the enemy of regression, so it is progress we constantly strive for. Without progress there is no growth. If you're not growing you're regressing. **You must commit to progress.** This is the only way to make the changes you've made permanent and avoid losing ground.

Acts 14:26

<u>New International Version (©1984)</u>
"From Attalia they sailed back to Antioch, where they had been ***committed to the grace of God*** for the work they had now completed."

2 Chronicles 16:9

<u>New Living Translation (©2007)</u>
"The eyes of the LORD search the whole earth in order to strengthen those whose hearts are ***fully committed to him...***"

You Can Change

Create, Connect, Commit is the revolutionary process that will create enduring change in your life and break the negative cycles of behavior that are holding you back, stealing your dreams, hindering your relationship with God and may even be driving you into depression. It is the only system of self help that has ever worked for me, and believe me I've tried them all. I not only tried self help, I tried professional help, but nothing worked until I learned this process and committed to living it every day. I sank so far into depression that I feared I would never be able to hold a job and if not for intervention may have committed suicide. **Create, Connect, Commit** helped me conquer my fears, break free from negative cycles of thought and behavior, put my depression in check and created a rewarding, productive life for me. **Create, Connect, Commit** is a life changing experience and I believe in it so much that I am dedicating my life to getting it into the hands of everyone who needs it.

New Converts will find **Create, Connect, Commit to God** gives them the process they need to make their lifestyle changes permanent and commit to becoming a new creation and living a spirit filled life. **Long time followers of Christ** will find **CCC to God** renews their spiritual life and empowers them for success in their personal lives. This journey of self discovery will lead to a spiritual awakening and give them the tools they need to become the dedicated, successful Christians they've always wanted to be. They'll also experience personal growth through introspection, reframing and goal setting. **Churches** will find that **CCC to God** provides the necessary tools for genuine conversion and they will see their attendance increase and their retention levels peak when they incorporate **CCC to God** into their programs. The goal of implementing **CCC to God** churchwide is to bring *Shalom* to your church. **CCC to God** will create a sense of purpose and order in the church and create peace among members and peace with God.

I'm not a doctor or psychologist and I do not have a PhD. I am an ordained and licensed minister whose battle with depression cost him his ministry, career, marriage and nearly his life. I recovered from a level of depression most never return from. I started from scratch and built a new career. I started writing about the process I discovered for creating enduring change in my life, pursued my dreams and reached my goals. After wandering in the wilderness for 4 years, I came to terms with my faith. I realized that I was a born again child of God and there was nothing I could do to change that fact. I rededicated myself to God, but freed myself from the unattainable standard of perfection which I tried to adhere to during my ten years in ministry.

I tried everything to cure my depression, but nothing worked. Therapy was ineffective and medications were hit and miss. When I decided to beat depression once and for all I studied everything I could about psychology and the process of change. **Create, Connect, Commit** is the process I developed out of my need for something that worked. I desperately needed something that would work and this process works so well I want to make sure it is available to **everyone who suffers from depression, anxiety, codependency, the fear of failure, addiction, low self esteem, obesity or who just wants to change.** Nearly all psychological issues have at least one thing in common; **the inability to change the negative behavior.**

  This is not the first time that someone has *asked* you to change, but it is the first time that someone has *told* you **how to change.** No one has ever given you step by step instructions to show you exactly what to do in order to create enduring change in your life. Follow the step by step instructions laid out in this book and you will change your life forever. Visit blog.createconnectcommit.com and createconnectcommit.com to stay posted on current issues related to personality typing, depression, change and Christianity. **Create Connect Commit to God** is available at createconnectcommit.com.

Chapter Two

Personality Typing

Personality typing is a tool which the **Create, Connect, Commit Philosophy** incorporates. The self analysis involved helps to unlock the mysteries of our behavior. Underlying fears, motivations and desires are revealed, and give us specific areas which we need to work on if we are going to change. This is a crucial step in the self discovery process. Analyzing our beliefs through the lens of scripture, logical thinking and truth along with understanding our personality type help create the framework by which we shift our mental frames, create new boundaries and create a new self image.

I began studying personality types as a way of examining my behavior and trying to make improvements in my life long before I ever realized I had a problem with depression. Theories of personality type are as diverse as religious sects, and proponents of the different theories can be just as dogmatic as religious zealots. I have found the study of personality types to be a useful tool for self discovery, understanding behavior, and making necessary changes based on our inherit tendencies, strengths and weaknesses. I found the **Enneagram of Personality** to be the most insightful and useful model and I discuss it in detail later in this chapter. The Enneagram is an ancient system. The people encountered by Ulysses in The Odyssey, perhaps the oldest work in western literature, are character types derived from the Enneagram. Anyone who has seen the film "O Brother Where Art Thou" can also recognize the Enneagram types in the film, since it is based on The Odyssey. We'll examine four different typing systems.

The first theory dealing with different types which I studied was the Four Temperaments Theory. I found the description of my temperament blend to be somewhat accurate and helpful, but not nearly as accurate as the Enneagram.

The Four Temperaments

Four Temperaments is a theory of psychology that stems from the ancient medical concept of humorism. I first read about the four temperaments in the book "Why You Act the Way You Do" by **Tim LaHaye.** The book includes a self test you can take to determine what your blend of temperament is. This book was a great tool in helping me to understand my behavior and gave me the first real indication that I had a problem with depression. Lahaye is a Christian author, and expresses those beliefs in his books. There are personality tests that you can access and take for free on the internet and I'll provide the URLs to sites that I have used.

The Four Temperament Types

Humorism is the theory of the makeup and workings of the human body adopted by Greek and Roman physicians and philosophers. From Hippocrates onward, Humorism was adopted by Greek, Roman and Islamic physicians, and became the most commonly held view of the human body among European physicians until the advent of modern medical research in the nineteenth century.

This theory taught that the human body was filled with four basic substances, called four humors, which are in balance when a person is healthy. All diseases and disabilities resulted from an excess or deficit of one of these four humors. The four humors were identified as black bile, yellow bile, phlegm, and blood .Each of the four types of humors corresponded to a different personality type.

Sanguine

Sanguine are most likely the life of the party. They are funny and relish the limelight. They are affectionate, enjoy social activities, and make friends easily. They are imaginative and creative, and are often the one who enthusiastically promotes new ideas on the job. People call them vivacious, generous, and light-hearted. They wear their emotions on their sleeve, but are always quick to "forgive and forget." They struggle with follow-through, are chronically late, and tend to be forgetful. They have a short attention span and are easily distracted. As quickly as they discover a new hobby or pursuit, they can also lose interest--when it ceases to be engaging or fun. They can talk to anyone and make them feel that they are genuinely interested in them, and they are, until they turn their attention to the next person. Sanguine are natural salesman, preachers, motivational speakers and excel in any profession that requires an outgoing personality and dealing with people. Sanguine is the lowest level of my temperament, but I have at times had some characteristics of the Sanguine, for instance when I was preaching. The preacher at the church where I was a Youth Minister is a sanguine and it makes him perfect for the job in many ways. His charismatic, charming, magnetic personality makes him well liked and much sought after. He is a dynamic speaker and loves the limelight. He could sell ice to an Eskimo and his sanguine qualities make him a lovable figure. He would have been more suited at Evangelism as he is easily bored by the everyday routine of pastoring, calling on the sick and attending to the details and the business of running a church. His borderline ADD personality and occasional lack of follow through make him a classic sanguine and he has a way of making you love him in spite of his weaknesses.

Choleric

A person who is choleric is a doer. They have a lot of ambition, energy, and passion, and try to instill it in others. They can dominate people of other temperaments, especially phlegmatic types. Many great charismatic military and political figures were choleric. Choleric tend not to see potential problems or obstacles when working on a project. They can only see the finished project and keep chipping away at it until it they get it done. Choleric is my secondary temperament. Both my ex-wife and her stepfather are choleric. They are workaholics and see problems as a challenge to be mastered. My ex-wife cannot be still, and when she does try to relax and watch a movie, she quickly falls asleep. She is constantly doing, and expresses her love for others by doing for them. Her stepfather loves doing for others and gets excited when someone else has had some difficulty and asks for his help. He has never seen a problem he can't overcome when it comes to getting the job done. He constantly takes on new projects and studies new subjects. Doing is being for a choleric. Choleric is my secondary temperament.

Melancholic

A person who is a thoughtful ponderer has a *melancholic* disposition. Often very kind and considerate, melancholic can be highly creative as artists, writers, musicians and actors - but also can become overly pre-occupied with the tragedy and cruelty in the world, thus becoming depressed. A *melancholic* is also often a perfectionist, being very particular about what they want and how they want it in some cases. This often results in being dissatisfied with one's own artistic or creative works and always pointing out to themselves what could and should be improved. They are often loners and most times choose to stay alone and reflect. They are highly motivated when working on a project, but easily depressed when the project is finished. They tend to foresee problems and can point out everything that could possibly go wrong when considering a potential project. Melancholic is my primary temperament. I often get overly involved and singularly focused on a particular project and tend to work on that project at the exclusion of all else. I have a high degree of energy and enthusiasm while working toward my goal, and then often feel depressed once the task is completed. I have perfectionist tendencies when it comes to my work, can point out every potential problem and am never satisfied with my performance. I tend to focus on what I should have done. My melancholy temperament predisposes me to depression.

Phlegmatic

While phlegmatic are generally self-content and kind, their shy personality can often inhibit enthusiasm in others and make themselves lazy and resistant to change. They are "steady as she goes" types. People with a Phlegmatic temperament slowly proceed through life expending as little energy as possible. Since they have no temperament needs, they have no need to regenerate. So expending energy doing anything would seem like a waste. Phlegmatic tend to be observers of life rather than doers. Phlegmatic take few chances, break few rules and generally lead safe but boring lives. They are very consistent, relaxed, rational, curious, and observant, making them good administrators and diplomats. The phlegmatic has many friends, is reliable and compassionate. Phlegmatic are generally quiet and very even tempered, competent and steady, peaceful and agreeable, have administrative ability, mediate problems, avoid conflicts, are good under pressure and usually find the easy way of doing things. Phlegmatic is my third strongest temperament. My supervisor when I was a K-9 Officer at the Police Department was a phlegmatic. He is the most even tempered person I have ever known. He is one the best friends I have ever had, but he was often cold to people he had no interest in. Some people could talk to him and he would say nothing in return. Several times while searching buildings with his dog we encountered burglars and I never was able to understand how he remained so calm, it was uncanny. He was interested in the dogs, his wife and daughter and little else. He was a bit of a recluse, but overcame this tendency when he got interested in lifting weights and became a personal trainer. All around he is a great person and phlegmatic make loyal, caring friends.

Temperament in the Gospels

Many Christian writers have speculated about the temperaments of the Gospel writers, as each seems to reflect a unique--and slightly different--perspective. To the extent that each of the Gospels offers a slightly different perspective of the life of Christ, it may be possible to characterize each one's "temperament."

Matthew demonstrates definitively that Christ is the Messiah, the fulfillment of all the prophecies of the Old Testament and emphasizes the Kingdom of God. Luke highlights Jesus' relationship with the Father, especially through prayer, as well as the poor, women, the lowly and the suppressed. Mark is the least "scholarly" and tells a straightforward fast-paced story; he shows Christ's urgency and his conquering action. John is the most mystical, poetic, and theoretical of all the four. You might surmise that Matthew is choleric, Luke the relationship-oriented sanguine, Mark the straight story, simple and unadorned in phlegmatic style, and John, the truth will set you free; the only Gospel where Christ carries the cross alone, the most poetic and mystical of all four gospels, the idealistic, melancholic I can relate to.

Which Temperament Are You?

1.) Are you an extrovert? If so you are predominantly sanguine or choleric.
2.) If yes to 1, do you lean toward being a super extrovert? Are you usually the first to speak? If so you are a sanguine.
3.) If yes to one, are you a good salesman? If so you are predominantly sanguine.
4.) If yes to 1 but no to 2 and 3, are you a natural leader? If so you are choleric.
5.) If no to one, are you a perfectionist, analytical and somewhat critical? If so you are predominantly melancholy.

6.) If no to one, are you known by others as being very quiet? Do you rarely get angry but experience many fears and worries? If so you are phlegmatic.

Temperament Blends

LaHaye believes there are twelve mixtures of the four temperaments, representing people who have the traits of two temperaments, called Mel-Chlor, Chlor-San, San-Phleg, Phleg-Mel, Mel-San, Chlor-Phleg; and the reverse of these: Chlor-Mel, San-Chlor, Phleg-San, Mel-Phleg, San-Mel, and Phleg-Chlor.

I am a melancholic choleric (Mel-Chlor). I have recently tested as melancholic phlegmatic (Mel – Phleg) which is consistent with Lahaye's theory that you can have more than one underlying subtype and that we all have some level of each type making up our personality. You can take a temperament test at no charge at **http://www.oneishy.com/personality/personality_test.php** or at many other sites available on the internet.

Temperament and Personality

Temperament consists of the traits we were born with. Personality is a combination of our temperament and life experiences, Temperament is determined by our unique neurological characteristics and unlike personality, it cannot be changed. Our personalities can change over time. We could say that temperament is our hardware and personality is our software. To fully understand what motivates us and why we think and act the way we do, we should examine both temperament and personality.

16 Personality Types

After getting interested in Personality Typing, I researched other theories and found that many variations of the Personality Types theory exited. One of the most popular is the 16 Personality Types model. The sixteen personality types are based on the well-known research of Carl Jung, Katharine C. Briggs, and Isabel Briggs Myers. Basically an individual is primarily **E**xtraverted or **I**ntroverted; **S**ensing or i**N**tuitive; **T**hinking or **F**eeling; and **J**udging or **P**erceiving. The possible combinations of these basic preferences form 16 different Personality Types, generally known as the Myers Briggs Personality Types or MBTI Personality Types.

ISTJ, ISTP, ISFJ, ISFP, INFJ, INFP, INTJ, INTP,

ESTP, ESTJ, ESFP, ESFJ, ENFP, ENFJ, ENTP, ENTJ

<u>David Keirsey</u> expanded on the ancient study of temperament by Hippocrates and Plato. In his works, Keirsey used the same names coined by Plato: **Artisan, Guardian, Idealist, and Rational.** Keirsey divided the four temperaments into two categories (roles), each with two types (role variants). The resulting 16 types correlate with the 16 personality types. You can take the Keirsey Temperament Sorter Test at**; http://www.keirsey.com/**

I typed as Guardian SJ after taking the sorter. The personality description is similar to the results of another test I took which I will describe later in this chapter, so I won't go into detail here.

The type descriptions of Isabel Briggs Myers differ from the character descriptions of David Keirsey in several ways:

- Myers primarily focused on how people think and feel; Keirsey focused more on behavior.
- Myers' descriptions use a linear four-factor model; Keirsey's descriptions use a systems field theory model.
- Myers, following the teaching of Carl Jung, emphasized the extraversion/introversion dichotomy; Keirsey's model placed greater importance on the sensing/intuition dichotomy.
- Myers grouped types by 'function attitudes'; Keirsey grouped types by temperament.

I frequently get different results when I test for the Meyers Briggs Personality Types. My latest test typed me as ISTJ. I have also typed as

ISFJ. You can take various Personality Tests including MBTI at no cost online at **http://similarminds.com/** Brief descriptions of each of the 16 types follow.

MBTI Personality Types

ISTJs are internally focused; they take things in via their five senses in a literal, rock-solid fashion. Their secondary mode is external, where they deal with things rationally and logically.

ISTJ types are serious and quiet. They are interested in security and tranquil living. They are extremely thorough, responsible, and dependable. They have well-developed powers of concentration. They are usually interested in supporting and promoting traditions and established organizations. Well-organized and hard working, they work steadily toward their goals. They can usually accomplish just about anything once they have set their mind to it. I have typed ISTJ on some of the tests I have taken. Some of the characteristics fit. The IT types correspond to Enneagram type Five. Five is the wing of my personality subtype.

Jungian functional preference ordering:

Dominant: Introverted Sensing
Auxiliary: Extraverted Thinking
Tertiary: Introverted Feeling
Inferior: Extraverted Intuition

ISTPs, are internally focused, they deal with things rationally and logically. Their secondary mode is external, where they take things in via their five senses in a literal, rock-solid fashion.

ISTPs are generally quiet and reserved. They are interested in how and why things work. They like to take things apart to see how they work. They have excellent skills with mechanical things. Risk-takers who live for the moment they are usually interested in and gifted at extreme sports. Uncomplicated in their desires, they are loyal to their peers and to their internal value systems, but not overly concerned with respecting laws and rules if they get in the way of getting something done. Detached and analytical, they excel at finding solutions to practical problems. My nephew is an ISTP and seems to have been born that way. Even as a toddler, he liked to take things apart and if anyone was working on something he had to be in the middle of it. Corresponds to Enneagram Type Five.

Jungian functional preference ordering:

Dominant: Introverted Thinking
Auxiliary: Extraverted Sensing
Tertiary: Introverted Intuition
Inferior: Extraverted Feeling

ISFJs are internally focused. Their secondary mode is external, where they deal with things according to how they feel about them, or how they fit into their personal value system.

ISFJs live in a world that is solid and kind. They are truly warm and kind-hearted, and want to believe the best about people. They value harmony and cooperation, and are likely to be very sensitive to other people's feelings. People like ISFJs for their consideration and awareness, and their ability to bring out the best in others by their sincere desire to believe the best about everyone.

Quiet, kind, and conscientious, they can be depended on to follow through. They usually put the needs of others above their own. Stable and practical, they value security and traditions. They are extremely perceptive of other's feelings and genuinely interested in serving others. I am an ISFJ. Corresponds to Enneagram type Six.

Jungian functional preference ordering:

Dominant: Introverted Sensing
Auxiliary: Extraverted Feeling
Tertiary: Introverted Thinking
Inferior: Extraverted Intuition

ISFPs are internally focused, where they deal with things according to how they feel about them, or how they fit into their value system. Their secondary mode is external, where they take things in via their five senses in a literal, rock-solid fashion.

ISFPs live in the world of possibilities. They are keenly in tune with the way things look, taste, sound, feel and smell. They have a strong aesthetic appreciation for art, and are likely to be artists in some form, because they are unusually gifted at creating and composing things which will strongly affect the senses. They have a strong set of values, which they strive to consistently meet in their lives. They need to feel as if they're living their lives in accordance with what they feel is right, and will rebel against anything which conflicts with that goal. They're likely to choose jobs and careers which allow them the freedom of working towards the realization of their value-oriented personal goals.

ISFPs tend to be quiet and reserved, and difficult to get to know well. They hold back their ideas and opinions except from those who they are closest to. Quiet, serious, sensitive and kind, they avoid conflict. They are loyal and faithful friends. They have extremely well-developed senses, and aesthetic appreciation for beauty. They are not interested in leading or controlling others. Flexible and open-minded, they are likely to be original and creative. They live in the moment and tend to enjoy it. IF types correspond to Enneagram type Six.

Jungian functional preference ordering:

Dominant: Introverted Feeling
Auxiliary: Extraverted Sensing
Tertiary: Introverted Intuition
Inferior: Extraverted Thinking

INFJs are internally focused; they take things in primarily via intuition. Their secondary mode is external, where they deal with things according to how they feel about them, or how they fit into their personal value system.

INFJs are gentle, caring, complex and highly intuitive individuals. Artistic and creative, they live in a world of hidden meanings and possibilities. Only one percent of the population has an INFJ Personality Type, making it the rarest of all the types.

Quietly forceful, original, and sensitive, they tend to stick with things until they are done. They are extremely intuitive about people, and concerned for their feelings. They have well-developed value systems which they strictly adhere to. They are well-respected for their perseverance in doing the right thing. They tend to be individualistic, rather than leading or following. IF types correspond to Enneagram type Six.

Jungian functional preference ordering:

Dominant: Introverted Intuition
Auxiliary: Extraverted Feeling
Tertiary: Introverted Thinking
Inferior: Extraverted Sensing

INFPs are internally focused; they deal with things according to how they feel, or how things fit into their personal value system. Their secondary mode is external, where they take things in primarily via their intuition.

INFPs, more than other iNtuitive Feeling types, are focused on making the world a better place. Their primary goal is to find out their purpose in life and how they can best serve humanity. They are idealists and perfectionists, who drive themselves hard in the quest for achieving their goals.

Quiet, reflective, and idealistic they are interested in serving humanity. They have well-developed value systems, which they strive to live in accordance with. They are extremely loyal, adaptable and laid-back unless a strongly-held value is threatened. They are usually talented writers, mentally quick, able to see possibilities, interested in understanding and helping people. IF types correspond to Enneagram type Six.

Jungian functional preference ordering:

Dominant: Introverted Feeling
Auxiliary: Extraverted Intuition
Tertiary: Introverted Sensing
Inferior: Extraverted Thinking

INTJs are internally focused; they take things in primarily via their intuition. Their secondary mode is external, where they deal with things rationally and logically.

INTJs live in the world of ideas and strategic planning. They value intelligence, knowledge, and competence, and typically have high standards in these regards, which they continuously strive to fulfill. To a somewhat lesser extent, they expect the same of others.

With Introverted Intuition dominating their personality, INTJs focus their energy on observing the world, and generating ideas and possibilities. Their mind constantly gathers information and makes associations about it. They are tremendously insightful and are usually quick to understand new ideas. However, their primary interest is not *understanding* a concept, but rather *applying* that concept in a useful way. Unlike the INTP, they do not follow an idea as far as they possibly can, seeking only to understand it fully. INTJs are driven to come to conclusions about ideas. Their need for closure and organization usually requires that they take some action. IT types correspond to Enneagram type Five.

Jungian functional preference ordering:

Dominant: Introverted Intuition
Auxiliary: Extraverted Thinking
Tertiary: Introverted Feeling
Inferior: Extraverted Sensing

INTPs are internally focused; they deal with things rationally and logically. Their secondary mode is external, where they take things in primarily via their intuition.

INTPs live in the world of theoretical possibilities. They see everything in terms of how it could be improved, or what it could be turned into. They live primarily inside their own minds, having the ability to analyze difficult problems, identify patterns, and come up with logical explanations. They seek clarity in everything, and are therefore driven to build knowledge. They highly value intelligence and the ability to apply logic to theories to find solutions. They typically are so driven to turn problems into logical explanations, that they live much of their lives within their own heads. They may not place as much importance or value on the external world. Their natural drive to turn theories into something clear and easy to understand may turn into a feeling of personal responsibility to solve theoretical problems. INTPs help society move towards a higher understanding. IT types correspond to Enneagram type Five.

Jungian functional preference ordering:

Dominant: Introverted Thinking
Auxiliary: Extraverted Intuition
Tertiary: Introverted Sensing
Inferior: Extraverted Feeling

ESTPs are externally focused; they take things in via their five senses in a literal, concrete fashion. Their secondary mode is internal, where they deal with things rationally and logically.

ESTPs are outgoing, straight-shooting types. Enthusiastic and excitable, ESTPs are "doers" who like action. Blunt, straight-forward risk-takers, they are willing to plunge right into things and get their hands dirty. They live in the here-and-now, and place little importance on introspection or theory. They analyze the facts of a situation, quickly decide what action should be taken, execute the action, and move on to the next situation that presents itself.

They are friendly, adaptable, action-oriented "Doers" who are focused on immediate results. Living in the here-and-now, they're risk-takers who live fast-paced lifestyles. They quickly grow impatient with long explanations. They are extremely loyal to their peers, but not usually respectful of laws and rules if they get in the way of getting things done. ESTPs are likeable and have great people skills. ET types correspond to Enneagram Type One.

Jungian functional preference ordering:

Dominant: Extraverted Sensing
Auxiliary: Introverted Thinking
Tertiary: Extraverted Feeling
Inferior: Introverted Intuition

ESTJs are externally focused; they deal with things rationally and logically. Their secondary mode is internal, where they take things in via their five senses in a literal, concrete fashion.

ESTJs live in a world of facts and needs. They live in the present, with their eyes constantly scanning their environment to ensure everything is running smoothly and systematically. They honor traditions and laws, and have a clear set of standards and beliefs. They expect the same of others, and have no tolerance or understanding of individuals who do not value their beliefs. They value competence and efficiency, and like to see quick results for their efforts.

Practical, traditional, and organized they are likely to be athletic. They are not interested in theory or abstraction unless they can see the practical application; they have clear visions of the way things should be. They are loyal and hard-working but like to be in charge. Exceptionally capable in organizing and running activities, they are "Good citizens" who value security and peaceful living. ET Types correspond with Enneagram Type One.

Jungian functional preference ordering:

Dominant: Extraverted Thinking
Auxiliary: Introverted Sensing
Tertiary: Extraverted Intuition
Inferior: Introverted Feeling

ESFPs are externally focused. They take things in via their five senses in a literal, concrete fashion. Their secondary mode is internal, where they deal with things according to their feelings, or how things fit into their personal value system.

ESFPs live in the world of people possibilities. They love people and new experiences. They are lively and fun, and enjoy being the center of attention. They live in the moment, and relish excitement and drama in their lives.

People-oriented and fun-loving, they make things more fun for others by their enjoyment. Living for the moment, they love new experiences. They dislike theory and impersonal analysis. Interested in serving others they are likely to be the center of attention in social situations. They are known for their common sense and practical ability. EF types correspond to Enneagram Type Two.

Jungian functional preference ordering:

Dominant: Extraverted Sensing
Auxiliary: Introverted Feeling
Tertiary: Extraverted Thinking
Inferior: Introverted Intuition

ESFJs are externally focused; they deal with things according to how they feel about them, or how they fit into their personal value system. Their secondary mode is internal, where they take things in via their five senses in a literal, concrete fashion.

ESFJs are people oriented, they love people. They are genuinely interested in others. They use their Sensing and Judging characteristics to gather specific, detailed information about others, and turn this information into supportive judgments. They want to like people, and have a special skill at bringing out the best in others. They are extremely good at reading others, and understanding their point of view. The ESFJ's strong desire to be liked and for everything to be pleasant makes them highly supportive of others. People like to be around ESFJs, because the ESFJ has a special gift of invariably making people feel good about themselves. Their people skills tend to make ESFJs successful at whatever they do.

Warm-hearted, popular, and conscientious, they tend to put the needs of others over their own needs. They have a strong sense of responsibility and duty, value traditions and security and are interested in serving others. They need positive reinforcement to feel good about themselves. They have a well-developed sense of space and function. EF types correspond to Enneagram Type Two.

Jungian functional preference ordering:

Dominant: Extraverted Feeling
Auxiliary: Introverted Sensing
Tertiary: Extraverted Intuition
Inferior: Introverted Thinking

ENFPs are externally focused; they take things in primarily via their intuition. Their secondary mode is internal, where they deal with things according to how they feel about them, or how they fit into their personal value system.

ENFPs are warm, enthusiastic people, typically very bright and full of potential. They live in the world of possibilities, and can become very passionate and excited about things. Their enthusiasm lends them the ability to inspire and motivate others, more so than other types. They can talk their way into or out of anything. They love life, seeing it as a special gift, and strive to make the most out of it.

Enthusiastic, idealistic, and creative they are able to do almost anything that interests them. They have great people skills and a need to live life in accordance with their inner values. They are excited by new ideas, but bored with details. They are open-minded and flexible, with a broad range of interests and abilities. EF Types correspond to Enneagram Type Two.

Jungian functional preference ordering:

Dominant: Extraverted Intuition
Auxiliary: Introverted Feeling

Tertiary: Extraverted Thinking
Inferior: Introverted Sensing

ENFJs are externally focused; they deal with things according to how they feel about them, or how they fit into their personal value system. Their secondary mode is internal, where they take things in primarily via your intuition.

ENFJs are people-focused individuals. They live in the world of people possibilities. More so than any other type, they have excellent people skills. They understand and care about people, and have a special talent for bringing out the best in others. ENFJ's main interest in life is giving love, support, and a good time to other people. They are focused on understanding, supporting, and encouraging others. They make things happen for people, and get their best personal satisfaction from this.

Popular and sensitive, they have outstanding people skills. They are externally focused, with real concern for how others think and feel. They usually dislike being alone. They see everything from the human angle, and dislike impersonal analysis. They are very effective at managing people issues, and leading group discussions. Interested in serving others they probably place the needs of others over their own needs. EF Types correspond to Enneagram Type Two.

Jungian functional preference ordering:

Dominant: Extraverted Feeling
Auxiliary: Introverted Intuition
Tertiary: Extraverted Sensing
Inferior: Introverted Thinking

ENTPs are externally focused; they take things in primarily via their intuition. Their secondary mode is internal, where they deal with things rationally and logically.

With Extraverted Intuition dominating their personality, the ENTP's primary interest in life understands the world in which they live. They are constantly absorbing ideas and images about the situations they are presented in their lives. Using their intuition to process this information, they are usually extremely quick and accurate in their ability to size up a situation. With the exception of their ENFP cousin, the ENTP has a deeper understanding of their environment than any of the other types.

Creative, resourceful, and intellectually quick, they are skilled in a broad range of areas. They enjoy debating issues, and may be into "one-up-manship". They get very excited about new ideas and projects, but may neglect the more routine aspects of life. Generally outspoken and assertive, they enjoy people and are stimulating company. They have an excellent ability to understand concepts and apply logic to find solutions. ET types correspond to Enneagram Type One.

Jungian functional preference ordering:

Dominant: Extraverted Intuition
Auxiliary: Introverted Thinking
Tertiary: Extraverted Feeling
Inferior: Introverted Sensing

ENTJs are externally focused; they deal with things rationally and logically. Their secondary mode is internal, where they take things in primarily via their intuition.

ENTJs are natural born leaders. They live in a world of possibilities where they see all sorts of challenges to be overcome, and they want to be the ones responsible for overcoming them. They have a drive for leadership, which is well-served by their quickness to grasp complexities, their ability to absorb a large amount of impersonal information, and their quick and decisive judgments. They are "take charge" people.

Assertive and outspoken - they are driven to lead. They have an excellent ability to understand difficult organizational problems and create solid solutions. Intelligent and well-informed, they usually excel at public speaking. They value knowledge and competence, and usually have little patience with inefficiency or disorganization. ET Types correspond to Enneagram Type One.

Jungian functional preference ordering:

Dominant: Extraverted Thinking
Auxiliary: Introverted Intuition
Tertiary: Extraverted Sensing
Inferior: Introverted Feeling

David Keirsey created the theory of temperament associated with type. In his research, he made observations that allowed him to combine two of the four sets of preferences, into four distinct temperament categories. Each of the sixteen personality types fits into one of these temperament categories.

SJ - "The Guardians"

Keirsey describes the SJ group's primary objective as "Security Seeking". The SJ grouping includes the types:

- ESTJ - "The Supervisors"
- ISTJ - "The Inspectors"
- ESFJ - "The Providers"
- ISFJ - "The Protectors"

SP - "The Artisans"

Keirsey describes the SP group's primary objective as "Sensation Seeking". The SP grouping includes the types:

- ESTP - "The Promoters"
- ISTP - "The Crafters"
- ESFP - "The Performers"
- ISFP - "The Composers"

NT - "The Rationals"

Keirsey describes the NT group's primary objective as "Knowledge Seeking". The NT grouping includes the types:

- ENTJ - "The Field Marshals"
- INTJ - "The Masterminds"
- ENTP - "The Inventors"
- INTP - "The Architects"

NF - "The Idealists"

Keirsey describes the NF group's primary objective as "Identity Seeking". The NF grouping includes the types:

- ENFJ - "The Teachers"
- INFJ - "The Counselors"
- ENFP - "The Champions"
- INFP - "The Healers"

I have found the Enneagram to be a more accurate tool in mapping personality than either of the 16 type models. I tested ISFJ and ISTJ on MBTI tests and Guardian SJ on the Keirsey temperament sorter. ISTJ is my most frequent test result. There is some truth in the ISTJ description, but it is nothing like The Type 6 description I got from the Enneagram. That was like reading my autobiography. You can read about how I used this information and self discovery to effect enduring change in my life in "Change Anything" at createconnectcommit.com

The Enneagram provided me with the best personality profile of all the systems I have studied, hands down. It provides a tool for self improvement (integration) as well as a model for behavior we should avoid (disintegration). Where this system actually originated is a matter of dispute. While I do not agree with the religious and spiritual beliefs associated with the Enneagram by some, whoever developed it really understood human behavior.

Jungian Types

Carl Jung posited that there are two general psychological attitudes (introversion and extroversion) and four psychological functions (thinking, feeling, intuition and sensation). This produces eight psychological types.

The Enneagram types correlate to Jung's types as follows;

One –extroverted thinking.

Two – extroverted feeling.

Three – does not correspond to any Jungian type. Elements of the Three exist within other Jungian Types.

Four – introverted intuitive.

Five – introverted thinking.

Six – introverted feeling.

Seven – extroverted sensation.

Eight – extroverted intuitive.

Nine – introverted sensation.

Psychiatric Designations Of The Enneagram

Type One corresponds to Compulsive Personality Disorder

Type Two corresponds to Histrionic Personality Disorder

Type Three corresponds to Narcissistic Personality Disorder

Type Four corresponds to the Avoidant Personality Disorder

Type Five corresponds partly to the Paranoid Personality Disorder and partly to the Schizotypal Personality Disorder

Type Six corresponds partly to the Passive Aggressive Personality Disorder and partly to the Dependent Personality Disorder.

Type Seven corresponds partly to the Manic Depressive Personality Disorder and partly to the Histrionic Personality Disorder.

Type Eight corresponds to the Antisocial Personality Disorder.

Type Nine corresponds partly to the Dependent Personality Disorder and partly to the Passive Aggressive Personality Disorder.

The Wing

No one is a pure personality type. Everyone is a mixture of two types, the basic type and the wing, which are adjacent on the Enneagram. Once you have determined your personality type, the next step is to determine which wing you have. The wing is one of types on either side of your basic personality type. You can determine your wing through the descriptions; one of them will fit you better than the other. As integration occurs, the wing integrates also. As I move into the healthier state for example, I am a Six with a Five wing becoming a Nine with an Eight wing.

Chapter Three

The Enneagram

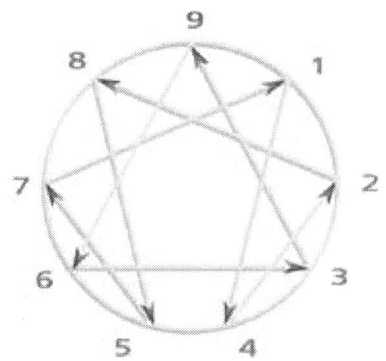

The most striking result I got from a personality test was when I took the Enneagram of Personality test. I had studied many other personality typing systems than just those listed in this book, and the Enneagram gave me the most accurate and useful information of all. It opened the door to self discovery and led me to make dynamic changes in my life. While no system of personality typing is perfect, the Enneagram has been the most useful to me.

The Enneagram *symbol* has roots stretching into antiquity and can be traced back at least as far as the works of Pythagoras. The circle symbolizes unity, the inner triangle symbolizes the "law of three" and the hexagon represents the "law of seven". These three elements constitute the Enneagram figure. The symbol was reintroduced to the modern world by George Gurdjieff. Gurdjief was a Greek-Armenian mystic and spiritual teacher. He called his discipline "The Work"(connoting "work on oneself"). Gurdjieff's principles and instructions later became known as the "Fourth Way". At one point he described his teaching as **"esoteric Christianity".** Although Gurdjieff used the Enneagram to describe possibilities of human development, his concept of it was principally related to the symbolic communication of ancient knowledge and the "self-work" process through which people can acquire insight; not for the categorizing of personality styles. Gurdjieff did *not* teach a system of types associated with the symbol.

Author Robin Amis claims a Christian orthodox origin for the Enneagram symbol Gurdjieff used, known as the Fourth Way Enneagram. Amis claims that Gurdijeff developed his teaching with insights gained from visits to Mount Athos, politically known in Greece as the **Self-governed Monastic State of the Holy Mountain**. There are twenty sovereign monasteries on Mount Athos and 12 sketes. A skete is a community of Christian hermits following a monastic rule, allowing them to worship in comparative solitude.

Many early Enneagram enthusiasts mistakenly attributed the system of the nine types to Gurdjieff, however Gurdjieff never taught anything about a system of understanding character related to the Enneagram symbol. The person credited with originally putting the Enneagram of Personality system together is Oscar Ichazo. Ichazo is the Bolivian-born founder of the Arica School which he established in 1968. In developing his Enneagram theories, Ichazo drew upon the ancient idea of the nine divine forms. This idea was discussed by Plato as *the Divine Forms* or *Platonic Solids,* qualities of existence that are essential, that cannot be broken down into constituent parts. This idea was further developed by the Neo-Platonic philosophers, particularly Plotinus in his work, *The Enneads*.

The primary difference between Ichazo's theories and modern psychology is that he has proposed a model of the components of the human psyche from which aberrations develop, whereas modern psychology has preferred to focus on observed behavior. In 1992 intellectual copyright for the Enneagram of Personality was denied to Ichazo on the basis that he had published claims that his theories were factual and factual ideas cannot be copyrighted. (Arica v. Palmer, court case, provided by *Information Law Web)*

Claudio Naranjo, a Chilean-born, American-trained psychiatrist who extensively explored the theories of personality, studied with Ichazo in Chile. He then took Ichazo's teachings and further developed them, articulating nine personality types in Western psychological terms. Naranjo then brought his understanding of the Enneagram system to Berkeley, California, where he taught it to private students in the context of his own program of self-development work in the early 1970s. Naranjo cross referenced Enneagram character styles with other typing systems, including the *Diagnostic and Statistical Manual of Mental Disorders,* the most common source of psychiatric diagnoses. Although he spoke in psychiatric language, Naranjo's efforts failed to penetrate professional mental health circles. Instead, The Enneagram became popular in Catholic and Christian networks before eventually emerging into the popular culture.

Based on material first taught by Claudio Naranjo, authors such as Helen Palmer, Don Riso, Russ Hudson, Patrick O'Leary, Richard Rohr and Elizabeth Wagele began to publish the first widely read books on the Enneagram of Personality beginning in the 1980s and 1990s.

Some claim the " Enneagram of Personality" only dates back to the 1960's when Ichazo was first teaching it; others say that it dates back earlier than the 4th Century A.D. when **Evagrius of Pontus** described nine personality types or styles. Evagrius of Pontus (c.345-399) was one of the most prominent figures among the monks of the desert settlements of Nitria, Sketis, and Kellia in Lower Egypt. Through the course of his ascetic writings he formulated a systematic presentation of the teaching of the semi-eremitic monks of these settlements. The works of Evagrius had a profound influence on Eastern Orthodox monastic teaching and passed to the West through the writings of John Cassian.

The philosophy behind the Enneagram contains components from mystical Judaism, Kabbalah, Christianity, Islam, Taoism, Buddhism, and ancient Greek philosophy, particularly the philosophy of Socrates, Plato, and the Neo-Platonists. Perhaps the history of the Enneagram explains why the system is often presented in humanistic terms. However efforts to use the system to diagnose pathology and predict potential are still popular. Because the Enneagram has become popular through human potential and spiritual venues, traditional psychotherapists have been slow to recognize its value. Presently, there are a number of researchers in psychology who are applying scientific methods to prove the validity of the system. But it already has a life of its own outside the culture of psychology

While I am in no way interested in the spiritual and mystical aspects related to the Enneagram, I am interested in its Christian roots and applications. I am most interested in learning why I think and act the way I do and using that information to improve my quality of life, and helping others to do the same. The Enneagram of Personality is the best tool I have found for determining personality type, giving a model for improvement as well as a model for behavior one should avoid, understanding how different personality types interact in a relationship and applying the information in order to make lasting changes in one's life.

Understanding my underlying fears and motivations helped me to resolve my emotional insecurities and learn to face my anxieties. I came to believe in myself and developed self confidence. I ignored my fear of failure and began to reach my goals, like writing books for instance. I quit worrying that they wouldn't be good enough, disregarded the fear that they would never be published, and quit worrying about what people would think of them. I just did what I had a knack for, I wrote about what I was passionate about. I began to ignore the fear and do it anyway in all areas of my life, and it was the self discovery that came from studying the Enneagram of Personality that led to these positive steps in my recovery from depression.

The Enneagram exists on the boundary between secular and spiritual psychology. Spiritual psychology holds that each human being has a sacred gift to offer, but as we react defensively to the pain of human experiences, our gift is obscured. An individual's defense can resemble their gift, but it is actually a protective mask, often referred to as a *persona, false self, fixation* or a *trance.* People labeled co-dependent for example, are usually gifted at being compassionate; however, they may warp the capacity to disguise and protect their early wounds.

All the main theories of personality are rooted in ancient philosophy and/or mythology. The 4 Temperaments and the 16 Personality theories are both rooted in ancient Greek and Roman philosophy. Even though I myself am a Christian, I don't discount the practicality and usefulness of personality typing simply because of the roots of the theories or how other people may choose to apply them. It has been a powerful tool which has aided in my recovery. There is no conflict between my beliefs and the use of personality typing, The Enneagram symbol itself may hint of God's creation of man in his own image.

I separate the Enneagram of Personality theory from the mystical teachings of the Enneagram. My practical application of personality typing should in no way be construed to be an endorsement of the teachings of George Ivanovich Gurdjieff, Oscar Ichazo, The Fourth Way, the **Arica School**, the Enneagram Institute or any other teachings of the spiritual or mystical aspects related to the Enneagram.

The Enneagram of Personality

Courtesy of The Enneagram Institute
Copyright 2005, The Enneagram Institute. All Rights Reserved. Used with Permission.

The **Enneagram of Personality** includes nine types. The term "enneagram" derives from two Greek words, *ennea* (nine) and *grammos* (something written or drawn). The enneagram figure consists of a nine-pointed diagram, usually within a circle.

Each Enneagram personality type expresses a distinctive and habitual pattern of thinking and emotions. The behavioral characteristics of the personality types are less distinctive. By recognizing their personality pattern a person may be able to use the Enneagram as an effective method for self-understanding and self-development.

Ichazo identified nine ways in which a person's ego becomes fixated within the psyche at an early stage of life. For each person one of these 'ego fixations' then becomes the core of a self-image around which their psychological personality develops. Each fixation is also supported at the emotional level by a particular 'passion' or 'vice'. The principal psychological connections between the nine ego fixations can be 'mapped' using the points, lines and circle of the enneagram figure. (Palmer, *The Enneagram in Love and Work*, pp.24-26)

We each are endowed with specific instinctual intelligences that are necessary for our survival. These instincts compose our "subtypes" or secondary personality traits. We each have a *self-preservation* instinct, a *sexual instinct*, and a *social instinct*.

One of the instincts is the dominant focus of our attention and behavior. We each also have a second Instinct that is used to support the dominant Instinct, as well as a third Instinct that is the least developed.

Courtesy of The Enneagram Institute
Copyright 2005, The Enneagram Institute. All Rights Reserved. Used with Permission.

The Nine Types

The 9 personality types of the Enneagram are given various names by different practitioners of Enneagram theory but the characteristics of the types remain consistent. The 9 types are;

1 The Reformer or Perfectionist - "produces order". Dominant Functions; Objectivity and Social Responsibility. Underdeveloped Relating; Ones underdevelop the ability to relate to the environment as they feel less than the perfection they strive for.

2 <u>Helper</u> or Giver - "<u> must help others.</u>" Dominant Functions; Empathy and Altruism. Overdeveloped Feeling; Twos express only positive emotions while suppressing negative ones.

3 Achiever or Motivator "<u> needs to succeed.</u>" Dominant Functions; Self-Esteem and Self-Development. Most out of touch with Feeling; Threes project an image which substitutes for true feelings.

4 Individualist or <u>Romantic</u> - "<u>unique.</u>" Dominant Functions; Self-Awareness and Artistic Creativity. Underdeveloped Feeling; Fours underdevelop the personal expression of feelings and reveal themselves through some sort of art or aesthetic lifestyle.

5 Investigator or <u>Thinker</u> "<u>needs to understand the world.</u>" Dominant Functions; Open-Mindedness and Original Thinking. Underdeveloped Doing; Fives substitute thinking for doing.

6 Loyalist or <u>Skeptic</u> – "<u>affectionate and skeptical.</u>" Dominant Functions; Commitment and Social Affiliation. Most out of touch with Doing; Sixes are most out of touch with the ability to act on their own without the approval of an authority figure,

7 <u>Enthusiast</u> – "<u>happy and open to new things.</u>" Dominant Functions; Enthusiasm and Practical Action. Overdeveloped Doing; Sevens overdevelop the ability to act, becoming hyperactive and manic,

8 Challenger or <u>Leader</u>- "<u>must be strong.</u>" Dominant Functions; Self-Assertion and Leadership. Overdeveloped Relating; Eights overdevelop the ability to relate to the environment, seeing themselves as bigger than everyone else.

9 Peacemaker or Mediator - "at peace." Dominant Functions; Acceptance and Receptivity. Most out of touch with Relating; Nines are most out of touch with their ability to relate to the environment as an individual since they identify with another.

Enneagram Tests

The scientifically validated RHETI test is available at http://www.enneagraminstitute.com/

1. To install on your PC desktop (free)
2. To host on your website (free)
3. To print out as hardcopy ($25, unlimited use)

The following tests are also available at The Enneagram Institute's website;

The Free RHETI Sampler 10 minutes, free

The Free Brief QUEST 5 minutes, free

The RHETI—independently validated full test 40 minutes, $10

The QUEST-TAS
The Quick Enneagram Sorting
Test &Type Attitude Sorter 40 minutes, $10

<u>The IVQ</u>
<u>The Instinctual Variants</u>
<u>Questionnaire</u> 20 minutes, $8

You can take a free Enneagram test at:

http://similarminds.com/ - the Enneagram –Jung test at this site gives an accurate MBTI type which you can then check in this book in the section on 16 personality types and see which Enneagram type corresponds to the MBTI type

http://www.enneagraminstitute.com/

http://www.eclecticenergies.com/enneagram/test.php or at many other sites on the internet. *I caution you to only use the Enneagram as a tool for discovering your personality type. Be aware of the New Age philosophy and Eastern mysticism associated with some of these sites.*

1 Corinthians 1:21

<u>**New Living Translation**</u> **(©2007)**
"Since God in his wisdom saw to it that the world would never know him *through human wisdom,* he has used our foolish preaching to save those who believe."

There is no path to God through human wisdom. As Eph. 2:8 states "For it is by grace you have been saved, through faith--and this not from yourselves, it is the gift of God." While I differ in my religious convictions from many of those who espouse the wisdom of the Enneagram, most of them do share at least one common goal with me; to help people discover their personality type, their inner fears and motivations, their strengths and weaknesses and to use the information to become the best people they can possibly be.

Since the Enneagram reflects all the different personality types, I believe it can also be used as a model of completeness for any process. I explain this further in the section *"The Enneagram of Change."* That's as far as my use of the Enneagram goes.

My use of the Enneagram of personality is no different from Lahaye's use of temperament theory. So take the tests but be wary of the content of some of the sites where the test is available.

You may mistype based on these short tests. When you get the results read the description of your personality type and if the information is not shockingly accurate, you have most likely mistyped. For this reason I recommend paying the small fee and taking the scientifically validated test provided by the Enneagram Institute

I took the test at **http://similarminds.com/** and typed as 6, the Loyalist. Type Sixes correspond to Jung's introverted feeling type, and I tested type 6 with a Type 5 Wing at **http://www.eclecticenergies.com/enneagram/test**.php. Type Five corresponds to Jung's introverted thinking type. This would explain my testing as both ISFJ and ISTJ. When I initially searched for Ennegram Type 6 on the internet I found the following site;
http://www.enneagraminstitute.com/TypeSix.asp

The Enneagram Institute is a Service Mark of Enneagram Personality Types, Inc.
All Images, Content and Layout Copyright The Enneagram Institute 1998-2010.

The information was so accurate it shocked me. The site had a section on different levels of the personality types that was especially helpful to me. I could see that I had been at various levels at different times in my life. This led me to purchase the book "Personality Types: by Don Richard Riso."

My type description in the book was so accurate, it was downright scary. There was a lifetime's worth of self analysis, describing my problems to a tee, and explaining the beliefs and behaviors that were at the root of those problems. Such information could only have come from years of therapy, yet here it was in black and white, in a book written by someone who had never even heard of me. How could someone paint such an accurate description of me with no knowledge of who I was? It was amazing.

Personality Typing, The Enneagram and Christianity

Some Christian writers have criticized personality typing and even associated it with divining, fortune telling and astrology; practices forbidden in the Bible. I disagree. By assessing our individual personality types we are not attempting to predict the future or seeking divine knowledge from some mystical force. We are simply using a tool to help determine why we think and act the way we do. This knowledge is critical information in the **Create, Connect, Commit** process and I'm open to using whichever system of personality typing produces the most accurate and helpful results.

Tim LaHaye is a well known Christian author and speaker. He is the author of the tremendously popular "Left Behind" series and an expert on Bible Prophecy. His book "Why You Act The Way You Do" was referenced in the earlier section on personality types and introduced us to the theory of the *Four Temperaments*. LaHaye explained how we all have blends of those four basic temperaments which determine many of the ways in which we think and act. LaHaye is a well respected authority on the Bible and a leading figure in Evangelical Christianity. Even though The Four Temperaments Theory is rooted in ancient Greek and Roman philosophy, LaHaye finds no fault in using the theory to help people discover their inner strengths and weaknesses. This information can be used to facilitate change and foster self development. Indeed, LaHaye's book even contains a section on temperament and how it affects your relationship with God.

If one takes an objective look at the systems of personality typing and temperament analysis, one cannot deny that the characteristics described in the systems exist to some extent in every individual. I do not know which system of personality typing is the correct one; I only know which system has been the most accurate and helpful to me and others who have used it.

If temperament and personality exist (and they do) then they had to have come from somewhere. Are we born with these qualities? Yes, to some extent we are. Temperament consists of the traits we were born with. Personality is a combination of our temperament and life experiences, Temperament is determined by our unique neurological characteristics and unlike personality, it cannot be changed. Our personalities can change over time. We could say that temperament is our hardware and personality is our software.

Still, for enough characteristics of behavior to be present in all individuals to the extent that they can be categorized and organized into certain distinct personality types and temperaments; it leaves us with an unanswered question; **Where do these behaviors stem from?**

If you are a Christian and accept the biblical account of creation in the book of Genesis then you believe that we all have one common ancestor, Adam. As such, Adam is the father of all races. According to your belief; as many different races of people as there are in the world, the DNA to create all those races existed in Adam. It only stands to reason then, that all personality types and temperaments are rooted in Adam. Whichever the correct models of personality types and temperaments actually are, the templates had to have existed in Adam. God is the designer and creator of those templates. God created man in his own image, therefore, before The Fall, Adam was complete. All the temperaments and personality types must have existed in perfect balance in Adam. He was in a perfect relationship with his creator, unhampered by sin and was as perfect as any man can be. Jesus Christ is often referred to as "The Second Adam" denoting his Immaculate Conception and sinless perfection. Indeed, Christ came to fix what Adam had broken.

1 Corinthians 15:45-49

New Living Translation (©2007)
"The Scriptures tell us, "The first man, Adam, became a living person." But the last Adam--that is, Christ--is a life-giving Spirit. What comes first is the natural body, then the spiritual body comes later. Adam, the first man, was made from the dust of the earth, while Christ, the second man, came from heaven. Earthly people are like the earthly man, and heavenly people are like the heavenly man. Just as we are now like the earthly man, we will someday be like the heavenly man."

After The Fall, Adam became self conscious and alienated. He became "self aware" and as such we are all self conscious and alienated to this day.
Rom 5:19 - "For as by one man's disobedience many were made sinners, so also by one Man's obedience many will be made righteous."

The study of personality typing therefore, does not conflict with my religious belief or my convictions in Christianity.

The Ennegram symbol and the study of the Enneagram are sometimes associated with mysticism or other forms of New Age spiritualism. My use of the symbol in no way implies a belief in such philosophies or an endorsement of such practices. I do not believe it is the path to enlightenment or to God as some may claim. As I've already stated, there is no path to God through human wisdom.

I do believe the Enneagram is the most accurate system of personality typing and a powerful tool which we can use to help us become the best we can be. I believe in the words of Christ *"I am the way, the truth, and the life. No one can come to the Father except through me."* Salvation is through accepting Christ as Lord and Savior, there is no other path to God. As Eph. 2:8 states "For it is by grace you have been saved, through faith--and this not from yourselves, it is the gift of God."

Due to the apparent connection between the symbol and New Age practices I had to ask myself if there was anything wrong with my use of the symbol or the Enneagram of personality. I had to examine the symbol through the lens of logic and truth and determine if there was anything about the symbol itself which was inherently evil or which contradicted with my own personal beliefs. I had to ask myself the following questions;

1.) "What does the symbol represent?"

The Enneagram symbol is composed of three parts, the circle, the inner triangle, and the "periodic figure." The circle symbolizes unity, the inner triangle symbolizes the "law of three," and the hexagonal periodic figure represents the "law of seven." These three elements constitute the Enneagram. There are nine points on the Enneagram.

2.) Do the concepts of unity, the law of seven, the law of three or the number nine represent anything that contradicts with my beliefs?

What does the Bible have to say about unity?

Psalm 133:1
1. How good and pleasant it is when brothers live together in unity!

John 17:23
23. I in them and you in me. May they be brought to complete unity to let the world know that you sent me and have loved them even as you have loved me.

1 Corinthians 1:10
10. I appeal to you, brothers, in the name of our Lord Jesus Christ, that all of you agree with one another so that there may be no divisions among you and that you may be perfectly united in mind and thought.

1 Corinthians 12:12

12 The body is a unit, though it is made up of many parts; and though all its parts are many, they form one body. So it is with Christ.

Ephesians 4:3

3. Make every effort to keep the unity of the Spirit through the bond of peace.

Ephesians 4:11-13

11. It was he who gave some to be apostles, some to be prophets, some to be evangelists, and some to be pastors and teachers, 12. to prepare God's people for works of service, so that the body of Christ may be built up 13. until we all reach unity in the faith and in the knowledge of the Son of God and become mature, attaining to the whole measure of the fullness of Christ.

Colossians 3:14

14 And over all these virtues put on love, which binds them all together in perfect unity.

What about the law of three and the law of seven?

Three : 3 - Biblical Meaning of the Number is approval, entire and solid. This number is also used when describing the Trinity or the Godhead (divine perfection). This number has also been associated with spirit and life.

Seven : 7 - Biblical Meaning of the Number is spiritual perfection and spiritual completeness. This number has also been used when describing the covenant between man and God.

One : 1 - Biblical Meaning of the Number is the number of God. Independence is also attached to this number as well, for it excludes all things that are different. This number is also used when marking the beginnings of things. **Unity** is very common when defining this number, for it stands alone and cannot be divided.

Nine : 9 - Biblical Meaning of Number is judgment or finality. Basically, it's used when judging man and all of his works. This number has also been used to describe the perfect movement of God.

The Trinity

"Trinity" is a term that is not found in the Bible but a word used to describe what is apparent about God in the Scriptures. The Bible clearly speaks of God the Father, God the Son (Jesus Christ), and God the Holy Spirit...and also clearly presents that there is only one God.

Thus the term: "Tri" meaning three, and "Unity" meaning one, Tri+Unity = Trinity. It is a way of acknowledging what the Bible reveals to us about God, that God is yet three "Persons" who have the same essence of deity.

God the Son (Jesus) is fully, completely God. God the Father is fully, completely God. And God the Holy Spirit is fully, completely God. Yet there is only one God.

Seven Spirits

The Bible tells us there are seven Spirits of God. The "seven spirits of God" are mentioned in Revelation 1:4; 3:1; 4:5; and 5:6. Revelation 1:4 mentions that the seven spirits are before God's throne. Revelation 3:1 indicates that Jesus Christ "holds" the seven spirits of God. Revelation 4:5 links the seven spirits of God with seven burning lamps that are before God's throne. Revelation 5:6 identifies the seven spirits with the "seven eyes" of the Lamb and states that they are "sent out into all the earth." Isaiah 11:2 says, "The Spirit of the LORD will rest on him — the Spirit of wisdom and of understanding, the Spirit of counsel and of power, the Spirit of knowledge and of the fear of the LORD." ...(1) Spirit of the LORD, (2) Spirit of wisdom, (3) Spirit of understanding, (4) Spirit of counsel, (5) Spirit of power, (6) Spirit of knowledge, (7) Spirit of the fear of the Lord.

3 Persons, 7 Spirits, 1 God; the triangle, the hexagon, the circle. God created man in His own image. Therefore the Enneagram could be a symbol of God's perfect creation of man; Adam as he existed before The Fall. This is merely conjecture, but could explain why the Enneagram of personality is such an accurate tool for assessing personality.

The Number Three

The Hebrew word for God "**Elohim**" is made up of three separate words: "**El, Ela and Elim**" which means God, Goddess and Gods. The numerological value of the Hebrew word for the word three (Shalosh) is 333. The numerological value of the Hebrew word "Alef", which is the first letter of the Hebrew alphabet, is 111. The Hebrew alphabet has 27 letters (22+5 final letters) which is 3x3x3

The recurrence of the number three is found throughout the Bible.

Noah had three sons (Gen 6:10) and Job had three daughters (Job 1:2; cf. 42:13); The Ark of the Covenant contained three sacred objects 'The gold jar of manna, Aaron's staff that had budded, and the stone tablets of the covenant" (Heb. 9:4). Solomon's Palace of the Forest of Lebanon was designed with windows "placed high in sets of three facing each other. All the doorways had rectangular frames; they were in the front part in sets of three, facing each other" (1 Kgs 7:4-5). In John's vision a triple entrance way marked all four sides of the city of the New Jerusalem (Rev 21:13). David "bowed down before Jonathan three times, with his face to the ground" (1 Sam 20:41) and Daniel regularly prayed three times a day giving thanks to God (Dan 6:10, 13). Israelite men were required to appear before the Lord three times in a year: "Three times a year all your men must appear before the LORD your God at the place he will choose: at the Feast of Unleavened Bread, the Feast of Weeks and the Feast of Tabernacles" (Deut 16:16). Jesus answered Satan's threefold temptation by citing three scriptural passages Matt 4:1-11). Paul experienced three shipwrecks (2 Cor 11:28) and prayed three times to the Lord for the removal of his "thorn in the flesh" (2 Cor 12:7-8). In the New Testament Jesus told the Jewish populace at the Temple, "Destroy this temple, and I will raise it again in three days" (John 2:16).

Moses' mother was able to conceal her baby for three months (Exod 2:3; cf. Acts 7:20; Heb 11:23) and the ark remained at the house of Obed-Edom for three months (1 Chron 13:14). Support for the priests of Hezekiah's day was gained by means of a tithe which began "in the third month and finished in the seventh month" (2 Chron 31:7). Ezekiel received a message from the Lord concerning the fate of Egypt in the third month of the eleventh year of his exile (Ezek 31:1) and the Lord revealed through Amos, "I also withheld rain from you when the harvest was still three months away" (Amos 4:7).

Jesus' mother Mary visited Elizabeth, Zechariah's wife, and stayed for three months (Luke 1:56). Paul stayed in Ephesus for three months and "spoke boldly" in the synagogue there (Acts 19:8), and subsequently stayed three months in Greece (Acts 20:3). Still later after the ship that was carrying him to Rome to stand trial was wrecked in a storm, he and his captives stayed on the island of Malta for three months (Acts 28:11).

The Number Seven

The recurrence of the number seven-or an exact multiple of seven- is found throughout the Bible and is widely recognized. The Sabbath on the seventh day, the seven years of plenty, and the seven years of famine in Egypt, the seven priests and seven trumpets marching around Jericho, The Sabbath year of the Land are well-known examples.

Also, Solomon's building the Temple for seven years, Naaman's washing in the river seven times, and the seven churches, seven seals, seven trumpets, seven bowls, seven stars, seven spirits and so on in the Book of Revelation, all show the consistent use of the number seven. Seven is used over 700 times in the Bible. It is used 54 times in the Book of Revelation.

The Number Nine

There are nine fruits of the Spirit. "The fruit of the Spirit is love, joy, peace, patience, kindness, goodness, faithfulness, gentleness and self-control. Against such things there is no law." **(Galatians 5:19-23, New International Version)**

The Enneagram symbolizes the Nine Fruits of the Spirit listed in the *Epistle to the Galatians*. This star is sometimes depicted with the Latin initials for each of the fruits placed within the points: caritas, gaudium, pax, longanimitas, benignitas, bonitus, fides, mansuetudo and continentia.

How The Enneagram Works

Nine points of the Enneagram

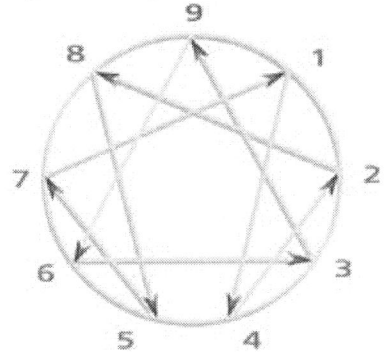

If we were to focus on the **nine points of the Enneagram** and numerically signify them (1-9), we will discover that one triangle connects the numbers 3, 6, 9 (all extensions of three) while the hexagon connects the numbers 1, 4, 2, 8, 5, 7 (follow the arrows)

Divide the number one by the number seven (=.142857142857...), and you get an infinitely recurring pattern (1,4,2,8,5,7), a never-ending but regular process. When you connect those points, in that order, on a circle with nine points that are equally spaced, you trace the six-pointed shape that is one of the two figures that make up the enneagram.

Divide two by seven, and one gets the same pattern, but starting with the number 2 (=.285714...). The same thing happens if one divides any of the remaining numbers up through seven, by the number 7. But, interestingly, the symmetrical six-pointed figure that results from this mathematical 'ritual' only occurs when the circle on which the figure is traced is broken up into NINE equally-distant points. Connect the 142857 dots on a seven or eight pointed figure, and, you just have a mess.

It is as if a nine-pointed grid is necessary to reveal the symmetry within the seven-stage process. Seven and nine are intimately related numbers psychologically speaking.

1/7 = .142857

This equation is movements in thirds, 1-8, 4-5, 2-7. At this point the relationships invert, 8-1, 5-4, 7-2. Pairing the number with the third number from it, the sum of each pair will give you 9.

This can be seen if one repeats the equation:

$$\begin{array}{r}142857\\+857142\\\hline=999999\end{array}$$

These are not only number sequence partners, but interval inversions too. The 3rd and the 6th are taken out, and together they equal 9, as do all inversions. 1&8, 4&5, 2&7. The digits 1-9 equal 45; 4 plus 5 equals 9.

The central figure of the Enneagram, the **equilateral triangle** comprised of points 3, 6, and 9, can be taken to be 'outside' of the process represented by the 1-4-2-8-5-7 sequence. It represents an entirely different 'order of existence', one that is indeed incommensurable with the order that is suggested by the 6-pointed figure. The 1-4-2-8-5-7 sequence is understood as representing the mundane 'prevailing' order, **the 6 pointed figure represents man;** man was created on the 6th day, he was instructed to work for 6 days, 6 is the biblical number of man and his works. This same sequence traces the six sided figure along the paths of integration and disintegration. In stress 1-4-2-8-5-7-1. In growth the reverse 1-7-5-8-2-4-1

The 369 triangle may be understood as a representation of an extra-ordinary order, outside of the realm of the 'mundane' world. These 3 points of the triangle could represent the Trinity. So within the Enneagram we find 7 and 3 existing in one, as we do in God and we find 3 existing within but separate from 6 as we do in the believer. The Holy Spirit fills the believer, the body is the temple of the Holy Spirit; **1 Cor. 6:19 New Living Translation (©2007)**

"Don't you realize that your body is the temple of the Holy Spirit, who lives in you and was given to you by God? You do not belong to yourself," The Enneagram symbol could be seen as representing God and at the same time representing man and his relationship with God. I believe it symbolizes God's perfect creation of man, man before The Fall.

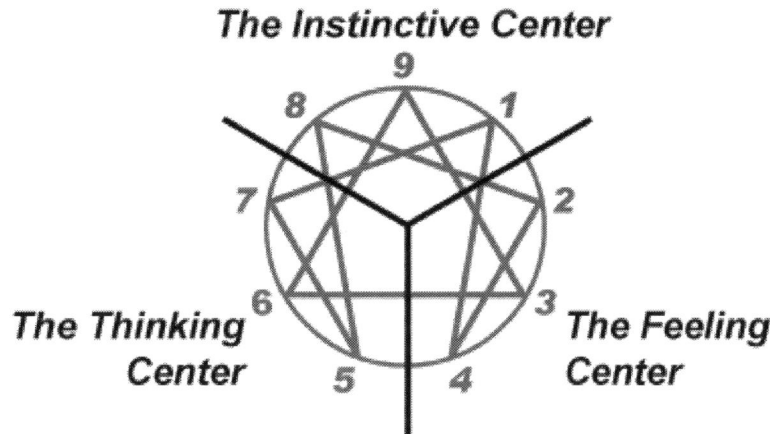

The Centers

The Enneagram is a 3 x 3 arrangement of nine personality types *in three Centers*. There are three types in the *Instinctive Center*, three in the *Feeling Center*, and three in the *Thinking Center*, as shown above. Each Center consists of three personality types that have in common the assets and liabilities of that Center. For example, personality type Four has unique strengths and weaknesses involving its feelings, which is why it is in the Feeling Center. Likewise, the Eight's strengths and weaknesses involve its relationship to its instinctual drives, which is why it is in the Instinctive Center, and so forth for all nine personality types.

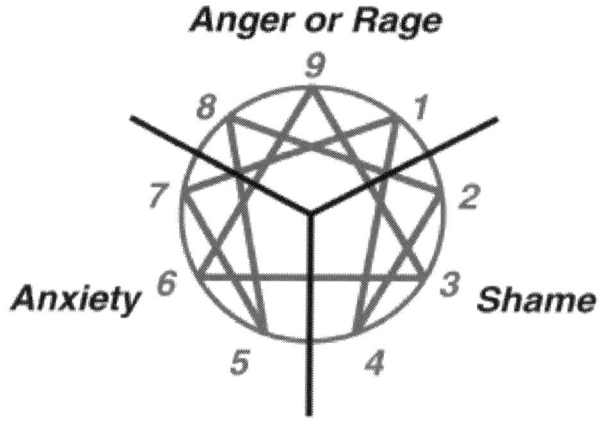

Each center has a dominant emotion. In the Instinctive Center, the emotion is *Anger* or *Rage*. In the Feeling Center, the emotion is *Shame*, and in the Thinking Center, it is *Anxiety* or *Dread*. Of course, all nine types contain all three of these emotions, but in each Center, the personalities of the types are particularly affected by that Center's emotional theme.

Id, Superego and Ego

Sigmund Freud believed there were three structures of the psyche or personality:

- **Id**: a selfish, primitive, childish, pleasure-oriented part of the personality with no ability to delay gratification. "The Child".
- **Superego**: internalized societal and parental standards of "good" and "bad", "right" and "wrong" behavior. "The Parent".
- **Ego**: the moderator between the id and superego which seeks compromises to pacify both. It can be viewed as our "Sense of Self." "The Adult".

Frued's structural terminology can be applied to the Enneagram types, depending on whether the ego, id or superego in each of the nine basic types is the focus of its problem area. The types whose imbalance is in their *egos* are the *withdrawn* types. The types whose imbalances are in their *ids* are the *aggressive* types, and the types whose imbalances are in their *superegos* are the *compliant* types.

Fours, Fives and Nines are all **withdrawn** from the direct expression of their **egos**. They compensate for it in characteristic ways. Fours by dissociating from reality through their imaginations, Fives by dissociating from reality through their all engrossing thought process and Nines by dissociating with reality through an intense association with others.

Ones, Twos and Sixes are all **compliant** to an internalization of someone or something in their superegos which exerts a dominant influence in their behavior. Ones are compliant to their idealistic obligations which are impressed upon them by their **superegos**. Twos are compliant to the demand of their superegos that they always be loving, and Sixes are compliant to an authority figure they have internalized through their superegos.

Threes, Sevens and Eights are all **aggressive**, that is, their **ids** are aggressively oriented to various aspects of their environments. Threes harness their aggressiveness as competition with other people to whom they seek to compare themselves favorably. Sevens are aggressive (acquisitive) toward their environment, from which they try to obtain more satisfaction for themselves, and Eights are aggressive, (self assertive) toward their environment, constantly trying to project themselves in the environment so that it will become a reflection of them.

Integration And Disintegration

The ***Direction of Stress*** or ***Disintegration*** for each type is indicated by the sequence of numbers 1-4-2-8-5-7-1. This means that an average to unhealthy One under stress will eventually behave like an average to unhealthy Four; an average to unhealthy Four will act out their stress like an average to unhealthy Two; an average to unhealthy Two will act out under stress like an Eight, an Eight will act out under stress like a Five, a Five will act out like a

Seven, and a Seven will act out like a One. 1-4-2-8-5-7—and the sequence returns to 1 and begins again. Likewise, on the equilateral triangle, the sequence is 9-6-3-9: a stressed out Nine will act out like a Six, a stressed out Six will act out like a Three, and a stressed out Three will act out like a Nine.

The Direction of Disintegration

1-4-2-8-5-7-1

9-6-3-9

We are often tempted to move in our Direction of Disintegration because the normal and neurotic conflicts we get into compel us to find a quick fix for our emotional needs. The type which is in the Direction of Disintegration seems to be the solution, though it never is.

The ***Direction of Integration*** or ***Growth*** is indicated for each type by the *reverse* of the sequences for disintegration. Each type moves toward integration in a direction that is the opposite of its unhealthy direction. Thus, the sequence for the Direction of Integration is 1-7-5-8-2-4-1: an integrating One goes to Seven, an integrating Seven goes to Five, an integrating Five goes to Eight, an integrating Eight goes to Two, an integrating Two goes to Four, and an integrating Four goes to One. On the equilateral triangle, the sequence is 9-3-6-9: an integrating Nine will go to Three, an integrating Three will go to Six, and an integrating Six will go to Nine.

The Direction of Integration

1-7-5-8-2-4-1

9-3-6-9

The Three Instincts

The three Instincts are a third set of distinctions that are extremely important for understanding personality. A major aspect of human nature lies in our instinctual "hard wiring" as biological beings. We each are endowed with specific instinctual intelligences that are necessary for our survival as individuals and as a species. We each have a *self-preservation* instinct (for preserving the body and its life and functioning), a *sexual instinct* (for extending ourselves in the environment and through the generations), and a *social instinct* (for getting along with others and forming secure social bonds).

Neo-Platonism

I have found very little information in other personality typing systems to explain how personalities change over time, or a model which gives us a goal for improvement (integration) and shows us trends in behavior which we should avoid (disintegration). The Enneagram of personality is a complete model, and is the best tool I have found for understanding human behavior. Knowing why we think, feel and act the way we do and having a model to show us how we can improve can only be helpful. If we understand our strengths and weaknesses and move in the direction of integration, we become healthy. We become better people. We think, feel and act in healthier ways. Is there anything inherently wrong in that?

New Age practitioners who incorporate the Enneagram of personality see integration as the path to spiritual enlightenment. They practice "Releases and Affirmations for each type as practices that can awaken them to higher spiritual qualities." These practices stem from the philosophy of Neoplatonism. **Neo-Platonism** is the modern term for a school of religious and mystical philosophy that took shape in the 3rd century CE, founded by Plotinus and based on the teachings of Plato and other Platonists.

The philosophy teaches that the primeval Source of Being is the One and the Infinite, as opposed to the many and the finite. It is the source of all life, and therefore absolute causality and the only real existence. However, the important feature of it is that it is beyond all Being, although the source of it.

Directly or indirectly, everything is brought forth by the "One." In it all things, so far as they have being, are divine, and God is all in all. Each lower stage of being is united with the "One" by all the higher stages, and receives its share of reality only by transmission through them. All derived existence, however, has a drift towards, a longing for, the higher, and bends towards it so far as its nature will permit.

Neoplatonists believed human perfection and happiness were attainable in this world, without awaiting an afterlife. Perfection and happiness— seen as synonymous— could be achieved through philosophical contemplation.

They did not believe in an independent existence of evil. They compared it to darkness, which does not exist in itself but only as the absence of light. So too, evil is simply the absence of good

Neo-Platonism strongly influenced Christian thinkers (such as St. Augustine, Boethius, Pseudo-Dionysius, John Scotus Eriugena, and Bonaventure). Neoplatonism was also present in medieval Islamic and Jewish thinkers such as al-Farabi and Maimonides, and experienced a revival in the Renaissance with the acquisition and translation of Greek and Arabic Neoplatonic texts.

I do not share these beliefs. Although interesting and having some similarity to Christian beliefs, (one God, the soul and even the existence of Hades) I do not encourage anyone to take the paths of Platonism, Neo-Platonism, Pantheism, Gnosticism or any other path to God other than faith in Jesus Christ.

I believe salvation is by grace through faith in Jesus Christ as Lord and Savior. I am a sinner who needed a Savior, all my works are as filthy rags and I will never be perfect. I strive to the best I can be but only the Blood of Christ makes me Holy and acceptable to God. Spiritual growth comes through Bible study, prayer and the work of the Holy Spirit. Personal growth comes from an awareness of who we are, where we are in life and how we got there. Simply having this knowledge is meaningless without action. We must take steps to improve ourselves and our position in life. Asking God to do it for us while taking no action on our own will not solve our problems, improve our lots in life, or create spiritual growth. The Bible teaches both God's sovereignty and man's responsibility. We have a responsibility to act. God told Noah how to build the ark; He didn't build it for him.

Determining our personality type, our strengths and weaknesses and evaluating our belief systems; then moving toward integration, correcting our premises and forming new belief systems based on scripture, logical thinking and truth are the essence of Create, Connect, Commit to God.

New Age beliefs, Neo-Platonic practices, Gnosticism, Mysticism nor any other religion other than Christianity are not part of the CCC to God philosophy. Self improvement, spiritual growth, connection to God and his people, commitment to God and putting our faith into action by serving are. Any questions?

3.) Does personality typing conflict with my beliefs?

I've already addressed this question.

4.) If others connect the Enneagram to New Age beliefs, Neo-Platonism, Kabbalah and Eastern mysticism, then why do you use it?

Because it is the most accurate and helpful personality typing system I have found and what others use the Ennegram for is of little concern to me. I cannot control what other people do, but this is not going to prevent me from utilizing a tool to self discovery which has nothing inherently wrong with it.

5.) Aren't the teachings found in scripture sufficient? Why do you need to use personality typing?

God's people have always been able to reap the benefits of teachings other than their own without being led astray. Moses and Daniel are perfect examples. Moses was educated in all the wisdom of Egyptians. The writing skills he gained as an Egyptian helped him to pen the first five books of the Bible. Daniel became Chief of the Magi, the hereditary priesthood of the Medes, yet remained faithful and committed to serving God.

Acts 7:22

New International Version (©1984)
Moses was educated in all the wisdom of the Egyptians and was powerful in speech and action.

Daniel 1:4

New Living Translation (©2007)
"Select only strong, healthy, and good-looking young men," he said. "Make sure they are well versed in every branch of learning, are gifted with knowledge and good judgment, and are suited to serve in the royal palace. *Train these young men in the language and literature of Babylon.*"

New International Version (©1984)

Mat 2:1 After Jesus was born in Bethlehem in Judea, during the time of King Herod, ***Magi*** from the east came to Jerusalem
Mat 2:2 and asked, "Where is the one who has been born king of the Jews? We saw his star in the east and have come to worship him."

Who were the wise men or **Magi**?

Magi; In Latin plural of *magus*, in ancient Greek *magos*, in Persian "مغ", in English singular 'magian', 'mage', 'magus', 'magusian', 'magusaean'. Magi is a term, used since at least the 4th century BCE, to denote a follower of Zoroaster, or rather, a follower of what the Hellenistic world associated Zoroaster with, which was – in the main – the ability to read the stars, and manipulate the fate that the stars foretold. Zoroaster, who was perceived by the Greeks to be the **"Chaldean"** "founder" of the Magi and "inventor" of both astrology and magic. The meaning prior to the Hellenistic period is uncertain. In English, the term "magi" is most commonly used in reference to the Gospel of Matthew's "wise men from the East", or "three wise men" (though that number does not actually appear in Matthew's account.)

Most of what we associate with the "Magi" is from early church traditions. Most have assumed that there were three of them since they brought three specific gifts. They are called "Magi," from the Latinized form of the Greek word *magoi*, transliterated from the Persian for a select sect of priests. (Our word "magic" comes from the same root.)

The ancient Magi were a hereditary priesthood of the Medes credited with profound and extraordinary religious knowledge. After some Magi, who had been attached to the Median court, proved to be expert in the interpretation of dreams, Darius the Great established them over the state religion of Persia. It was in this dual capacity whereby civil and political counsel was invested with religious authority, that the Magi became the supreme priestly caste of the Persian Empire, and continued to be prominent during the subsequent Seleucid, Parthian, and Sasanian periods.

One of the titles given to Daniel (Belteshazzar) was *Rab-mag*, the Chief of the Magi.

(English Standard Version (©2001)
O Belteshazzar, chief of the magicians, because I know that the spirit of the holy gods is in you and that no mystery is too difficult for you, tell me the visions of my dream that I saw and their interpretation. **Daniel 4:9**

Daniel's career included being a principal administrator in two world empires: the Babylonian and the subsequent Persian Empire. When Darius appointed him, a Jew, over the previously hereditary Median priesthood, the resulting repercussions resulted in the plots leading to the lion's den. Daniel apparently entrusted a Messianic vision (to be announced in due time by a "star") to a secret sect of the Magi for its eventual fulfillment.

Living six centuries before the birth of Christ, Daniel certainly received an incredible number of Messianic prophecies. In addition to several overviews of all of Gentile world history, the Angel Gabriel told him the precise day that Jesus would present Himself as King to Jerusalem.

It is interesting that Daniel's founding of a secret sect of the Magi also had a role in having these prominent Gentiles present gifts at the birth of the Jewish Messiah. The gifts of gold, frankincense, and myrrh were also prophetic, speaking of our Lord's offices of king, priest, and savior. Gold speaks of His kingship; frankincense was a spice used in the priestly duties. Also, God stipulated in Exodus 30:34-36 that frankincense was to be prepared for the "purpose of sacrificial fumigation". Jesus Christ was killed on Calvary as the Perfect Sacrifice which would be acceptable to God to take away the sins of all who would accept it.; and myrrh was an embalming ointment anticipating His death.

After finding the young child Jesus and presenting their prophetic gifts, the Magi "being warned in a dream" (a form of communication most acceptable to them) departed to their own country, ignoring King Herod's request to keep them informed.

If Daniel could be trained in the language and literature of Babylon and be appointed Chief of the Magi yet retain absolute faith in God to the point that he would surrender his life and be thrown into a den of lions before giving up his convictions; can't we utilize the wisdom of the Enneagram without giving heed to the superstitions and false teachings of others who use the Enneagram for a purpose other than personality typing?

Be Not Deceived

Luke 21:8

<u>King James Bible</u>
"And he said, Take heed that ye be not deceived: for many shall come in my name, saying, I am Christ; and the time draweth near: go ye not therefore after them."

Many times in the Bible we are commanded to *"be not deceived."* The Bible makes it clear that this is our responsibility. Many others will claim to be Christ or show us "another path." These paths lead to destruction.

One of the ways in which we can avoid being deceived is to make absolutely certain that we understand that Jesus is the Way, the Truth and the Life and that no one comes to the Father except through Him. There is no other path to God.

Human wisdom is for our benefit, understanding who we are and why we think, act and feel the way we do will help us take action to correct our weaknesses and improve ourselves. There is nothing wrong with being the best we can be, but salvation is only by grace through faith in Jesus Christ.

1 Corinthians 1:21

<u>New Living Translation (©2007)</u>
"Since God in his wisdom saw to it that the world would never know him *through human wisdom*, he has used our foolish preaching to save those who believe."

Before going any further in the Create, Connect, Commit process, be absolutely certain that you are saved, trusting Jesus as Lord and Savior.

<u>1 John 5:11-12</u> And this is the testimony: God has given us eternal life, and this life is in his Son. The one who has the Son has this eternal life; the one who does not have the Son of God does not have this eternal life.

<u>Isaiah 59:2</u> But your sinful acts have alienated you from your God; your sins have caused him to reject you and not listen to your prayers.

<u>Romans 5:8</u> But God demonstrates his own love for us, in that while we were still sinners, Christ died for us.

According to <u>Romans 5:8</u>, God demonstrated His love for us through the death of His Son, Jesus Christ. Why did Christ have to die for us? Because Scripture declares all men to be sinful. To "sin" means to miss the mark. The Bible declares "all have sinned and fall short of the glory (the perfect holiness) of God" (<u>Rom. 3:23</u>). In other words sin separates us from God who is Holy (righteous and just) and God must therefore judge sinful man.

<u>Habakkuk 1:13</u> You are too just to tolerate evil; you are unable to condone wrongdoing.

Scripture also teaches that no amount of human goodness, human works, human morality, or religious activity can gain acceptance with God or get anyone into heaven.

Romans 3:9 What then? Are we better off? Certainly not, for we have already charged that Jews and Greeks alike are all under sin, **10** just as it is written: "**There is no one righteous**, **not even one**.

Ephesians 2:8-9 For by grace you are saved through faith, and this is not of yourselves, it is the gift of God; it is not of works, so that no one can boast.

Titus 3:5-7 he saved us, not by works of righteousness that we have done but on the basis of his mercy, through the washing of the new birth and the renewing of the Holy Spirit, whom he poured out on us in full measure through Jesus Christ our Savior. And so, since we have been justified by his grace, we become heirs with the confident expectation of eternal life.

Romans 4:1-5 What then shall we say that Abraham, our ancestor according to the flesh, has discovered regarding this matter? For if Abraham was declared righteous by the works of the law, he has something to boast about (but not before God). For what does the scripture say? "Abraham believed God, and it was credited to him as righteousness." Now to the one who works, his pay is not credited due to grace but due to obligation. But to the one who does not work, but believes in the one who declares the ungodly righteous, his faith is credited as righteousness.

God is not only Holy (we can never attain His Holy character on our own or by our works of righteousness) He is also perfect love and full of grace and mercy. Because of His love and grace, He has not left us without hope and a solution.

Romans 5:8 But God demonstrates his own love for us, in that while we were still sinners, Christ died for us.

God's own Son became a man (the God-man), lived a sinless life, died on the cross for our sins, and was raised from the grave proving both the fact He is God's Son and that His death was a substitute for our own.

Romans 6:23 For the wages of sin [is] death, but the gift of God [is] eternal life in Christ Jesus our Lord.

This is why He is called our Kinsman Redeemer. He had to become a man in order to be a substitute for us, yet He had to remain God, Holy; perfect and sinless. His perfect sacrifice is the only one God would accept to cover our sins. Jesus is the perfect lamb without spot or blemish sacrificed on the Passover. We are redeemed by His blood; The Blood of The Lamb.

Col 2:13 When you were dead in your sins and in the uncircumcision of your sinful nature, God made you alive with Christ. He forgave us all our sins,

Col 2:14 having canceled the written code, with its regulations, that was against us and that stood opposed to us; he took it away, nailing it to the cross.

Col 2:15 And having disarmed the powers and authorities, he made a public spectacle of them, triumphing over them by the cross.

Col 2:16 Therefore do not let anyone judge you by what you eat or drink, or with regard to a religious festival, a New Moon celebration or a Sabbath day.

Col 2:17 These are a shadow of the things that were to come; the reality, however, is found in Christ.

On the cross Jesus fulfilled the law. The righteous demands of the law were satisfied in the death of Jesus Christ. The law righteously demanded that the sinning soul should die. Under the ordinances of the Old Testament (the old covenant) believers had the provision that they could take an animal as a substitute and thus cover their sins. But the righteousness of the law had to be satisfied. It was satisfied in the death of Jesus Christ, and so there He brought an end to the law and its authority over man, because the law has now been totally satisfied through His death (and we have a new covenant.)

Romans 1:4 who was appointed the Son-of-God-in-power according to the Holy Spirit by the resurrection from the dead, Jesus Christ our Lord.

Romans 4:25 He was given over because of our transgressions and was raised for the sake of our justification.

2 Corinthians 5:21 God made the one who knew no sin to be sin for us, so that in him we would become the righteousness of God.

1 Peter 3:18 Because Christ also suffered once for sins, the just for the unjust, to bring you to God, by being put to death in the flesh but by being made alive in the spirit.

Because of what Jesus Christ accomplished for us on the cross, the Bible states "He that has the Son has life." We can receive the Son, Jesus Christ, as our Savior by personal faith, trusting in the person of Christ and His death for our sins.

John 1:12 But to all who have received him--those who believe in his name--he has given the right to become God's children

John 3:16-18 For this is the way God loved the world: he gave his one and only Son that everyone who believes in him should not perish but have eternal life. 17 For God did not send his Son into the world to condemn the world, but that the world should be saved through him. 18 The one who believes in Him is not condemned. The one who does not believe has been condemned already, because he has not believed in the name of the one and only Son of God.

If you would like to receive and trust Jesus as your personal Savior, express your faith in Him by praying a sincere prayer acknowledging your sinfulness, accepting His forgiveness and putting your faith in Him for your salvation. There is no other way to be saved. Jesus truly is The Way, The Truth and The Life and no one comes to the Father but through Him.

"Lord, I confess I am a sinner. I ask forgiveness of those sins in the name of Jesus. I believe that Jesus is who He said He was. I believe He died on the Cross for my sins, was buried and rose again on the third day. I accept Jesus as Lord and Savior. Jesus, I ask you to come into my heart right now, and make me a new creation in Christ. I ask this in Jesus name, Amen.

PLAN – DO – STUDY – ACT

God had a perfect **plan**. He created Adam in His own image and fellowshipped with him in a perfect relationship. Adam sinned, fell from grace and ruined the perfect fellowship. Because of Adam's sin, every man's relationship with God fell from its perfect state.

God became a man **(do)**. He walked where Adam walked, He ate what Adam ate, He felt what Adam felt **(study)**. He went to the cross, died for our sins, saved us from damnation and restored the fellowship between man and God **(act)**.

Description of Each Type

Healthy, average and unhealthy refers to a person's psychological state. The goal is to achieve a healthy psychological state. The Enneagram is a model for achieving this state. Being healthy, average or unhealthy has nothing to do with salvation. Salvation is by grace through faith, blood bought by the sacrifice of divine substitution. A person can be saved and still be psychology unhealthy. A lost person can be psychologically healthy, productive and successful. Integration towards the healthy state is a goal for personal growth, not the path to God. But being healthy will allow the spiritual side of one's personality type to flourish. There is a section on prayer for each type, a concept unique to Create, Connect, Commit to God. The prayers focus on improving the unhealthy aspects of each personality type. A section on ministering to each type follows. This information is helpful for ministers, counselors and mental health professionals, as well as the individual. Recognizing behavior trends will help the individual know what type of therapy or counseling they are best suited for. Once you have taken a test to determine your type, read the type description and see if it describes you. If not you have mistyped. If you mistype, you need to pay the fee to take the full RHETI test at **http://www.enneagraminstitute.com/** The Enneagram-Jung test at similarminds.com is good for determining your MBTI type, then you can read your description in this book and see which Enneagram type corresponds.

1
THE REFORMER

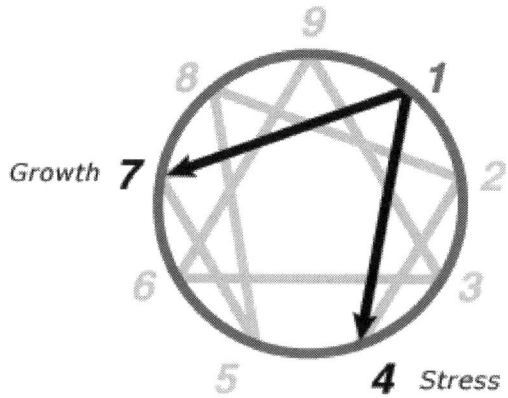

Enneagram Type One

Ones are conscientious and highly ethical people. They have strong morals and a keen sense of right and wrong. They are teachers, organizers and crusaders for change. They are constantly striving to improve things, but afraid of making a mistake. Well-organized, orderly, and fastidious, they try to maintain high standards, but can slip into being critical and becoming perfectionist. They often have problems with resentment and impatience. At their best they are wise, discerning, realistic, and noble.

Basic Fear: Of being corrupt/evil, defective
Basic Desire: To be good, to have integrity, to be balanced
Characteristic role: The Reformer
Ego Fixation: Resentment
Holy Idea: Perfection
Temptation: To be hypocritical
Vice/Passion: Anger
Virtue: Serenity

Key Motivations: Ones want to be right, to ascend to higher levels and to improve everything and everyone. They need to be consistent with their ideals, to justify themselves and to be above reproach so as not to be condemned by anyone.

The Meaning of the Arrows
Stress/Disintegration point: Four. Angry and critical Ones may become moody and irrational like unhealthy Fours
Security/Integration point: Seven. Objective and principled Ones may become more spontaneous and joyful like healthy Sevens

Healthy Ones grow wise, discerning and tolerant of others. They develop a realistic and balanced approach to life. They become rational, conscientious and principled, always being fair and objective. They value truth, justice and personal integrity.

Average Ones are high minded idealists. They strive for excellence in all they do. They are too controlled and see emotions as weakness. They are critical, judgmental, opinionated perfectionists and tend to be workaholics. They can be intolerant, angry and abrasive toward others.

Unhealthy Ones are dogmatic, intolerant, self – righteous and uncompromising. They hate to be proven wrong. They often have obsessive compulsive disorder but act hypocritically doing the opposite of what they preach. They are cruel and condemning toward others, subject to nervous breakdowns and sudden severe depression.

Description

Ones are essentially looking to make things better, because they feel that nothing is ever quite good enough. This makes them perfectionists who desire to reform and improve. Ones are often driven and ambitious, and are sometimes workaholics. They are natural born organizers who make lists and finish everything on them, the last ones to leave work and the first ones to return. They tend to be rational, idealistic, principled, purposeful, self controlled, conscientious and ethical. They have a strong sense of right and wrong and will stand up for a cause they believe in. They are opinionated and outspoken, but often don't realize it. Ones have a fine eye for detail. They are always aware of the flaws in themselves and others. They are teachers, reformers, and advocates for change: always striving to improve things, but afraid of making a mistake. They are well-organized, orderly, meticulous and hypercritical. They try to maintain high standards, but can slip into being critical and judgmental, constantly striving for perfection. Always falling short of the perfection they desire feeds their feelings of guilt and fuels their burgeoning anger against an imperfect world. They tend to feel guilty about their anger however; anger is "bad" and Ones strive sincerely and wholeheartedly to be "good." They generally see emotionality as a sign of weakness and lack of control. They suppress their anger, resulting in impatience, frustration, annoyance and judgmental criticality. For this reason, Ones can be difficult to live with, however they tend to be loyal, responsible and capable partners and friends. They follow the rules and expect others to do so as well. Because they believe so thoroughly in their convictions, they are often excellent leaders who can inspire those who follow them. At their worst they are resentful, impatient and judgmental. At their best they are wise, discerning, realistic, and noble.

Recognizing Type One

Ones may shift attention from their imperfections by making comparisons. They may display a cold anger while denying it. They see anger as wrong, so rather than admit their anger, they will turn a cold shoulder or be passive aggressive while in denial about their behavior. They may ask for criticism and take it seriously. It is a familiar form of love to Ones. They may be more critical of themselves than others. They try to make certain their responses are appropriate at all times. They may resent the expectations of others which they take so seriously. They may be darkly suspicious of sensual pleasure. They may have a black/white, either/or view of many things. Ones live in a small but perfect world. They may be unable to discriminate between big rules and little ones and want to do everything "by the book".

How you can help

Challenge their ideas of perfection. Ask them why it is so important that others follow all their rules, get them to see this about themselves. Bodywork like massage is particularly helpful for Ones. It relieves pent up stress and negative energy. Poetry and art should be included in their prayers, introduce them to the "My Vision" poem in this book. Help them integrate pleasure and fun into their lives, there is more to life than trying to be perfect. Help them learn to criticize their habit of criticism. Help them accept imperfection in themselves and others (this may be your biggest challenge.) Help them make their important norms/rules/obligations relative to the situation. Point out their nit picking in a friendly, constructive way. Show them that it is okay to have emotions and weaknesses. Help them realize that no one is perfect and never will be. Show them that they need to let their values serve them, not to serve their values. **This is the key to becoming a healthy One.** *The Sabbath was made for man, man was not made for the Sabbath.* If they can grasp this principle, they are on their way to integration.

Scripture

Mark 2:27 New Living Translation (©2007)
Then Jesus said to them, "The Sabbath was made to meet the needs of people, and not people to meet the requirements of the Sabbath.

Relating

Ones appear confident, but it is their ideas they have faith in, not themselves. They see themselves as being less than the perfect ideas they strive toward. They subordinate themselves to a value or belief, such as truth or justice and they seek to be as perfect as the value. Ones believe these values are not actually a part of themselves; rather they are ideas they must work toward and can never fully attain. Attempting to reach these standards gives average to unhealthy Ones a sense of superiority.

This is where problems arise. As they move toward disintegration (neurosis) average Ones begin to identify with their values so much that unhealthy Ones think they have ascended to their values and that everyone who has not should be chastised. Unhealthy Ones know they are not perfect yet they think and act as if they were. They want to appear perfect in order to avoid being condemned. They believe they are made righteous by their attempt to become perfect. The more zealous the effort the more righteous they become in their own minds. They believe that by aligning themselves with their values they will always be justified no matter how badly they fail. Aligning themselves with their values also makes them feel they are better than the rest of us. They feel they are among the "Chosen Few" because they know the correct path, the right way of doing things and the way everything "should" be.

Repression and Aggression

Being in the relating triad, Ones typically have a problem with the repression of some part of their psyches. Ones repress their emotions. Their attempts to redirect their emotions result from their quest for perfection. Emotions take a backseat as Ones struggle with the conflict between striving after values and implementing them in the real world. They see themselves as being less than the values they strive for yet give the impression they are greater than the environment which they feel obligated to improve. They constantly compare themselves to the values they strive toward and measure the difference between their present perfection and where they fell short in the past.

Ones also have an internal conflict. They struggle between the calm, cool, rational appearance they put on for the world to see and their repressed feelings. Even though they are not emotional or passionate they are well aware of their emotions. They strive to keep their feelings in check, particularly their aggressive and sexual impulses, but are never quite satisfied with their attempts

Average to unhealthy Ones always feel trapped in these conflicts. There is constantly a conflict between the perfection of their values and their own imperfections, between feeling righteous and feeling sinful, between their desire for order and perfection and the disorder and imperfection they see everywhere, between good and evil, between right and wrong.

The Type One personality corresponds to Jung's extraverted thinking type. They are governed by their values. Whatever high minded ideas they ascribe to become the ruling principles by which they live. Everything that agrees with their principles is right, everything that conflicts with them is wrong.

"This type of man elevates objective reality or an objectively oriented intellectual formula into the ruling principle not only for himself but for his whole environment. By this formula good and evil are measured and beauty and ugliness determined. Everything that agrees with his formula is right, everything that contradicts it is wrong. Because this formula seems to embody the entire meaning of life it is made into a universal law which must be put into effect everywhere all the time; both individually and collectively. Just as the extraverted thinking type subordinates himself to his formula, so for their own good everybody around him must obey it too, for whoever refuses to obey it is wrong – he is resisting the universal law, and is therefore unreasonable, immoral and without a conscience. His moral code forbids him to tolerate exceptions, his ideal must under all circumstances be realized. This is not from any great love of his neighbor, but from the higher standpoint of justice and truth…..."Oughts" and "Musts" bulk large in this programme. If the formula is broad enough, this type may play a very useful role in social life as a reformer or public prosecutor or purifier of conscience……But the more rigid the formula, the more he develops into a martinet, a quibbler, and a prig, who would like to force himself and others into one mold. Here we have the two extremes between which the majority of these types move. (C.G.Jung, *Psychological Types*, 347)

What Jung is describing are various points along the continuum of the One's traits. When they are healthy One's are the wisest, most objective and principled of all the personality types. They deal fairly with others without regard for personal feelings. They are deeply concerned with their values, namely justice, not only for themselves but for everyone else as well.

But when they are unhealthy they try to apply their values to every conceivable situation. They have no room for anyone who disagrees with them. They are convinced that they alone know the truth and their lives stem from that fact. Anyone or anything that contradicts their version of the truth is condemned and deserves to be punished in their minds. The problem for unhealthy Ones is the fact that they are merely human. They cannot control themselves as perfectly as they feel they must. Their impulses can only be repressed for so long; eventually the flesh will win out. This is the inner conflict of the One.

Origins

As children, Ones identified negatively with their father figure. They learned to avoid criticism and condemnation by attempting to be perfect. My ex-wife is a Two with a One wing, and as a child she did no wrong. Little Miss Suzy Homemaker, she aimed for perfection and tried to please everyone by being blameless and doing for them.

Even as an adult she sought her father's approval and strived to have a close relationship with him. Ones got the impression from their fathers or father figures that they didn't quite measure up and must constantly strive to be better. They pushed their own feelings and wishes inside and tried to please everyone else in order to avoid criticism and condemnation. Their own emotions were repressed. They often become obsessive, compulsive and anal retentive; with such attention to detail that the obsession becomes an annoyance to others.

Their fathers may have been absent from the family, abusive or unfair. In my ex-wife's case, her parents divorced when she was young and her father was absent. She had a negative relationship with her stepfather in her teen years. Ones may have a negative relationship with God the Father, fearing eternal punishment, afraid of offending God and being condemned. My ex-wife was overly active in church from an early age. As a child Ones may fear being sent to Hell for natural behaviors like impulsiveness, pleasure seeking, selfishness and other normal childhood behaviors.

Ones were never allowed to be children but were forced to become little adults at an early age. This was definitely the case with my ex-wife, buying groceries, cooking, cleaning house and doing all the yard work at 14 years old. She acted as the mother type for her friends as well. While still 14 she was caught by a State Trooper driving to the store to buy groceries for her mother. We started dating when she was 15 and she was forced to grow up even more, as she was the adult in our relationship.

Because of their childhood situations, Ones determine to be better than their fathers. My ex-wife was determined to be at every school play, sporting event and any other activity my son was involved in and to make sure he had the support and everything else that she never had. She stayed married to me for my son's sake, not wanting him to suffer through divorce as she had. To avoid condemnation Ones feel they must be better than their fathers.

Ones did not rebel against the restrictions placed on them; rather they repressed their impulses and felt guilty about their transgressions. They also come to resent the fact that the burden of perfection was placed on them.

They become jealous and angry at those who do not have this burden placed on them.

Anger

Ones become angry at themselves for their own imperfections and vent their anger by taking it out on others. Instead of resolving their own issues, average to unhealthy Ones make themselves feel better by finding fault with everyone else. This self righteousness could be seen as aggressiveness however Ones are not an aggressive Type. They live by their values and their aggression is the result of a perceived failure to live up to those values; either by themselves or others.

Their anger stems from putting more on themselves than they can bear; perfection is an impossible burden to carry. The fact that they are imperfect conflicts with their value of perfection and they feel guilty, fearing condemnation for anything less than Christ like perfection.

When they are healthy Ones become objective and they accept human imperfections, including their own. They become discerning, moral, tolerant and reasonable. They realize that their values may not apply equally to everyone in all circumstances. But when they are unhealthy they punish others for the least of their faults while rationalizing their own imperfections. They become merciless, having lost their humanity. They serve their values rather than having their values serve humanity

The Healthy One

Healthy Ones allow themselves to be human, they are not afraid of their impulses. They only repress their feelings to a healthy level. Their feelings come into balance and they achieve a healthy state in their psyches. Their subjective and objective sides come into balance and they become objective, realistic and tolerant. They become extraordinarily wise and discerning. By accepting what is, they become transcendentally realistic, knowing the best action to take in each moment. Humane, inspiring, and hopeful: the truth will be heard.

They become conscientious with strong personal convictions: they have an intense sense of right and wrong, personal religious and moral values. They wish to be rational, reasonable, self-disciplined, mature, moderate in all things. Extremely principled, always wanting to be fair, objective, and ethical: truth and justice primary values. They have a sense of responsibility, personal integrity, and of having a higher purpose often make them teachers and witnesses to the truth.

Descriptive Terms; Disciplined, Conscientious, Consistent, Advocate, Idealistic, Crusader, Ethical, Tolerant, Principled, Moral, Just, Good, Fair, Realistic

The Average One

Ones are guided by their consciences. They feel guilt and anxiety when they contradict their values. If they feel they have not met their moral principles and values as perfectly as they should, they begin to strive after an extremely high standard of excellence in everything they do. They want to make everything better. They become people with a mission; propelling themselves and others toward perpetual improvement. The difference between healthy and average Ones is that average Ones want to improve the world according to their own values. They feel the obligation to strive after their values in everything. They relate to the world from a position of moral superiority. They feel they know the way things should be and everyone should listen to them.

Their values define what should be the norm for everyone else. They are convinced they know how everything should be. They feel they should live by their values and so should everyone else. They are on a mission to right wrongs, educate the ignorant, guide the aimless, and instruct others of the "right" view, the world according to their values. They do not trust other people to do the right thing.

They feel they must make the rules which everyone else should follow. Nothing is too small or incidental to be exempted from the imposition of their values. They proselytize their values on others in every area of life; smoking, drinking, use of seat belts, television, music, pornography, nothing is too trivial to be ignored. Even when they are truly right, they do not allow others to find out for themselves. They impose their values instead of letting others decide for themselves.

They are constantly evaluating how they measure up to their values. They want to measure their improvement in all areas. They are extremely purposeful always striving for a higher value or goal. Everything they do must be related to their quest for perfection. They only have time for education, not entertainment. They associate themselves with and often lead high minded causes.

Average Ones know exactly where they stand on every issue, and can argue their position with the skill of an experienced attorney. They love to debate and can present their augments effectively. They have tremendous self confidence because they truly believe that their cause is right. They want to shape the world with their values and this is where they run into trouble.

Descriptive Terms; Appropriate, Impersonal, Orderly, Controlling, Right, Proper, Tense, Fixer, Critical, Purist

Unhealthy Ones

Unhealthy Ones will never allow themselves to be proven wrong. Facts and intelligent arguments don't matter, they are never wrong. They are completely and utterly convinced that they are right about whatever they say or do. Their values have become unbending absolutes and unhealthy Ones have no tolerance for any ideas that do not match their own.

Their values are rigid dogmas from which they cannot deviate. They see everything as black or white, right or wrong, good or evil, saved or lost.

There is no gray area and absolutely no room for compromise. The slightest imperfection ruins the whole and in their worlds they must mercilessly root out all imperfection. Trying to live with such standards negates their own humanity. The higher they climb the more of humanity they leave behind. They claim to love humanity, but they despise individuals.

Average Ones include themselves in their criticism and feel guilty when they fail to attain perfection, but not unhealthy Ones. They exclude themselves from their criticism and condemnation. They are supremely self righteous. Their belief in their values justifies them even if they don't put their values into action. They feel that they are right so everything they say and do is right.

Anger is their only emotion. They would like to think that they are impartial in judging wrongdoers but they are motivated by vindictiveness. They would never admit it though; they could never see themselves as being motivated by anything less than perfection.

They are completely intolerant of the beliefs and actions of others. Anyone who disagrees with them is immoral and evil. Their values define what is right for everyone and they feel they must force everyone to live by their values. They will use religion, justice, truth or whatever means available to make others feel guilty or sinful. Their arguments become contradictory and even absurd. For instance; arguing that it is justifiable to murder a doctor who performs abortions, that slavery was a necessary evil for religious conversion and other ridiculous, contradictory positions. They rationalize everything they do; no matter how much their actions contradict their stated values. Their inner conflict makes them angry, and even unhealthy Ones try to repress their anger. They see anger as a weakness and try to stifle it. They attempt self control but their repressed feelings could surface at any time and their anger erupt at even the slightest provocation.

Descriptive Terms; Opinionated, Self-righteous, Inflexible, Compulsive, Non-adaptable, Resentful, Indignant, Nit Picking , Obstinate, Scolding, Punitive, Abrasive, Dogmatic, Obsessive

Subtypes

One With A Nine Wing

The personalities of the One and the Nine reinforce each other. They are both removed from their environments in a sense. The One relates to values and ideas other than the environment and the Nine relates to idealizations of people rather than people themselves. Ones with a Nine wing are somewhat disconnected. William F. Buckley and Peter Jennings are classic examples of this subtype.

Healthy; Unusually moderate and objective in dealing with others, they tend to be dispassionately involved. They have a spiritual, mystical side and are attracted to nature, art and animals rather than humans. They are rational, fair minded, and concerned with truth and justice. They tend to be cold and impersonal but intellectually brilliant and unselfconsciously devoted to principles.

Average; They believe that whoever claims to be noble must conduct himself nobly . One must act in a fashion that conforms to one's position, and with the reputation that one has earned. Combined with the conservatism of Nines, this produces the aristocratic elite, the classic preppie comfortable with the Establishment. Notions of class, privelige and public responsibility are important to them. Their high minded values may lead them into causes either for or against their social backgrounds. They relate more to abstract ideas than to individuals. The One's impersonalness combined with the Nine's disconnectedness makes for people who preach to others from their abstract notions while trying to remain entirely impersonal. Their emotions are subdued, and they have a tendency to be unconcerned about human nature in general. Their mental world is compartmentalized; areas of interest and disinterest, conviction and indifference, discipline and laxity, consistency and inconsistency manifest themselves.

Unhealthy; Completely disassociated from their emotions and contradictions. They resist seeing what does not fit into their world view. They tend to have stifled emotions, intellectually barricading themselves behind stubbornly held opinions. They have little compassion for or identification with others. Unhealthy ones with a Nine wing are extremely intolerant and self-righteous. They readily identify what they see as the evil doing of others and are obsessed with taking measues to rectify it while disassociating themselves from their own hypocrisy. They cause a great deal of harm to others because they do not understand the nature or extent of suffering they inflict on others.

One With A Two Wing

Healthy; The personalities of the One and the Two are somewhat in conflict with each other. Ones are rational and impersonal, while Twos are emotional and involved with people. Although One is the primary type, there is a noticeable degree of warmth and interpersonal focus in this subtype that compensates for the One's emotional control. The Two wing eases the One's tendency to be overly harsh and judgmental. Ones with a Two wing will attempt to be caring and personal; they try to temper the rigor of their values so they can take the needs of individuals into consideration. They mix tolerance with compassion, integrity with genuine concern, and objectivity with empathy. The Two wing offsets the One's demeanor making them generous, helpful, kind and good humored. They are often found in service professions such as nursing and teaching, Tom Brokaw and Jane Fonda are classic examples of this subtype.

Average; They have a desire to exert a personal influence over others; they often proselytize others, though they have good intentions. They are convinced that they are right and well meaning. They feel a sense of personal responsibility for the welfare of others and are frequently involved in public causes. Average Ones want to control themselves while average Twos want to control others; these motives reinforce each other making it difficult for those around this subtype to break away from their influence.

Ones with a Two wing allow themselves clearly defined emotional outlets as a reaction to their self control. They tend to be perfectionist, have a strict conscience, and seek self satisfaction from their own goodness and self importance. They tend to lecture and scold people more than their counterparts with a Nine wing. They are prone to anger and resentment when others don't listen to them. They are thin skinned and do not like their values, ideals, motives or lives to be questioned.

Unhealthy; May be intolerant and condescending to those who disagree with them. May attempt to manipulate others emotionally, making them feel guilty for being less than perfect. They have a tendency toward self deception about their motives and self righteousness when their motives are questioned. They can be hypocritical, guilty of the very faults they condemn in others. Self deception and feelings of entitlement make their defenses difficult to break. The repressed aggression of the One combined with the indirect aggression of the Two build a tremendous amount of covert aggression in this subtype. They may have physical problems, compulsive habits or nervous breakdowns as a result of the anxiety generated by their contradictions.

Disintegration; The One Goes To Four

When neurotic Ones go to four the repulsiveness of their punitive attitudes and actions comes crashing down on them. They see their own corruption and hypocrisy and are rightly horrified. They fear they have sinned to the point that they cannot be forgiven.

They succumb to their subconscious processes, although they are completely unprepared for it. What they discover about themselves fills them with horror, disgust and self loathing. They become shamed of self, fatigued and unable to function. They are tormented by delusional self-contempt, self-reproaches, self-hatred, and morbid thoughts: everything is a source of torment. They suddenly see their emotional chaos and the evil they have done. The values by which they've lived and controlled themselves are no longer of any help.

Their convictions now convict them. They see clearly their hatred, intolerance and cruelty but they go too far and condemn themselves as harshly as they have condemned others. They go from finding nothing good in others to finding nothing good in themselves.

They become depressed, hopeless and emotionally disturbed. They are prone to extreme guilt, self hatred, and emotional torment from which it is difficult to recover. There seems to be nothing worthwhile outside of themselves to which they can reattach, no values or ideals they feel worthy of associating, thus they identify more with the unhealthy four; self loathing, self shamed, self contemptuous, self reproachful, self hating, tormented by self.

They realize that they themselves are the source of their problems; their hypocrisies, hatred, contradictions and twisted passions. It seems the only way to resolve what is tearing them apart is to do away with self. Complete and incapacitating breakdown and suicide are very real possibilities.

Integration; The One Goes To Seven

Ones exercise too much control over their feelings and impulses. When they go to Seven, they learn to relax and take delight in life. They learn to trust themselves. They are more in touch with reality, becoming life affirming, rather than controlled and constricted. They develop a positive outlook on life. They learn that people can please themselves without sinking into the morass of sensuality; pleasure is possible without becoming irresponsible or selfish.

Integrating Ones no longer feel they must make everything perfect. They progress from obligation to enthusiasm, from constraint to freedom of action. They are more relaxed and able to express their feelings spontaneously, thus becoming more productive. They are more in touch with the world, playful and happy.

The burden of perfection has been lifted from them, no longer obsessed with an unattainable standard they realize they can enjoy what is good in life without constantly feeling obligated to improve it. Things do not have to be perfect to be good. They realize much in life is already good and that it is not up to them to improve upon it. They marvel at nature, the beauty of the arts, or the extraordinary accomplishments of others who (though imperfect) make valuable contributions to the world. They realize that people (including themselves) places and things can be less than perfect and still be valuable. They discover that it is frequently possible for them to be flexible without compromising their values. They stop preaching from their abstract values and notions and experience life as it is. They have come down from their heavenly thrones and decided to join the human race.

Prayers for Type One

Lord, deliver me from the feeling that it is up to me to fix everything. Help me to stop focusing on everything that is wrong with things. My desire for order and efficiency no longer controls my life, you do. In Jesus name I ask this, let it be so, amen.

Lord help me to stop fearing and disowning my body and my feelings. I give this fear to you and ask for your guidance in dealing with my feelings. I refuse to be angry, impatient and easily annoyed. I trust you to deal with my emotional and physical distress. In Jesus name I ask this, amen.

Lord, release me from driving myself and others to be perfect. Only you are perfect. Although I strive to follow your example I accept the fact that I am only human and all humans are imperfect. Help me to stop imposing my standards and values on others. In Jesus name I ask this, amen.

Lord, help me not to judge others. Release me from the fear that other people's beliefs and values threaten my own. Take away my bitterness and disappointment with the world. Help me to accept and to stop obsessing over the things I cannot change. Help me to change the things I can and give me the strength I need to make this possible. Release me from rationalizing my own behavior. In Jesus name I ask this, let it be so, amen.

Lord help me to see my own contradictions. Release me from my fear of being condemned for being wrong. Help me to overcome my fear of losing control and becoming irrational. I am through holding myself and others to impossible standards. I know you love me just as I am and I accept your unconditional love. In Jesus name I ask this, amen.

Lord, give me the peace to allow myself to relax and enjoy the life you have given me. I know you accept me and love me unconditionally. I know salvation is by grace through faith and not by works, please release me from my relentless quest for perfection. I accept that the best I can do is good enough. Thank you Jesus, amen.

Lord, I am grateful that others have much to teach me and I have much to learn. Help me to be able to make mistakes without condemning myself. I accept that mistakes are your way of teaching me and release myself from condemnation over them. Thank you for forgiveness Father. I accept my feelings; help me to understand that they are legitimate and that it is normal to feel this way. I am gentle and forgiving of myself, help me to treat others with tenderness and respect. In Jesus name, amen

Lord, help me to be compassionate and forgiving of others. Life is good and all good things come from you. Help me to see the miracles unfolding before my eyes in each day you give me. I love you Lord. Amen.

Counseling

Sections on counseling are intended as advice for licensed therapists and counselors. The information is in no way meant as a substitute for therapy or counseling provided by a licensed professional. The sections are provided for information purposes only. The information is not meant to diagnose, treat, or cure any illness. If you have symptoms of depression or any mental illness, seek professional help.

I recommend having the counselee take the Riso-Hudson Ennegram Type Indicator, the test comes in the book, "Discovering Your Personality Type" and is also available online at The Enneagram Institute's website for a small fee. Both you and the counselee should be comfortable that they have correctly typed before beginning counseling.

Counselors should also read the entire book and incorporate Create, Connect, Commit into counseling. CCC is a scientifically based complete system of change and is effective for helping all personality types. CCC creates enduring change in the lives of followers, and is effective for creating change no matter what the underlying issue. The author assumes no responsibility/liability for the use of the information. The choice of the application of the information is up the reader. No claims or warranties are made and the content is for information purposes only.

Counseling Ones

Ones can be self-critical and self-deprecating. They tend to avoid or analyze emotions. They may be workaholics. They may be depressed or have relationship problems. They can be prone to compulsive behaviors, anxiety disorders, or obsessive-intrusive bad thoughts. They are often egodystonic.

Egodystonic is a psychological term referring to thoughts and behaviors (e.g., dreams, impulses, compulsions, desires, etc.) that are in conflict, or dissonant, with the needs and goals of the ego, or further, in conflict with a person's ideal self-image.

The concept is studied in detail in abnormal psychology, and is the opposite of egosyntonic. Obsessive compulsive disorder is considered to be an ego-dystonic disorder, as the thoughts and compulsions experienced or expressed are often not consistent with the individual's self-perception, causing extreme distress. Ones typically distant themselves from their anger, overcompensating for it with kindness, or engaging in passive aggressive behavior while denying it.

You may find many of the traits of the One when dealing with a Two with a One wing. Keep this in mind for all types. It is important to know their subtype. Traits of the Nine or the Two may be present in the One depending on the wing. Be familiar with the unhealthy descriptions of both subtypes and the path of disintegration.

Ones may abuse substances in an effort to quiet their over active super-ego. It also allows them to express the flip side of being so moral (trap door behavior).Their personal stories may center on comparing themselves to others or resentment for being overlooked. They can deny their pain by comparing it to something worse. They will also deny their anger and aggressiveness. Often aggressiveness is disguised as "fixing the problem."

In marriage counseling, keep in mind they may act self righteous and portray their partner as the one who needs help.

When unhealthy, Ones are obsessive about what seems wrong and how it should be corrected. They become angry, critical of themselves and others and unable to let in any perspective other than the one they think is right. They may picture themselves as alternately good and bad in their either/or, black/white, good/evil world. They fixate on ethics, values, fairness and work before play. They feel the need to fix what they see wrong with the world.

They may express their moral intensity through political action. They fall on either end of the political spectrum.

Childhood Experiences

As children, Ones' basic trust in their own value was interrupted. They were wounded because they were caught off guard by criticism. They took criticism hard, it was humiliating, a blow to the ego that felt more like a blow to the gut. Many Ones remember being criticized for responding spontaneously to pleasure and sensation, or feeling guilt or self condemnation for doing so. They began to distrust their emotions and instincts and relied on their minds instead to discern the rules of survival.

To avoid criticism, Ones learned to internalize values of rightness and goodness. A strong super-ego resulted, sometimes referred to as the "inner critic". Ones were often "good" little boys and girls who were overachievers. Although some remember being rebellious, they were still driven by trying to be good and right according to their values.

In the service of being good, Ones disown their anger. They direct their overt behavior or attitudes into precisely the opposite direction of their underlying unacceptable impulses. This defense mechanism of reaction formation protects them from recognizing their anger or other feelings incongruent with their perfectionist ideals. In other words they can work when they really want to play, or overcompensate for being angry by acting especially pleasant.

Typical Problems for Ones

Many Ones have made personal growth efforts through books or self improvement models before they ever come to a minister or counseling. Their interest in self improvement, their trust in external authority and their often painful internal premises make them receptive to changework. The exceptions are those who turn their internal critic toward others. These "chosen few" don't seek counseling except to improve the people around them.

The problem for Ones is living their values instead of living their lives. It is easier for them to try to be better than they are than to be who they are. Living by values, they are constantly plagued by a sense of unreality. Too many "musts" and should've, could've, would'ves. When they are hit with reality they will recognize that in trying to live out their values, they lost their own identity. This kind of existential crisis, accompanied by symptoms of depression and loss, sometimes brings Ones to counseling.

What To Avoid

Conspiring with the One and their righteous story line or too quickly challenging the One's inner critic are mistakes to avoid. Keep in mind that Ones are hyper alert to criticism; be aware that you may come off sounding more negative to them than you actually are. In transference, Ones may either idealize or criticize the counselor. Idealization will lead to less honesty while being critical can lead them to abandon counseling.

Under stress Ones are unaware of the aura of rage they radiate. They can look tense and rigid, perhaps frowning or clenching their jaw. This can be intimidating. Caught in counter transference, the counselor could feel defensive or anxious because of this. Remember, Ones are not aware that they are projecting this anger.

Ones may not be comfortable in counseling until they understand the "rules". They need to know the formula. If the counselor ignores this need, counseling may come to an abrupt and unnecessary end.

Ones need the counselor to understand how difficult it is for them to ask for what they need. The counselor will have to read into the One, in most cases, they will not directly ask for what they need. If they do, and the request is denied, they may feel ashamed and withdraw. If you turn down a request, always explain why to Ones. Remember they are very sensitive to ethical concerns.

Remember that Ones are authority compliant, usually polite, and come across as strong, all of which can mask their vulnerability. Counselors who overlook this may find that Ones quit their counseling sessions with minimal discussion. Look for cues that they are being defensive, and most of all, listen to them. When they get down to their real feelings, these feeling may turn to anger; then they may feel ashamed of the anger. It is difficult to get to their real feelings, because they may be ashamed of them. Their tendency is to bury their feelings because they make them less than perfect.

Try not to be critical of them; they already have an inner critic at work within themselves. Try to get to their real feelings and help them understand that it is okay to have these feelings. Ones may be charming and intellectual, quickly shifting the conversation to interesting subjects to avoid feelings. This will lead to engaging conversation that avoids any real issue. Your counseling sessions could end up being no more than a friendly chat.

What Works For Ones

Ones need to trust the process before trying to achieve any goals. Most of them are familiar with goal setting; the real work in counseling is about being in the process, regardless of the outcome, and learning that everything is not about control.

Ones need structure and a dependable schedule. They need a regular time for their sessions and a schedule they can depend on. They need to be able to trust the process and have faith in it.

Ones may have difficulty knowing how they feel or what they should feel, help them articulate their feelings. Pose a possibility about their feelings and ask if it fits. Be patient in this process. Use logic and non-judgmental questions. Show that you are interested and most of all that you care.

Since their attention is usually focused on what they are not doing well, it helps when counselors acknowledge their progress. They want to see progress and be rewarded. Help them to feel and accept your positive feedback. Remember that they are gut based people who act as if they are thought based people.

Help them identify the physical signs of emotions; the body sensations connected to emotional states. Ask them what they physically feel when they are emotionally angry and help them to recognize the physical signs. Other habitual inner states have physiological effects that can be identified and worked with. Asking Ones to tune in to their body feelings can shift their focus off their "shameful" anger and can help them step outside of themselves and observe their feelings from a neutral standpoint. It can also help them link their reactions to their habitual driving emotions and childhood beliefs.

Ones will have to address anger in some way, but working effectively with the anger hidden in reaction formation is challenging to say the least. Ones may have as many words for anger as Hindus have for cow, but they will not want to talk about it. They tend to overcompensate for their anger, for instance saying good things about someone who has just wounded them. Although most people would react with anger, Ones tend to put a positive spin on what they believe are unjustified feelings. This spin is unconscious and feels safer than risking a more authentic response.

Exploring with Ones how it feels to uphold the standards of their values can help them admit their true and immediate feelings. But they have to trust that they won't be judged by the counselor the way they judge themselves. When you give feedback, be aware of the One's strong internal critic. If the One's dispossessed anger is exposed prematurely, they may react with denial, defensiveness and shame, widening the gap between what they feel and what they "should" feel. Understand how devastating Ones think their own anger is. Approach it by saying something like "I would like for you to notice something here....." Try to enlist their ability to dispassionately observe themselves.

The anger in a One's reaction formation may take the form of specific complaints or just generalized irritation. Most Ones will admit their feelings of irritation. They see it as a low grade justified sense of anger that supports self righteousness. They don't like to admit their anger however. Angry Ones can devalue the subjects of their wrath and rationalize being unfair.

Ones accomplish much in an angry state of mind and it creates an energy that therapists can work with. Working directly with their anger in the safety of the counseling relationship can free a One from self imposed restrictions. They can move from neurotically trying to control life to appreciating the world as it is. They can also connect with driving issues that are unrelated to the problems they are presenting.

Counselors may need to reassure Ones that it is normal to have needs and even satisfy them. Their resentments often conceal their hidden desires. An angry One may in fact have a need to be appreciated, express sadness, or a need to have more pleasure and fun. If you ask them what they want, they may be stumped by the question. Because having personal needs may expose them to judgment or humiliation, Ones can be afraid to admit them, even to themselves.

When Ones recognize and experience their own displaced feelings they connect with their true selves and their resentful stories melt away. They may have a need that is not being met, like attention, and therefore be secretly jealous of another family member who they feel gets their attention. This jealousy may manifest itself in criticism. This was true in my ex-wife's case. The last 3 years of our marriage and after our divorce, she became just like the people she most criticized. There was an underlying envy or curiosity. She was also jealous of the attention I got from ministry, preaching, writing books and the website. She let it slip a couple of times that it was all about me. This jealousy manifested itself in hyper criticism of me and ultimately resentment.

Shifting a One from their head to their heart can bring a flood of emotions, most notably grief. Bodywork, massage, breathing techniques, dance, exercise, lifting weights, and painting, especially when done for self expression all help Ones connect with their feelings. Such practices can help Ones become more receptive. Recommend play, spontaneity, taking vacations, fun and time outdoors. Such activities create a space in the One's life for serenity. Ones also need to break from some of their self imposed rules. Encourage them to break the rules where it is harmless.

Helping a One uncover childhood beliefs and repressed experiences may reveal important information and promote change. Most Ones were forced to grow up early and be little adults, although they may paint a rosy picture of their childhood.

The Inner Critic

There are many ways to work with the inner critic in counseling. Using ironic humor can help. Having the One name the inner critic and have conversations with it through role playing or journaling can promote insight. If journaling is used, use a different color pen for the inner critic's comments, or have some way of distinguishing them.

Ones may also need to distinguish between their self observer and their inner critic. Encourage them to appreciate how helpful their critic has been in the past while questioning its present vigilance. Asking the inner critic to see an issue from the heart's perspective can also create a shift.

Childhood Origins and Relationships

"When asked what accounted for his success, Albert Einstein replied that he never grew up, and always saw the world through the eyes of a child."

Ones generally idealize their families and resist talking about them out of fear of being disloyal, unfair, or hindering the image they have created of an ideal childhood. Remind them that what they say in counseling is confidential and they can talk about difficult issues without betraying the good. Help them understand that by examining childhood situations, they are not judging the intentions of others; merely examining their experiences and how they shaped who they are.

Ones are afraid that if they fail to be hyper vigilant, their world will fall apart. They often take care of everyone else in their family to avoid looking inward. Counselors should help them make others take responsibility, and help them put true feelings into words. They are living a lie in most cases, exhibiting external power while inwardly being afraid. They fear not being in every situation and they need to put all things into concepts, they fear things such as feelings which they have no words for.

When counseling couples, be aware that Ones often attach new grievances to old resentments. When Ones have been hurt, they require a sincere apology as well as a change in the behavior of the other party before they can move forward. When this is not enough, it may help the unforgiven partner to feel less defensive if the counselor can expose the underlying vulnerability that is the driving force of the One's anger.

While they are slow to forgive they are quick to bring to an end any discussion of the consequences of their own unhealthy behavior in relationships. They use defense mechanisms such as rationalization or aggressively apologizing to prevent hearing about mistakes. They resist letting in new information once they have taken a position. It may be a good idea to schedule separate sessions so a One can ventilate feelings without damaging the relationship. Keep this balanced however. It is important not to make the One feel like he/she is the one who has the problem.

Ones have an inner need to be fair. Encourage them to listen to their bodies and to take time to reflect rather than react. To get past their "my way or the highway" mentality encourage them to brainstorm. When working on a problem, have them write down all possible scenarios and options. This allows the One to be creative.

As Ones shed their righteous images and their damaging behavior, they develop genuine humility and compassion. Help them detach from their perfectionist images and get in touch with who they really are.

Forgiveness

"Be kind to one another, tenderhearted, forgiving one another, as God in Christ forgave you." Ephesians 4:32 RSV

Remind Ones that forgiveness does not mean making the offense okay, acknowledging that they were done wrong is important. Let them know you are not overlooking this fact nor their pain from having been wronged. Explore what forgiveness means; forgiving themselves can be most difficult for Ones. Help Ones become more compassionate towards themselves and to get past their self chastising tendencies.

It can be devastating for Ones who have spent a lifetime doing everything right to have things go wrong. I am not a One, but empathize with this feeling; I was doing all the right things, still bad things happened. Divorce, illness, betrayals and other losses can all feel like a betrayal of their lifestyle of self sacrifice. In my case it felt as though my world had been turned upside down and everything I believed in had been destroyed.

Move them away from their helplessness in a seemingly cruel and unjust world and guide them to see the bigger picture. Evil and suffering exist in the world, and our faith gets us through it, it does not exempt us from it. A faith that cannot survive through evil and suffering is a weak, worthless faith that needs to be lost.

Ones can believe that they are good or bad. Counseling can allow their childhood wounds to be understood and dealt with. Repressed feelings can be accepted and understood. Compassion for themselves leads to compassion for others. Relationships can be observed from a wider perspective. They can become more comfortable with themselves and the inner critic less vigilant. Remind them that grace is the gift of God and they do not have to earn it.

"He who cannot forgive breaks the bridge over which he himself must pass." George Herbert

Final Thoughts

One can believe that they are either good or bad. The safety of counseling can allow their childhood wounds to be understood and grieved. Repressed feelings, including their needy angry feelings can be accepted. Compassion for themselves leads to compassion for others and softens the judgmental tendencies of the One. Relationships can be judged from a wider perspective. As Ones grow more comfortable with who they are, their comparing minds are less vigilant. Grace is especially relevant; they didn't have to earn it. The Sabbath was made for man; man was not made for the Sabbath. Help Ones see that what connects them with others is not perfection; what we share in common with others is our flaws.

2
THE HELPER
Enneagram Type Two

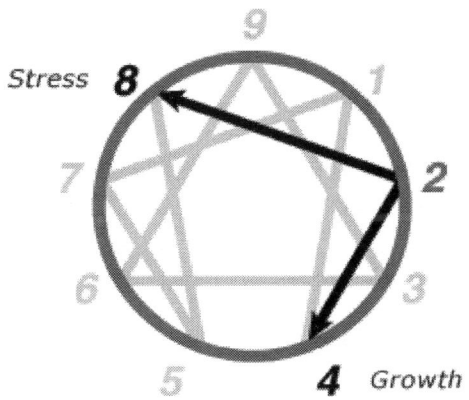

Type Two in Brief

Twos are empathetic, sincere, and warm-hearted. They are friendly, self-sacrificing and generous. They can also be sentimental, flattering, and people-pleasing. They mean well and are driven to be close to others, but can regress into doing things for others in order to feel needed. They typically have problems with possessiveness and with acknowledging their own needs. *At their Best*: unselfish and altruistic, they have unconditional love for others.

Characteristic role: **The Helper**
Ego Fixation: **Flattery**
Holy Idea: **Freedom**
Basic Fear: **Being unworthy of being loved**
Basic Desire: **To be loved unconditionally**
Temptation: **To manipulate others in order to get positive responses**
Vice/Passion: **Pride (specifically, Vainglory, the love of one's own goodness)**
Virtue: **Altruism**

Key Motivation: Twos want to be loved, needed and appreciated. They will coerce others into responding to themselves in order to meet these needs and feel vindicated.

The Meaning of the Arrows

Stress/Disintegration point: Eight (When Twos give without receiving back, they become manipulative and angry like unhealthy Eights. They fail to come to grips with their aggressive feelings)

Security/Integration point: Four (Helpful Twos become emotionally strong, caring, and authentic like healthy Fours when they get in touch with their feelings)

Healthy Twos; Become unselfish and altruistic, giving unconditional love to others. Empathetic, compassionate, warm and caring. Encouraging, selfless, helpful and loving.

Average Twos: Emotional, friendly, well meaning, full of good intentions. Becomes overly intimate and possessive. The self sacrificing parent type who cannot do enough for others. Becomes self important; feels indispensible, overrates actions on behalf of others. Can be overbearing and patronizing.

Unhealthy Twos: Manipulative and self serving; puts others in his/her debt and makes them feel guilty. Self deceptive about true motives and own behavior. Feels entitled to get whatever he/she wants from others. The martyr; feels abused, bitter, resentful and angry, can lead to health problem

Description

Twos are sincere and warm-hearted givers. They show their affection by doing for others. They are people oriented. They can be friendly, generous, and self-sacrificing, but can also be flattering, and people-pleasing; doing things for others in order to be needed. They typically have problems with intimacy and with acknowledging their own needs. They can be unselfish and altruistic, having unconditional love for others or become controlling and manipulative, creating needs in other peoples' lives so that they can fulfill them. They get their sense of self worth from being needed and appreciated by others.

They have a Basic Fear of being unwanted or unworthy of being loved. They want to be loved, needed and appreciated. Being generous and going out of their way for others makes Twos feel that theirs is the most fulfilling way to live. The love and empathy they feel and the genuine good they do gives them a sense of purpose and fulfillment. They have a hard time saying no and often wear themselves out doing for others, neglecting their own needs to take care of everyone else's.

They can be loving, helpful, generous, kind and considerate. People are easily drawn to them. They work so hard to be tactful and considerate of others that they often suppress their own feelings. They relate to people and make friends easily; they know what people need. They are generous, caring, warm, perceptive and sensitive to others' feelings. They are enthusiastic, fun loving and have a good sense of humor.

At their best they are the embodiment of "the good parent" that everyone wishes they had. At their worst they can be proud, self-deceiving about their true motives, have a tendency to become over-involved and controlling in the lives of others, and the tendency to manipulate others in order to get their own emotional needs met.

Recognizing Type Two

They may feel unappreciated, longing for approval and not receiving it. They may not be able to express the intense emotions they feel. They may lack an inner definition of self. They are often unable to distinguish their feelings from their social group's feelings. They may have difficulty making their own needs known. They do not see why they should be ashamed of manipulation. They are often unable to distinguish thoughts from feelings. They may experience betrayal of self in order to affiliate with others or hang on to a relationship. They may neglect their own health while taking care of others. They may not pay enough attention to recognize their inner confusion.

How You Can Help

Encourage solitude. It relieves the pressure to affiliate. Quiet reflection helps Twos find their own identities. Among all activities, help them find their true identity. Remember, "What you don't get up front, you get out back." Have them answer this question, "How do you take control?" In a constructive way, help them see that they try to control others. Help them to identify and understand their negative feelings.(You will have a hard time getting them to admit them) Help them face and work through their anger at not being appreciated, not getting approval, and not receiving strong enough emotional support. Their anger will show up when they realize they are angry at having given themselves away, such as in sexual relationships, but in other ways as well. Help them face their frustration at conforming to others' needs, whims, and expectations. Help them face their co-dependent nature. Contrast it with freedom. Ask who owns their friends' feelings. Watch out; they may answer in a way they think will win your approval. This is the challenge when working with a Two, they may just want to please you. Unhealthy Twos are the most difficult to help, as they cannot see any of their own behavior as a problem. They see everything they do as good. Let them know how much you love and appreciate them. Give warm thanks for their acts of kindness. Let them know when they overstep your boundaries. Show them your genuine love for them, not for what they do for you. In the Gospel of Luke, Martha was a Two, distracted by all the work she was doing to win Jesus' approval.

Scripture

Luk 10:38-42 As Jesus and his disciples were on their way, he came to a village where a woman named Martha opened her home to him.
 She had a sister called Mary, who sat at the Lord's feet listening to what he said.
 But Martha was distracted by all the preparations that had to be made. She came to him and asked, "Lord, don't you care that my sister has left me to do the work by myself? Tell her to help me!"
 "Martha, Martha," the Lord answered, "you are worried and upset about many things, but only one thing is needed. Mary has chosen what is better, and it will not be taken away from her."

Feeling

Twos are in the feeling triad. Twos have strong feelings for others but potentially have problems with their own feelings. They may express how positively they feel for others while ignoring their own negative feelings altogether. They see themselves as loving, caring people but more often than not there is an ulterior motive behind their caring and doing; they want to have others love them back for their actions. They show their love by doing, doing is being for a two. Their love is not free, expectations of repayment are attached.

Healthy Twos are the most considerate and genuinely loving of all the personality types. They have strong feelings and sincerely care about others. They go out of their way to help people, doing good and serving needs.

Unhealthy Twos deceive themselves about the presence and extent of their aggressive feelings, not recognizing their manipulative and domineering tendencies. Unhealthy Twos are among the most insidious of the personality types because they are extremely selfish. They do terrible harm to others while insisting and believing they themselves are utterly and completely good.

Even average Twos cannot see themselves as they really are. They are persons with mixed motives, conflicting feelings and personal needs they are trying to feel. Behind their seemingly generous nature is the desire to feel their own needs, and this need can lead to manipulation and co-dependency. They deny their ulterior motives and see themselves only in the most glowing terms. They ignore their negative qualities and become self deceptive. Twos' inner development may be limited by their "shadow side"—pride, self-deception, the tendency to become over-involved in the lives of others, and the tendency to manipulate others to get their own emotional needs met. CCC, reframing, creating new boundaries, and personal growth all entail going into the negative places in ourselves, and this very much goes against the grain of Twos, who prefers to see themselves in only the most positive, glowing terms. For example when confronting my ex-wife (a text book Two) about a situation in which she committed a terrible sin, her answer was "Talking about that does not help me hold my head up and go on with life." Admitting they are wrong is not in a Two's nature.

It's difficult to understand how Twos can deceive themselves so thoroughly. It is most difficult to deal with the manipulative way in which they go about getting what they want. The worse they get, the more difficult it becomes to square their totally virtuous perception of themselves with reality. They constantly exonerate themselves and demand that you do the same. They demand that you accept their interpretation of their actions against your better judgment even when it's contrary to the facts.

Twos correspond with Jung's extraverted feeling type;

"Depending on the degree of dissociation between the ego and the momentary state of feeling, signs of self disunity will become clearly apparent, because the originally compensatory attitude of the unconscious has turned into open opposition. This shows itself first of all in extravagant displays of feeling, gushing talk, loud expostulations, etc., which ring hollow: "the lady doth protest too much." It is at once apparent that some kind of resistance is being over-compensated, and one begins to wonder whether these demonstrations might not turn out quite different. And a little later they do. Only a slight alteration in the situation is needed to call forth at once just the opposite pronouncement on the self-same object. (C.G. Jung, *Psychological Types,* 357-358)

Hostility and Identity

Twos have a problem with hostility, although they deny it and conceal their aggression. Their self image prohibits them from being openly hostile. They convince themselves that their aggression is for the good of someone else and not in their own self interest. They fear doing anything openly that would keep others away from them. They live for relationships and their virtuous self image prohibits them from openly being selfish or aggressive. They are in denial about their selfish, aggressive motives and interpret their behavior in a way that fits their self image. This becomes habit and they become self deceived about the conflict between their self image and their true actions and motives. Unhealthy Twos can be very selfish and aggressive while believing they are incapable of either.

They are motivated by the need to be loved and appreciated. Yet they often have difficulty with intimacy. They are always in danger of letting their need to be loved deteriorate into their need to control others. By gradually making others dependent on them, they arouse resentment while demanding that others affirm how virtuous they are. When conflicts arise, average to unhealthy Twos see themselves as the victim. They always feel more sinned against than sinning. They can rationalize anything and when caught with logic will simply cease to discuss the matter. It's as though they feel ignoring the matter and not talking about it will make their behavior go away; if I don't talk about it, then it didn't happen. "I'm sorry" and "I was wrong" are phrases rarely uttered from the mouth of a Two. They see themselves as martyrs who have sacrificed themselves selflessly without being appreciated for it. Unhealthy Twos resentment at being unappreciated can manifest itself in psychosomatic illnesses which force others to take care of them.

Ironically, they do for others in order to gain their love, then fear that they are not loved for themselves alone. They feel they must earn love by being good and doing for others. They fear that others would not love them without them having to earn that love. This eventually leads to resentment and bitterness. It is perplexing to see how badly unhealthy Twos can treat others while justifying everything they do. No matter how unjustified or destructive their actions are they persuade themselves they have nothing but love and the best of intentions at heart. When I was going through my divorce, my ex-wife frequently tried to tell me how much better off I would be and how she was doing this for my best interest. Staying married was not "fair to me." She convinced herself she was acting out of love and the purest of intentions when it was her own act of selfishness that led to our marital problems and eventual divorce. When confronted with the facts, she simply wouldn't discuss it further. Any facts that did not fit neatly into her own virtuous self image were simply ignored and the subject was changed. You cannot reach an unhealthy Two with logic and truth. After our divorce, she became healthy again, and we became close friends.

Though known as the helper, servant type, seemingly unselfish one of the major ironies of all Twos is that unless they are very healthy the focus of their attention is essentially on themselves, although they neither give this impression to others nor think of themselves this way. The welfare of others is not their primary objective. Rather their positive feelings about themselves, reinforced by the positive reactions of others are the true motivation for their generous actions.

Perhaps the biggest obstacle preventing Twos, Threes, and Fours from becoming healthy is having to face their underlying fear of worthlessness. Beneath the surface, all three types fear that they are without worth in themselves, and so they must be or do something extraordinary in order to win love and acceptance from others. In the average to unhealthy Levels, Twos present a false image of being completely generous and unselfish and of not wanting any kind of reward for themselves, when in fact, they can have enormous expectations and unacknowledged emotional needs.

Average to unhealthy Twos seek validation of their worth by obeying their superego's demands to sacrifice themselves for others. They believe they must always put others first and be loving and unselfish if they want to get the love they desire. The problem is that "putting others first" makes Twos secretly angry and resentful, feelings they work hard to repress or deny. Nevertheless, they eventually erupt in various ways, disrupting their relationships and revealing the falseness of many of the average to unhealthy Two's claims about themselves and the depth of their "love."

Twos never see themselves as they really are and neither do others. There is an ever increasing disparity between the appearance of the saintly self-image and the reality of the selfish sinner.

Origins

As children Twos had ambivalent relationships to their fathers, or father figures. **Ambivalence** is a state of having simultaneous, conflicting feelings toward a person or thing. Stated another way, ambivalence is the experience of having thoughts and emotions of both positive and negative valence toward someone or something. A common example of ambivalence is the feeling of both love and hate for a person.

Twos have superego problems which result from their ambivalent orientation to their father figures. This helps explain the fact that the self esteem of a Two is conditional. They do not love themselves unconditionally (like Threes) nor do they lack self esteem (like Fours). Their self esteem is conditional upon their perception that they are absolutely good. They must see themselves as good so they can maintain self esteem and build an identity to which others will respond with the appreciation they desire. Doing is being, and doing for others is a means to get their own needs met.

There's nothing wrong with feeling good about being good, the problem is in needing to feel that they are good all the time. Twos must see themselves as good for others, even when they are anything but good. Ironically, their need to see themselves as good burgeons as they become more self-centered, manipulative and coercive.

Average to unhealthy Twos do everything in their power to be good in their own minds. They also seek reinforcement from others. Self deception is vital. They become destructive of the emotional lives of others while remaining convinced of their own virtue. Several months before our divorce my ex-wife started to express herself to me in what she called "honesty." She made comments to me that destroyed me emotionally, while she remained totally convinced that she was only being honest and her comments were meant to help me. The more cold, blunt, brutally honest and emotionally destructive she became, the more she was convinced that she was doing something good.

Healthy Twos are able to move beyond the needs of their egos and become caring and unselfish. They can express genuine love for others. In contrast, the love of an unhealthy Two is nothing more than a veneer for the desire to dominate others. They do not genuinely care for others or concern themselves with their welfare; they are only interested in their own neurotic needs. Unhealthy Twos do evil in the name of good and can no longer tell the difference.

Healthy Twos

Healthy Twos become deeply unselfish, humble, and altruistic: giving unconditional love to self and others. They feel it is a privilege to be in the lives of others. They are empathetic, compassionate, feeling for others. They are caring and concerned about the needs of others. They are thoughtful, warm-hearted, forgiving and sincere. They become encouraging and appreciative, able to see the good in others. Service is important, but they take care of themselves as well: they are nurturing, generous, and giving—a truly loving person.

Descriptive Terms: Compassionate, Sympathetic, Needed Caretaker, Nurturing, Caring, Tender, Warm, Helpful, Concerned, Giving, Loving, Physically Touching, Feels Needs of Others

Average Twos

They want to be closer to others, so they start "people pleasing," becoming overly friendly, emotionally demonstrative, and full of "good intentions" about everything. They give seductive attention: approval, "strokes," flattery. Love is their supreme value, and they talk about it constantly. They become overly intimate and intrusive: they need to be needed, so they hover, meddle, and control in the name of love. They want others to depend on them: they give, but expect something in return: they send double messages. They become enveloping and possessive: the codependent, self-sacrificial person who cannot do enough for others—wearing themselves out for everyone, creating needs for themselves to fulfill. Codependent best describes them.

Co-dependency is an emotional and behavioral condition that affects an individual's ability to have a healthy relationship. It is also known as "relationship addiction" because people with codependency often form or maintain relationships that are one-sided, emotionally destructive and/or abusive. The disorder was first identified as the result of years of studying interpersonal relationships in families of alcoholics. Co-dependent behavior can be learned by watching and imitating other family members who display this type of behavior or developed as a coping mechanism to compensate for actual or perceived inadequacies.

Co-dependent behavior may be a means by which a person compensates for low self esteem or other issues such as an addiction by a family member to drugs, alcohol, relationships, work, food, sex, or gambling; the existence of physical, emotional, or sexual abuse; or a relationship with someone who is suffering from a chronic mental or physical illness.

Co-dependents generally have low self-esteem and are looking for something external to make themselves feel better. They find it hard to "be themselves." Some try to feel better through the use of alcohol or drugs and become addicted. Others may develop compulsive behaviors like smoking, becoming a workaholic, gambling, excessive volunteering or indiscriminate sexual activity.

They have good intentions. They try to take care of a person who is experiencing difficulty, but the caretaking often becomes compulsive and defeating. Co-dependents often take on the role of a martyr and become "enablers" to individuals in need. They repeatedly bail the needy individual out of trouble therefore denying the needy individual the benefit of learning from the consequences of his/her mistakes.

These repeated bail out attempts allow the needy individual to continue on a destructive course and to become even more dependent on the unhealthy caretaking of the "enabler." As this reliance increases, the co-dependent develops a sense of reward and satisfaction from "being needed." When the caretaking becomes compulsive, the co-dependent feels trapped and helpless in the relationship, but is unable to break away from the cycle of behavior that causes it. Co-dependents view themselves as victims and are attracted to that same weakness in love and friendship relationships. They confuse love with pity. They have a tendency to "love" people they can pity and rescue. They have an unhealthy dependence on relationships, and will do anything to hold on to a relationship and avoid the feeling of abandonment.

Signs of co-dependency include the following;

- **Controlling behavior**
- **Distrust**
- **Hyper vigilance (a heightened awareness for potential threat/danger)**

- **Physical illness related to stress**
- A tendency to do more than their share, all of the time
- A tendency to become hurt when people don't recognize their efforts
- An extreme need for approval and recognition
- A sense of guilt when asserting themselves
- A compelling need to control others
- Caretaking behavior
- Lack of trust in self and/or others
- Fear of being abandoned or alone
- Difficulty identifying feelings or avoidance of feelings
- Rigidity/difficulty adjusting to change
- Problems with intimacy/boundaries
- Perfectionism
- An exaggerated sense of responsibility for the actions of others

From co-dependency they move to becoming increasingly self-important and self-satisfied, feel they are indispensable, although they overrate their efforts in others' behalf. Hypochondria, and psychosomatic pain and illness set in. They become a "martyr" for others. Overbearing, patronizing, presumptuous.

Descriptive Terms; Appreciative, Indispensable, Complimentary, Encouraging, Generous, People Focused, Emotional, Intimate, Catering, Affirming

Unhealthy Twos

They become manipulative and self-serving, instilling guilt by telling others how much they owe them. They abuse food and medication to "stuff feelings" and get sympathy. They undermine people, making belittling, disparaging remarks. They become increasingly negative and critical, criticizing others to make themselves fell more important. For example pointing out that others have obtained their wealth from inheritance or crooked means rather than hard work. Belittling the material possessions of others, they may come across as secretly jealous. Extremely self-deceptive about their motives and how aggressive and/or selfish their behavior is. Increasingly self important, feel that they are indispensible and inflate their own self worth, exaggerate their acts on behalf of others, exaggerate their role at work. They feel their place of employment could not function without them. Domineering and coercive: they feel entitled to get anything they want from others: the repayment of old debts, money, sexual favors. They are able to excuse and rationalize what they do since they feel abused and victimized by others and are bitterly resentful and angry. Somatization of their aggressions result in chronic health problems as they vindicate themselves by "falling apart" and burdening others. Generally corresponds to the Histrionic Personality Disorder. Symptoms include:

- Acting or looking overly seductive
- Being easily influenced by other people
- Being overly concerned with their looks
- Being overly dramatic and emotional
- Being overly sensitive to criticism or disapproval
- Believing that relationships are more intimate than they actually are
- Blaming failure or disappointment on others
- Constantly seeking reassurance or approval
- Having a low tolerance for frustration or delayed gratification
- Needing to be the center of attention (self-centeredness)
- Quickly changing emotions, which may seem shallow to others

Descriptive Terms; Manipulative, Dominating, Possessive, Manipulator, Patronizing, Repressive, Effusive, Prideful, Flatterer, Intrusive, Martyr-Victim-Guilt Producer, For more on this type in the unhealthy states check the provided link, search the internet or look for books on "The Jezebel Spirit." http://www.albatrus.org/english/church-order/women-matters/jezebel_in_our_society.htm

Subtypes

The Two With A One Wing

Healthy; The personalities of the Two and One are in conflict with each other. Twos are emotional, interpersonal and histrionic while Ones are rational, impersonal and self controlled. The two types counterbalance each other. This subtype has a strong conscience and a desire to act on principles. A person of this subtype will treat others fairly no matter what their emotional needs are. They will probably feel conflict between the heart and the head. Alan Alda and Mother Theresa are classic examples of this subtype.

They can do a great deal of good for others, teaching, improving the lives of others and working for a cause. They want to give the best possible service to others and do so with less self regard and more altruism than Twos with a Three wing. They make great teachers due to their objective, intellectual orientation to facts and values as well as the emotional warmth to bring ideas to life. They have a genuine concern for those entrusted to them.

Average; There is a tension between personalism and idealism. As Twos, they empathize with people, but if they have a strong One wing, their abstract values conflict with their feelings, making it difficult to wholeheartedly empathize with others. A part of them remains judgmental and pious. They can be very controlling, both of themselves and others. They are egocentric. Although this is hidden by their values, especially their abstract value of love. They want to be important to others yet be reasonable and objective. They are more subject to guilt and self condemnation than Twos with a Three wing. They tend to be critical of themselves when they don't live up to their own moral standards.

Unhealthy; Self righteous, inflexible and morallistic about whatever they feel is right. It almost impossible to change their minds. Self righteousness and self justification combine with self deception and manipulation to create a person who can never be convinced they are wrong and who always sees themselve as doing good. They are quick to comdemn others and able to justify themselves no matter what they do. They cannot allow themselves to be proven wrong or seen as selfish and they completely deny aggressive feelings. They are subject to hypochondria or body dysmorphic disorder.

The Two With A Three Wing

Healthy; Twos and Threes both relate easily to people, the traits of these two types tend to reinforce each other. They are charming, friendly and outgoing. They enjoy attention from others, are self assured and project a sense of well being and wholesome self enjoyment. They have genuine warmth about them. They tend to be more attractive than Twos with a One wing. Social qualities are valued more than moral or intellectual ones. Pat Boone and John Denver are classic examples of this subtype.

Average; Competiveness and the desire for success and prestige mix with the personality traits of the Two. Twos validate their goodness through others, threes validate their desirability through others; hence there is a calculating self consciousness in this subtype. They are highly aware of what others think of them and how they come across. They are social butterflies. Having the right friends and name dropping are important to them. They have a tendency to be self important and narcissistic, although this will be hidden by the Threes calculation and the Twos self sacrificing persona to some degree. They fear being humiliated and losing status rather than feeling guilty over their transgressions.

Unhealthy; Manipulative, exploitative, deceptive, self deceptive, opportunistic and neurotically entitled to get whatever they want from others. Beneath their apparent charm lies viciousness. They can become extremely hostile toward others. They are potentially psychopathic in the destructiveness they can wreak upon others. They seek to ruin what they cannot have, especially relationships. They are capable of pathological jealousy and violent crimes of passion.

Disintegration; The Two Goes To Eight

Unhealthy Twos fail to come to grips with their aggressive feelings. Even in the depths of their neurosis, they realize they are still coercing the attention of others, and this enrages them. They may become physically ill, but they are not deranged or dissociated from reality. Their consciousness exacerbates their problem with anger.

Illness and physical incapacitation take the possibility of violence out of their hands. Unconsciously, having a physical breakdown has been an adaptive response, but this form of adaptation may not last for long. They may recover and something else may trigger their move to Eight; the eruption of their aggressive feelings into seriously destructive behavior.

Being neurotic, they are in no position to deal constructively with their aggressive impulses. Their bitterness and desire for revenge are directed at those who have frustrated their desire to be loved. They still need to be seen as good however, and can only see themselves as good. Doing evil in the name of good becomes even more common.

When they move to Eight, Twos strike out at those who have not responded to them as they have wanted. Their suppressed hatred comes pouring out, and is openly expressed against those they feel have not loved them sufficiently in the past. Love turns completely into hate, and smoldering hatred into violence and destruction.

A Two at Eight can become physically violent, even murderous. The immediate family is most at risk, the very ones they are convinced they had nothing but good intentions and undying love for. The suffering saint becomes a vengeful monster, sacrificing others instead of doing for them.

Integration: The Two Goes To Four

Going to four allows healthy Twos to get in touch with their feelings, especially their aggressive ones. They become aware of themselves as they really are. They move from unwillingness to examine themselves and their motives toward self discovery. They accept their negative feelings as well as their positive ones. Because Twos at Four become emotionally honest, they are able to to express the full range of their emotions.

For the first time in their lives, integrating Twos unconditionally accept themselves, just as they unconditionally accept others. It becomes possible to give something deeper and more personal to others than they have ever done in the past. And when they are loved by others, it is more gratifying because it is not based on "doing"; others love them for who they are, not what they do.

They may become creative, expressing their feelings in new ways. They become deeper persons, having intuition into the depths of the human condition. Whatever they give to others is now all the more valuable, because integrating Twos are more genuine as human beings in every role of their lives; whether as artists, parents or friends.

Prayers for Type Two

Lord, help me to love others without expecting anything in return. I am grateful for all that you and others have done for me. Thank you for the joy and warmth that feels my heart. Amen.

Lord, grant me wisdom to understand that my happiness does not depend on pleasing others. Help me to let go of my need to do for others and nurture my own growth, development and relationship with you. Help me to accept that you love me for who I am, not what I do. Clear my conscience and my motives and allow me to own all my feelings without fear. In Jesus name I ask this, let it be so, Amen.

Lord help me to accept and acknowledge my negative feelings. Help me to be completely honest with you and with myself. Help me to be who I truly am, not the self image I have created. Release me from flattering others to make them feel good about me, doing things for others to make myself needed, and feeling possessive of others. Amen

Lord, free me from calling attention to what I have done for others and expecting others to repay my help in the way I want. Release me from feeling that others owe me for the things I have chosen to do for them. In Jesus name I ask this, Amen.

Lord, forgive me for making others feel guilty for not responding sufficiently to my needs. Forgive me for my attempts to force others to love me. Release me from the fear that I am unwanted and unloved. Amen.

Lord, release me from all attachment to feelings of victimization and abuse. Forgive me for attempting to justify my aggressive feelings. Release me from all feelings of rage and resentment toward others. In Jesus name, Amen.

Counseling Twos

Twos can be engaging, seductive and flattering towards counselors. They may be attractively dressed and use eye contact to establish a warm, engaging relationship. They may come to counseling wanting to help significant others, or bring them in to have the counselor work on them. This is characteristic of their caretaking role. They are usually focused on relationships and caretaking, relationships are everything to them, and unhealthy Twos will see more in some relationships than is actually there. They will do anything to keep from losing a relationship. They can give without boundaries which often leads to a panicky neediness, anger, exhaustion and demands. They can be disconnected from their own needs, while focused on relationships and caretaking. They may act emotional, prideful and sometimes histrionic.

Histrionic personality disorder (HPD) is defined by the American Psychiatric Association as a personality disorder characterized by a pattern of excessive emotionality and attention-seeking, including an excessive need for approval and inappropriate seductiveness, usually beginning in early adulthood. These individuals are lively, dramatic, enthusiastic, and flirtatious.

They may be inappropriately sexually provocative, express strong emotions with an impressionistic style, and be easily influenced by others. Associated features may include egocentrism, self-indulgence, continuous longing for appreciation, feelings that are easily hurt, and persistent manipulative behavior to achieve their own needs.

Despite the appearance that they are quite the socialites, many Twos feel social anxiety and report using substances before, during and after social events. The purpose is to repress unwelcome feelings, to mask feelings or to be a substitute for feelings.

Healthy Twos are in touch with their own feelings and easily connect with others in an emotional way. They are comfortable with themselves and faithfully follow what is in their own heart. They also recognize and support the best in others.

When they are unhealthy, Twos "give to get" giving other people what they themselves want while hiding the fact that they really want others to reciprocate. They can become controlling, angry and resentful when they don't feel appreciated. They can be indirect, disingenuous, and manipulative. The Two attention style fixates on relationships. They need to be appreciated and will do anything to hang on to a relationship, often seeing more in a relationship than is actually there. They fix on engagement with others, flattery, pleasing and supporting others selectively, being liked and looking good.

The Two persona fits the cultural female ideal. Being supportive, self sacrificing and attentive to others are highly valued feminine traits. Male Twos are not received as well and may find that integrating to Eight is a natural remedy to the feminized image.

Be aware of the wing and be familiar with the unhealthy descriptions of the wings and the path of disintegration.

Childhood Experiences

"Unless you become like a little child you cannot enter the Kingdom of God" Mark 10:15

As children, Twos had the inherent gift of emotional sensitivity and the ability to divine the needs of others. The Twos ability to read others and engage them is present from an early age. Knowing what others need and being able to provide it becomes a source of pride. In my ex-wife's case, being little miss "Suzy Homemaker" got her the attention and sense of importance she needed. When she worked as a babysitter, she would go the extra mile and also clean house. She thrived on the approval she got. In her career, she was an overachiever and her source of inspiration was the comment that she had achieved so much to be so young. As a mother, she was "Supermom", overachieving as in everything else.

These qualities were unconsciously exploited by needy family members. A depressed parent for example. The Two wants to fix the situation. They suppress feelings that might conflict with their giving role. As they get older, they are often drawn into relationships in which they are the caretaker or in which they are going to "fix" the situation. The locus of control is on the person the Two wants to please. Because their needs are met from the approval or appreciation of the people they do for, they are often starving in relation to themselves. They are not nourishing themselves and their own feelings are being unrecognized or denied. They are starving. They feel they have to perform perfectly in order to be loved. Their emotional stability is determined by another's reaction. One on hand they are being manipulated, on the other hand, they are the manipulator. The other person uses them, but they also use the other person to have their own needs met. They never see this though. They only see themselves as giving and as good. They feel they have to earn the love of others. They cannot depend on a love which accepts them for who they are. Whether the original manipulators are still in their lives doesn't matter; they are alive in their psyches. They either project them onto their loved ones or turn them against themselves.

As Twos play the Helper role, they grow prideful, believing they have no needs of their own while knowing what's best for others. They maintain this pride through the defense mechanism of repression. They banish unacceptable ideas or feelings into the subconscious. Twos describe pride as an inflated emotional state in which the needs of others can easily be understood and met. They are most likely not able to recognize pride until they experience the opposite; humiliation. When they don't feel appreciated or when others don't want what they are giving, it feels humiliating to be rejected or for them to realize that they have needs. Their aggressive sides might surface, often to the surprise of others.

By repressing their feelings, Twos deny being vulnerable and having normal needs. They often idealize the roles they play, in marriage for instance, doing the things they think the other person wants from them. They often have co-dependent relationships.

Typical Problems for Twos

The basic problem for Twos is that all their efforts in relationships have not led to getting their own needs met. In counseling, offer the Two the possibility of having their own needs recognized and help them to understand their compulsion to repress their own needs. My ex-wife told me that for years she had denied her own feelings and desires, pushed them inside, took care of everyone else and tried to make everyone else happy. This ultimately led to resentment.

Many Twos come to counseling through couples counseling where the partner was the identified recipient of the counseling. It is hopeful and exciting for Twos to work through their relationship problems since this is familiar territory for them. Some Twos feel that while their focus on relationships has helped them succeed, it doesn't always feel genuine. If the Two grew up with a critical parent, their present successes can feel like failures. Painful past experiences and the hurtful words of a critical parent can haunt them and rob them of the joy of their current success. The anxiety and shame is right behind the kudos.

What To Avoid

Twos are natural healers. They sometimes enter helping professions, they are naturals at it. They identify with the care giving role and may be critical of the counselor's skill. They may feel that they would be better suited to be the counselor. Another challenge is the interpersonal skills of the Two. They may flatter the counselor into thinking they are great. Twos are particularly talented at sensing someone's wound and acting as its healer. It is hard for the helper to be helped. The Two's focus on relationships may also lead to boundary confusion. Avoid becoming "friends", this actually creates work for the Two, and will make the professional boundaries fuzzy. Let the Two know that you like them, but maintain professional boundaries.

A Two's charm and pride, especially about relationships, can effectively mask their needs. They look better than they feel. They match perceived expectations and are easy to misjudge. They may tell you what they think will make you like them. They can look good and function well, hiding the depth of their pain. Twos will flatter and try to please the counselor in an effort to be special and therefore safe. This underscores the difficulty of getting honest feedback from Twos.

What Works For Twos

Ask Twos how they feel, don't assume they are fine just because they look fine. It is helpful to assign writing between sessions. Because they are tuned into the needs of others it's difficult for them to realize what they themselves feel. Have them write about anything that will help you work with them. Ask them to let you know anything that you are not discussing that you should be. Let them know they will be helping you in this manner, since it is in their nature to help.

In counseling, the relationship is always a large part of what helps people. The power of connecting cannot be overstated. This is particularly true with Twos; their wound is about relationships and so is their healing. Help them feel that the relationship with the counselor is a safe one. It is important for them to trust the counselor and believe that counseling will help.

Working With Pride

Good counseling with Twos will inevitably confront their pride. Pride creates a competitive, sometimes subtle dynamic in a Two's relationship. Others can feel overwhelmed from having the Two cast them into subordinate roles while playing the role of special caretaker themselves. This can bring others to distance themselves from the Two to keep from being overwhelmed and "managed" ironically having the opposite effect of what the Two desires. Learning to recognize the negative impact pride can have in a relationship is an important but difficult step for Twos. Then they can begin to understand their own motivation. After a Two's pride is exposed, the needs it covers up may also be revealed. The counselor can then help the client accept their human vulnerability. They need to see through their pride to recognize their underlying fears. It will be difficult to cut through their pride without provoking resistance. It helps to have Twos distinguish between the experience of pride and the experience of humility. Fear is the house of cards under the pride, and Twos are sometime giving out what they really want themselves. To feel humility, they need to get to a place where they can feel deeply loved by God. Quiet reflection in the presence of a loving God will help Twos become teachable and trust that only God can give them what they seek.

The counselor needs to recognize that shame plays an enormous role in having wants and needs. The shame is for not meeting the wants and needs of others perfectly. Twos feel they need to forgive themselves for having needs. Try to show them how normal this is, and teach them that their needs are important and there is no need to be forgiven for having them.

Working With Repression

As the safety of the counseling relationship grows, Twos become more truthful. It is also likely that they will discover feelings of remorse and sadness about the price they have paid for all their helpful behavior. They may have to grieve over the part of themselves they have lost on their way to reclaiming it.

Understand that it is difficult for Twos to recognize their own needs. Many Twos are shame driven. They are not willing or able to accept their own wants and needs, and they adapt to the wants and needs of others. Teach them to focus on themselves for a while.

Consciously spending time alone is essential for Twos. They need to face their fear of being disconnected with others and to reconnect with themselves. Learning to be comfortable with themselves and with their own company has spiritual and psychological benefits. As with all types be aware of the wing. Characteristics of the One or the Three may be present depending on the wing.

"Wonder connected with a principle of rational curiosity is the source of all knowledge and discovery, and it is a principle even of piety." -Horsley

Final Thoughts

Counseling should offer the Two a safe nurturing relationship with clear boundaries. Twos can examine their patterns and motivations and come to terms with their underlying needs. This helps them to become their true selves, independent of what others think. Letting go of the compulsion to do for others in order to be loved gives Twos the choice to nurture themselves as well as others. When their relationships are genuine and not co-dependent they become more fulfilling and the Two's gift of humility allows them to receive the genuine love and appreciation of others.

3
THE ACHIEVER

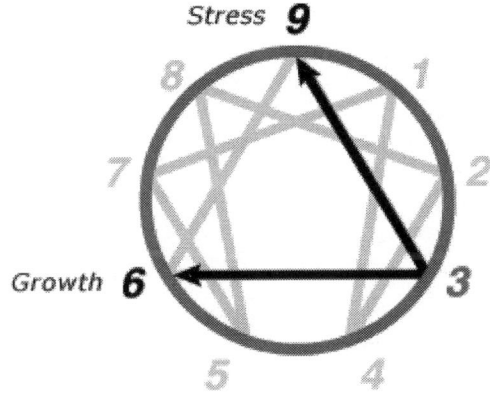

Enneagram Type Three

Threes arc the self-assured, attractive, and charming type. Ambitious, competent, success oriented and energetic, they can also be status-conscious and highly driven for achievement.. They are diplomatic and poised, but can become overly concerned with their image and what others think of them. They typically have problems with being workaholics and competitiveness. *At their Best*: self-accepting, authentic, everything they seem to be—role models who inspire others, CEOs, leaders, politicians, very successful people.

Characteristic role: The Achiever
Ego fixation: Vanity
Holy idea: Hope
Basic Fear: Being worthless
Basic Desire: To be valuable
Temptation: To please everybody

Vice/Passion: Deceit
Virtue: Truthfulness

Key Motivations: Want to be affirmed, to distinguish themselves from others, to have attention, to be admired, and to impress others.

Meaning of the Arrows;

Stress/Disintegration point: Nine (Burnt-out Threes start to disengage themselves from their relentless drive to success and look like unhealthy Nines. They are out of touch with their feelings.)

Security/Integration point: Six (Once they recognize being on top of everything is not all there is to life, Threes find it comfortable to commit themselves to others, like a healthy Six. The commitment to relationships also allows them to explore their emotions.)

Healthy Threes; Internally focused and authentic healthy Threes are everything they seem to be. Self confident, energetic, adaptable, attractive and popular. Driven to excel. The embodyment of many admired qualities and a role model for others.

Average Threes: Highly competitive, average threes are concerned with prestige and status. Success oriented. Image conscious and concerned about appearances. Pragmatic, goal oriented and efficient. Cold and calculating beneath the façade. Self promoting, conceited, make themselves sound better than they are. Narcissistic, arrogant, exhibitionist, hostile and contemptuous.

Unhealthy Threes: Exploitive and opportunistic, unhealthy Threes are out for themselves. Pathological liars, devious, deceptive, betraying. May become vindictive and attempt to ruin the good fortune of others. Sadistic, psychopathic tendencies; sabotage, murder, assassination. A former associate of mine who was also a law enforcement officer was an unhealthy three. He shamelessly and falsely promoted himself. He seemed to be a sociopath, having no conscience and only able to feel his own suffering. He made advances on the wives of other law enforcement officers, even exposing himself to his best friend's wife on one occasion. He had an affair with the wife of a friend who did extensive work for him free of charge and helped to advance his law enforcement career. He stole money from a drug dealer during a search warrant, and then tried to bribe a fellow officer because he thought he had been seen taking the money. The bribe money was turned in to the Sheriff, who as usual, did nothing about it. He used the stolen money to buy equipment for his business. He sabotaged the equipment of his competitors and vandalized their work. After I bought out his share of the business he was a partner in, he sabotaged my equipment and violated a non competition contract. He had an affair with his wife's younger sister who was under aged. He was involved in a shooting which occurred after a physical struggle. He was justified in the shooting, however he lied about how the incident started then tried to glorify himself and use the shooting as a tool for shameless self promotion. He submitted the video of the shooting to a TV program, attempting to glorify himself over this tragedy.

Description

Threes are the success oriented efficient type. They are adaptive, driven and image conscious. Threes are self-assured, attractive, charming often physically attractive and popular. Threes are socially competent, often extroverted, and sometimes charismatic. Ambitious, competent, and energetic, they can also be status-conscious and highly driven. Their confidence often motivates others to emulate them. They are diplomatic and poised, but can also be overly concerned with what others think of them. They need to be validated in order to feel worthy. They secretly fear being or becoming "losers." They can become narcissistic, arrogant, grandstanding and pretentious, allowing hostility for others to rise to the surface. They typically have problems with workaholism and competitiveness. They sometimes have problems with intimacy; their need to be validated for their image often hides a deep sense of shame about who they really are, a shame they unconsciously fear will be exposed if someone gets too close. Even the most "successful" Threes, who on the surface appear quite happy, often mask a deeply felt sense of meaninglessness. At their best they are self-accepting, authentic role models who inspire others. At their worst they are exploitive, vindictive, opportunistic, deceptive, cold blooded and ruthless in the pursuit of their goals.

Recognizing Type Three

Threes will not address their central problem: they are out of touch with their feelings. Their task is to remove their appropriated (false) feelings and replace them with their true ones; which they have but are most likely unaware of. They may be playing to an invisible audience. They often have severe mid-life crises. They often have a radical confusion between themselves and their social group. They may have difficulty separating feelings from roles. They may genuinely feel whatever role they play. They may appropriate a school of thought, spirituality or therapy instead of doing their own inner work. They may overly conform to religious or political party teachings. They think and feel with their community. They may want and overly depend on external signs of spiritual success. They may have an image of God (or some absolute authority) as terribly demanding.

How You Can Help

Invite them to move back into their true feelings. Help them pay attention to their body. Feelings are linked to physical condition and this type particularly links feelings to body image. Help them articulate feelings, especially of sexuality and anger. Help them acknowledge vulnerability. (This will be a major challenge.) Help them notice their conflict between intimacy and achievement. Help them understand that self worth is not determined by worldly success. Help them reframe their image of God and attitude toward authority. Find a group in which they must remain anonymous (like a choir). Help them do things counter to their image. Let them know it is okay to be who they really are, and that they do not have to feel shame for failing to live up to their inflated image. Help them to accept themselves and be authentic. Show them that being on top of everything is not everything. Engage in some non competitive activities. Help them see that everything does not have to be a competition.

Scripture

Mark 8:36 English Standard Version (©2001)
For what does it profit a man to gain the whole world and forfeit his soul?

Feeling

Threes are the primary personality type in the Feeling Triad, they are completely out of touch with their emotional lives. As a result, they suffer from an identity crisis. There is a huge difference between who they are and who they seem to be. The image they project to others is not the reality behind it. In time, their image becomes their only reality. What average Threes appear to be, the image they try to maintain, becomes who they are. This image can be different from moment to moment and from person to person. Their problem is that they have great difficulty in becoming inner-directed; developing themselves according to genuine feelings and realistic limitations.

When they are healthy, Threes are worthy of the admiration of others because they have worked diligently and taken great pains to acquire the skills they have mastered. Their positive self esteem is based in fact, and they are usually highly regarded by others. Healthy Threes embody the best in human nature.

Average Threes become intensely competitive. They want to maintain what they see as their natural superiority to others. Instead of developing themselves, they resort to projecting images that are meant to make good impressions on others. Pragmatic, cold and calculating, their image changes with their needs and their desire to get what they want. They hype themselves to attract admiration.

If they become unhealthy, Threes exploit others so they can maintain their sense of superiority. They become increasingly devious if they see themselves as losing the competition between themselves and others in which they envision themselves as constantly engaged. Extremely jealous, they try to ruin others to achieve the triumph their narcissistic personality desires.

Hostility and Narcissism

Threes are hostile toward anyone who is more successful than they are. This can range from verbal putdowns to outright sabotage and betrayal. They become psychopaths if they are unable to stay on top of others. Threes can get ugly if they do not get the limitless admiration they seek.

Average Threes are narcissists. They build their image upon their grandiose self regard. They seem to be genuinely in love with themselves, but it's actually their inflated images they have a passion for. Instead of loving who they really are, they love a false façade which far outshines the undeveloped person beneath.

Unhealthy Threes care only for themselves. Their interest in others is only to the degree they reflect well upon themselves. They are intensely self centered and have little ability to empathize with anyone else's feelings or needs. Relationships are one sided because both parties are in love with the same person; the Three.

Threes are in constant conflict. Convinced of their own superiority, average Threes are competitive with everyone, including those from whom they seek admiration. Other people are merely an audience that exists for the purpose of offering their endless applause. If they do not applaud, Threes tell them off, humiliate them or even resort to sabotage.

The narcissism of average Threes is not the same thing as genuine self esteem. Underneath the cool exterior, they are not really secure with themselves. Their false sense of self esteem is based on the ability to get the attention of others, not on the development of their true capacities. They project whatever image is needed at the moment to stay in the limelight. Everything they do is done for show.

They actually have a hidden dependency on others which they cannot acknowledge due to the demands of their narcissism. They cannot live with people and they cannot live without them. They are hostile toward the people they depend on and they are nobody without the attention of others. They secretly fear that others are and always will be superior to them.

"The need for a vindictive triumph then manifests itself mainly in often irresistible, mostly unconscious impulses to frustrate, outwit or defeat others in personal relations…

Much more frequently the drive toward a vindictive triumph is hidden. Indeed, because of its destructive nature, it is the most hidden element in the search for glory. It may be that only a rather frantic ambition will be apparent. In analysis alone are we able to see that the driving power behind it is the need to humiliate others by rising above them. (Karen Horney, *Neurosis and Human Growth*, 27-28)

Origins

As children, Threes identified with their mother figure. Their mothers lavished attention on them and they come to expect this from every relationship. They expect the world to admire them unconditionally, just as their mothers did. Because of the importance placed upon them by their mothers, they learned to regard themselves as superior beings, and grow up expecting that the world will require little more of them than to simply show up and receive the admiration and worship they feel they deserve.

The admiring look of approval they got from their mothers made them feel important, and it is the same look they seek from others. Admiration gives them a sense of worth, without they feel empty and hostile because their self image is threatened. By learning to relate to people in this way, Threes did not develop realistically.

The effortless affirmation made Threes feel they had no limitations. They did not develop a superego or a conscience. They developed a super id, so to speak and an overdeveloped persona. They invested their energy in themselves and their images. They envision themselves as people of limitless potential. Because of their belief in themselves, they go far, but they tend to allow their egos and their expectations to become inflated and are often hit with the crushing blow of reality.

Their upbringing and resulting psychological development is a mixed blessing. On one hand, it enables healthy to average threes to achieve their goals to a degree unmatched by other personality types. On the other hand, their lack of conscience and their inflated egos allow unhealthy Threes to exploit others, break the law, and engage in almost any behavior that furthers their agenda without any remorse. Nothing inside them restrains them from exploitive and immoral behavior. They use people shamelessly.

Ironically, while average to unhealthy Threes like to think they are superior to everyone else, in reality they are severely limited. Unless they develop themselves apart from their image and without regard for the approval of others, they will never know what it is to truly be themselves. Their task is to separate their feelings from their roles. This is difficult because they may genuinely feel whatever role they play. It also makes being able to relate to or love anyone nearly impossible. Unhealthy threes are empty. They may seem impressive because they are all advertising; they have learned to build a package designed to impress. They know how to push the right buttons to be admired. But by constantly seeking admiration, they make idols of themselves, worshipping themselves and expecting others to do the same. When others do not bow to them they strike out viciously, revealing their true colors; not as the angelic beings they portray themselves as, but as demons.

Healthy Threes

At their best, Threes are self-accepting, inner-directed, and authentic, everything they seem to be. Modest and charitable, they have a self-deprecating humor and a fullness of heart emerges. Gentle and benevolent, they are self-assured, energetic, and competent with high self-esteem: they believe in themselves and their own value. They become adaptable, desirable, charming, and gracious. They are ambitious to improve themselves, to be "the best they can be." They often become outstanding, a human ideal, embodying widely admired cultural qualities. Highly effective: others are motivated to be like them in some positive way.

Descriptive Terms; Admired, Practical, Creative, Efficient, Accomplished, Impressive, Outstanding, Goal-Oriented, Motivator, Self-starter, Empowering, Energetic, Highly Social, Got it all Together

Average Threes

Average Threes are highly concerned with their performance and doing a good job. They want to distinguish themselves from others. Average Threes want to establish their superiority over others through competition. Rising above others fuels their self esteem and the appearance of superiority makes Threes feel more desirable and worthy of attention and admiration. They outwardly appear grandiose while they inwardly suffer from an inferiority complex. Their drive to be superior to others stems from their need to not be inferior. Terrified of failure, they compare themselves with others in search of status and success. Average Threes create rivalries where none existed. Everything is turned into a contest; their looks, their career accomplishments, the attractiveness of their spouses, everything about them screams "Mine is better than yours." All their relationships end up in this self created competition because they constantly compare themselves to others. All their activity is geared toward winning this competition that is always on their minds. Enjoyment is not what drives the average Three, superiority is. They have and do things not because they enjoy them, but because they make them feel superior.

They constantly drive themselves to achieve goals as if self-worth depends on it. They pursue success with an efficiency unrivaled by any other personality type. The three things average Threes value most are prestige, status and success. Success means being number one. Average threes work hard to get and stay on top. They become careerists and social climbers, invested in exclusivity and being the "best." They are image-conscious; highly concerned with how they are perceived. They package themselves according to the expectations of others and become experts at marketing their images. Pragmatic and efficient, they are also premeditated; they lose touch with their own feelings beneath their glorified facade. They have problems with intimacy, credibility, and "phoniness." They want to impress others with their superiority: constantly promoting themselves, making themselves sound better than they really are. They are narcissistic, with grandiose, inflated notions about themselves and their talents. Exhibitionistic and seductive, they always want the attention focused on them. They live as though they were in front of the camera, acting out the role they must play to maintain their image. Arrogance and contempt is a defense against feeling jealous of others and their success.

Descriptive Terms; Adaptable, Career-Focused, Pragmatic, Opportunistic, Achiever, Ambitious, Image Conscious, Success Oriented, Competitive

Unhealthy Threes

Fearing failure and humiliation, they can be exploitative and opportunistic, covetous of the success of others, and willing to do "whatever it takes" to preserve the illusion of their superiority. Failure is one of the most humiliating prospects for Threes. Once they overextend themselves and are unable to make good on their claims, unhealthy Threes will attempt to maintain their grandiose images by exploiting others. They feel exploitation is necessary to maintain their grandiose self images. Ironically their quest to be superior has led to the development of an image that is not only superior to everyone else, but also superior to themselves. By overshooting the limits of their talents, they have created an image they cannot live up to. They are faced with the option of coming down to earth and recognizing their limitations or taking what they need to maintain their superiority from others. You can guess which one they choose.

The fear of failure and thus humiliation make unhealthy Threes more than willing to lie and cheat to get what they need to maintain the illusion of superiority. They have no principles other than "do whatever works for me." They are devious and deceptive so that their mistakes and wrongdoings will not be exposed. Untrustworthy, maliciously, they betray or sabotaging people to triumph over them. They become delusionally jealous of others and vindictive, attempting to ruin others' happiness. They are relentless and obsessive about destroying whatever reminds them of their own shortcomings and failures. Psychopathic, murder is possible.

Unhealthy Three generally corresponds to the Narcissistic Personality Disorder. The narcissist is described as being excessively preoccupied with issues of personal adequacy, power, and prestige. Theodore Millon identified five subtypes of narcissist:. Any individual narcissist may exhibit none or one of the following:

- **unprincipled narcissist** - including antisocial features. A charlatan - is a fraudulent, exploitative, deceptive and unscrupulous individual.

- **amorous narcissist** - including histrionic features. The Don Juan or Casanova of our times - is erotic, exhibitionist.

- **compensatory narcissist** - including negativistic (passive-aggressive), avoidant features.

- **elitist narcissist** - variant of pure pattern. Corresponds to Wilhelm Reich's "phallic narcissistic" personality type.

- **fanatic type** - including paranoid features. A severely narcissistically wounded individual, usually with major paranoid tendencies who holds onto an illusion of omnipotence. These people are fighting the reality of their insignificance and lost value and are trying to re-establish their self-esteem through grandiose fantasies and self-reinforcement. When unable to gain recognition of support from others, they take on the role of a heroic or worshipped person with a grandiose mission.

Descriptive Terms; Calculating, Defensive, Chameleon, Arrogant, Pretentious, Seeks Admiration, Self-deceptive, Lacks Self Awareness, Self-promoting, Prestige Conscious, Denies and Avoids Failure

Subtypes

The Three With A Two Wing

Healthy; The personality traits of the Three and the Two reinforce each other. Threes with a Two wing have extraordinary social skills; they like to be around people and to be the center of attention. They are charming, sociable and extremely popular. They also tend to be among the most physically attractive of the types. This adds to their social desirability as well as their stimulating effect on others. Arnold Schwarzenegger, Elvis Presley and Brooke Shields are notable example of this subtype..

Depending on how strong the Two wing is, they possess some degree of warmth and positive feelings for people. Threes are not completely without affection of course; they care about those few people they are genuinely close to. They are capable of encouraging and appreciating others, and their feelings can be touched and hurt. They seek affirmation from others; beside attention, they want to be loved. This encourages them to be more responsive to the needs and desires of others.

Average; Able to project their feelings or an illusion of their feelings; actors, models and singers. Histrionic, possessive, controlling, and self important. They care a great deal about what others think of them. Competiveness, comparing themselves to others and success in relationships are important to them. They want their significant other to be attractive, someone who reflects well on them (a trophy wife). Their children are often narcissistic extensions of themselves, as are their homes, hobbies, vacation homes, and other values in their lives. Narcissism is more open than it is in the Three with a Four wing. Enthusiastic and seductive.

Unhealthy; Deceptive about getting what they want from others. Can be self deceptive as well. Manipulative with a feeling of entitlement. They seek revenge against those who do not give them the love and attention they crave. Both the Three and the Two wing have a problem with aggression; Twos when they are unappreciated and Threes when there is any slight to their narcissism. This subtype is particularly hostile if they are not on top.

The jealous of unhealthy Twos and Threes motivates this subtype to coerce others to give them what they want. They become malicious to others, psychopathically destructive. They are deceptive and charming, attractive men and women who seem to have everything going for them until they suddenly become violent. The psychopath beneath the surface usually focuses his/her violence on those they are closest to, who have in some way frustrated their narcissistic needs.

The Three With A Four Wing

Healthy; The personality types of the Three and the Four conflict with one another. The three is interpersonal whereas the Four is withdrawn. Depending on the strength of the Four wing, some people of this subtype seem more like Fours than Threes. They can be quiet, subdued and rather private. They can have artistic interests and aesthetic sensibilities. Sylvester Stallone and Bryant Gumbel are notable examples.

They have some degree of intuition they can direct toward themselves and others. They have more potential for gaining self knowledge and developing their emotions that Threes with a Two wing. They may have an interest in art, though it is more likely to be self serving than creative. They are self assured and stand out, yet introspective and sensitive.

Average; Competitive with others, seeks success and prestige, yet in more subtle ways than Threes with a Two wing. Their imaginations will play a more active role and their feelings will likely be placed on objects rather than people. Threes with a Four wing are usually not as attractive as Threes with a Two wing. They tend to be more of the intellectual type. They tend to be pretentious, putting great stock in their ideals and expecting the same of others. Superiority and arrogance mix with exemption and self indulgence. They may be subtle show offs.

Unhealthy; Alternates between narcissism and self doubt. Subject to narcissism and grandiose fantasies. When anxious, they resort to the Fours depression and self contempt, if only briefly. Corresponds to bipolar disorder but the problem is not a chemical imbalance, it is the narcissism and the lack of fulfillment of their grandiose expectations. Possibly self destructive and suicidal if constantly frustrated by reality.

Disintegration; The Three Goes To Nine

The main problem with Threes is that they are out of touch with their feelings. Disintegration to Nine compound this problem and breaks down the Threes defenses. They deteriorate into neurosis, living in a dreamworld from which they never want to awake. Everything becomes unreal, including the terrible acts they may have committed. They no longer feel enraged, hostile or vindictive. Since those were the only true feelings they had, they feel nothing. They become flat, without interest in anything, not even themselves.

Their image has collapsed, exposing their emptiness. They sink into atypical depression, gaining weight and becoming vegetative. They may experience anxiety for the first time in their lives. If their condition worsens, they may deteriorate even further, into fragmented multiple personalities. Their multiple personalities are probably more accurate depictions of themselves than the false image they projected to others.

Integration; The Three Goes To Six

Going to six is uncomfortable for the Three. It means exposing themselves to the fear of being rejected. Genuine relationships bring the risk that their image will be blown. Intimacy brings the risk that the other will see through their image to the reality beneath, which may still be quite undeveloped.

When healthy Threes go to Six, they make a commitment to something outside of themselves. They face their fear of rejection. They realize that their value is not diminished by being part of something greater than themselves, in fact it helps them to grow within themselves. Solid values take root.

Their newfound commitment to others allows them to expose their true self to someone else, something they are afraid of doing. They may have a religious conversion when going to six. Tearing away the mask and exposing how underdeveloped they are to someone else is easier to do within a committed relationship, because they find they are still accepted.

Falling in love with someone who is clearly their superior will help healthy Threes go to and remain at Six. If they can admire and feel loved by someone they are not competing with, the relationship has a real chance of lasting. Once they have established a committed relationship, it helps them to remain healthy.

When they move to Six, Threes are no longer worried about impressing others with their prestige, success or status, or building themselves up at the expense of others. They use their talents to affirm the value of others rather than themselves. By recognizing the existence of values beyond themselves, integrating Threes develop their consciences.

Prayers for Type Three

Lord, help me to seek first your Kingdom and your Righteousness, then all the things I seek will be added unto me, for you will give me the desires of my heart. Give me a new heart, new desires and a hunger to seek your face. For what does it profit a man to gain the whole world and lose his own soul? In Jesus name, Amen.

Lord, help me to reveal myself without being afraid. Help me to develop the true talents you have given me by accepting who I am. Teach me to delight in the accomplishments and successes of others. I am happy to work for the good of others. I accept that I am responsible to those who look up to me. Help me to accept the love that others give me. In Jesus name, Amen.

Lord, I thank you that I am a New Creation in Christ and thank you for the new heart you have given me. Teach me to be caring and emotionally available. Help me to accept that I have value regardless of my achievements. Release me from driving myself relentlessly to be the best. Free me from comparing myself to others. Help me to stop hiding behind my image and concealing myself behind masks. In Jesus name, Amen.

Lord, free me from the desire to impress others with my performance. Release me from my insecurity; using arrogance to compensate for it, and from craving constant attention and affirmation. Free me from the grandiose expectations I have of myself. Forgive me for misrepresenting myself and my abilities. Forgive me for betraying my own integrity to get the admiration of others. In Jesus name, Amen.

Lord, help me to stop closing down my feelings in order to function. Free me from feeling that I must conceal my mistakes and limitations. Release me from fearing that I am inadequate and will be rejected and from my fear of failing and being humiliated. Forgive me for being jealous of others and their good fortune. Release me from my hostile feelings toward them. I no longer believe that sabotaging others will make things better for me. Amen.

Counseling Threes

Threes are the busy workaholic type. They often speak in slogans or positive thinking clichés. They may list all the things they are doing well, they like to impress and everything is a competition. Their social support system is often weak, although they may think otherwise. They are in an underlying competition even with their closest friends. They can come to counseling because their self image is damaged; they just lost a relationship or an important job. They are egomaniacs who are incredibly insecure. They often exhibit narcissistic characteristics. **Narcissistic personality disorder (NPD)** is a personality disorder defined by the Diagnostic and Statistical Manual of Mental Disorders, the diagnostic classification system used in the United States, as "a pervasive pattern of grandiosity, need for admiration, and a lack of empathy."

The narcissist is described as being excessively preoccupied with issues of personal adequacy, power, and prestige. Narcissistic personality disorder is closely linked to self-centeredness.

Threes avoid introspection, but respond well to suggestions and tasks. It takes more than a few questions to get to heart of the matter. They will respond well to the first few questions, and usefully get defensive or deflect the issue if you try to move beyond that. They may ask where you are going or what the purpose of your questions is if you make them feel uncomfortable. You have to build their trust gradually, remember they are very uncomfortable when the mask comes off. They do not like it when the insecurity behind their image is exposed. You have to read beneath the surface and dig to get to what is really going on, but you must be careful how you go about it.

 In couples counseling, they can demean the other with a competitive style of delivery. Remember that they are in competition with everyone, including their loved ones. Help them positively reframe their role in the relationship.

They may be run down, in poor physical health. When anxious, they can quickly swing to positive spin. Substance abuse can quiet the anxiety caused by neglecting their internal experience. They often have the energy for stellar performance even if their substance use becomes problematic. They are better than average at concealing their addictions.

Healthy Threes are able to tap into their creative sides and manifest what they want through a combination of visualization, positive thinking and hard work. They are flexible, willing to share their abundant energy and value the people in their lives, though sometimes for what the other can do for them or as objects to compete with. They are generally optimistic and accomplish whatever goals they set for themselves.

When unhealthy, they are self serving and competitive, needing all attention to be directed to their accomplishments – real or manufactured. They become dismissive, aggressive and cutting towards whoever obstructs their positive self image. Superficial image management is part of the American consumer culture. This culture supports the false image of the Three so much that it is difficult for them to feel motivated to change.

Be aware of the wing and be familiar with the unhealthy wing descriptions and the path of disintegration.

Childhood Experiences

Success humbles the great man, astonishes the common man, and puffs up the little man.

Threes are usually energetic and creative children, earnestly meeting the world. They are keenly observant of their parents and authority figures and are sensitive to family definitions of success and failure. Recognizing what gets rewarded and approved of by authority figures comes naturally to the Three child. Their accomplishments bring so much positive attention that they begin to think their self worth comes from an external source. They begin to sell what others will buy so to speak, and place their faith in their ability to achieve.

When the truth of their internal experience is in conflict with their external success, they unconsciously choose success. Anxiety over their internal feelings versus the expectations of the external world is assuaged by a compulsion to keep succeeding. They want approval and approval comes through accomplishment.

Most Threes had busy childhoods and many have scrapbooks that document their early successes. They may describe others in their family with an enthusiastic, positive spin, recounting their special qualities and successes. More often than not, feelings were repressed however and success was overvalued.

They are usually the star of their families, with much success and positive reinforcement. They may have played a precocious family role from the beginning, perhaps prompted by circumstances. They may have went to work at an early age or stood out in their families. For some, this role developed outside the family.

As a child, Threes learn to become an image of success by utilizing the defense mechanism of identification – unconsciously adopting the personality characteristics of others whom the Three envies or admires. They learn to feel whatever role they are playing. They identify with a winning image to keep their inner experience from threatening their outer persona. Success is everything to them and they are highly competitive, even with their friends.

Common Problems For Threes

Threes focus on the positive and screen out or discount negative feedback. The American culture amply rewards them for their achievement oriented drive. These facts make it unlikely Threes will seek counseling unless a major crisis provokes it. A serious blow to their inflated self image caused by a job, relationship or loss of status needs to occur before a Three will seek help. Interrupting drug and alcohol abuse or other compulsive behaviors can also precipitate such a crisis. A breakdown in health can also cause a Three to slow down enough to reflect and feel.

When a Three's activity slows, feelings they have repressed may surface, opening the door for inner work to take place. Health problems, an accident, a divorce, job loss or other major life event may cause a Three to slow down and their emotions to thaw. They begin to see through the façade and realize that success often has nothing to do with a person's character. This can lead to a mid life crisis of sorts which may bring them to counseling. When they are stuck in a place they are not successful they want to get out of it. They have a tremendous need to cling to the image of themselves they have shown to the world, and this is a challenge in counseling. To them, that image is who they are and they may not have developed a true self, instead just becoming whatever role they are playing. It takes a tremendous amount of energy to maintain that image, but they usually have the energy in abundance, until they break down. When they can't keep up the image, they are lost. Encourage them to find their true selves and to let go of the image. Let them know that counseling is a safe place to talk about feelings which they find unacceptable in social contexts. Tell them they can talk about all the things they don't want to burden their friends with. That's what you're there for.

What To Avoid

Threes want the counselor to alleviate their anxiety by garnering approval for their performance. What they really need is emotional safety. They may also quickly judge counselors as unlikely to help. Be careful not to respond with impatience, insensitivity or defensiveness. Their self-referencing and competiveness will try your patience. Counseling has to feel safe enough for the Three to drop their mask and reveal their vulnerabilities. They look strong but really need emotional support and TLC. It is easy to scare them away, especially if they expose their vulnerability and then don't feel safe. You have to make them feel comfortable with their guard down and this is not easy to do. Even though they appear confident and strong, they need compassion from the counselor. Be very careful with Threes; until they are ready to see through the farce of their images, being forced to do so can make them suicidal.

The challenge is to see past their camouflage of positivism and get to their real problems. They are motivated to be the most brilliant and successful person you've ever counseled. They may work at therapy like a workaholic. They will try to impress the counselor. Be careful not to buy into the image. They can tell what the counselor wants and will try to please the counselor. Giving tasks or offering a solution to soon should be avoided. Threes are task oriented and in counseling, they are looking for a quick fix. They are hard to read. False feelings done well can be difficult to distinguish from reel feelings. When they are most defended, they will compensate to avoid the appearance, smiling, giving the impression they are on top of everything and in control. They mask vulnerability in the same manner. Counseling could conflict with the Threes defenses. They approach counseling wanting to quickly get to the problem and fix it. One more thing they can do well.

Depression is masked and hard to spot in Threes. They have a lot of energy and depression is masked with high energy. They show the world what it wants to see and do a lot of masking. They have masks to cover pain, vulnerability, dreams, desires, old wounds and to manage intimacy in relationships. Pose a question such as, "Would you let it show if you were in pain or would you hide it?" This may open the door to talk about their masking behavior.

What Works For Threes

Don't settle for appearances with Threes. Probe and ask questions. It is difficult to break down their image and confronting them too quickly will result in them feeling trapped and playing the victim. You have to expose the image gradually and gently. Ask them directly "Is this the image or is this the real you?" That is confrontation enough. Once a Three can work with this distinction you can get to the core of their problems. But the layers have to be peeled back gradually, like an onion skin, one layer at a time to get down to what is real, be patient and kind. Threes can fool people and say the right things, they need a counselor who can stay with them as they work through each layer, and not be diverted by their successful image. As you ask questions let them know you hear what they are saying and ask if there is anything deeper. Give them time to go beneath the image and get to their heart. Remember that beneath the shiny exterior is a person who is really insecure inside and is compensating for this with the image they portray. Peeling away the layers and taking the mask off puts the Three in uncomfortable territory. Trust will have to be established first. Boundaries and rules are helpful for Threes, they like to know what the rules are and what is normal. This helps them feel safe.

Threes have generally not felt their own feelings while they were happening. They can feel encouraged and supported when they find their genuine emotional truth. But the inevitable void behind the Three's image will produce anxiety. The safety of their image is where they will run to when anxiety surfaces. If you begin to expose the emptiness behind their persona they will grow impatient and ask deflecting questions. Look for redirection.

Listen for the Three's unacknowledged feelings and give them feedback. Help them focus on their true feelings and learn to accept those feelings for what they are. If you can evoke the Three's capacity to self observe, their inherent honesty about their image making will often emerge. It will be a struggle to keep them from falling back into the habit of defending an image. Moving from presenting the image to just telling the truth will be difficult, but when Threes start telling the truth it can change the way they relate to others. Instead of always being in the performance mode and spinning everything into what they think the other person wants to hear, they can learn to be honest and be comfortable with who they are.

Being physically tense and deceiving themselves go hand in hand for Threes. As they get used to being honest, they'll recognize the physical signs that go along with deceit. They'll learn that living life without being image driven is a more peaceful existence. When they practice looking inside themselves they'll learn that it is more peaceful to tell the truth than to live a lie.

It helps for the counselor to gain the Three's trust by being honest about themselves. Honesty from the counselor is essential. Honesty from the counselor about their own human failings allows the Three to let go of their need to play a role.

It's a relief for Threes to realize that they are good enough without having to pretend. Help them look for good things they have done that do not depend on their image. Help them understand true friends will accept them for who they are and that letting the image go and being their true self will make them happier and give them energy for other things.

Pressure to Succeed

The competitive paradigm of success and failure is embedded in the American culture and amplified in Threes. Threes want counselors to be mindful of this when working with them. Seeing through the meaning of failure and success is important. Threes have been accustomed to achieving success then immediately moving to start working on their next success.

Being attached to goals interferes with being present, because they are already in the future, perhaps performing for an imaginary audience. Becoming aware of these different states of attention and how they feel in the body can strengthen a Three's self observer. They need to understand the difference in identification with competition and being authentically present. Truth is the most powerful thing. Counseling should provide a safe place to say anything, to feel comfortable, and for the Three to acquaint themselves with how they feel and have an emotional response. Teach them to revel in one success before moving on to the next. Allow them to take some time and learn to enjoy the feeling of accomplishment before setting the next goal and getting focused on that.

I am a firm believer in constantly setting new goals to stay motivated, but this is an obsession with Threes. They need to learn to enjoy success, one success at a time, and not obsess over what is next. They need to examine why success is important to them and look at the feelings underneath the success.

They need to look at failure too. They tend to rationalize it and gloss over it. Feeling the pain of failure is an opportunity to grow. They need to learn the value of having feelings and not just ignoring them. Threes often see beneath their image when they have a clear failure. It can be devastating to realize how competition and the need for approval have actually backfired and caused rejection. There is a battle going on between who they are and who society wants them to be. This is where the counselor can best be a witness for Christ. Helping the Three understand that God accepts them for who they truly are, that there is no need to wear a mask and try to impress God, and that they are not alone. God is with them and there for them to accept who they truly are and help them through their failures. God accepts us just as we are, and there is no pressure to perform or live up to an image. Create a safe place in counseling, where the Three can pray and experience Christ's unconditional love.

Family Origins

The Threes sense of being falsely valued usually has its roots in childhood experiences. Exploring family origins provides an opportunity to revise misunderstandings acquired in childhood. Understanding how they came to feel their value existed outside of themselves can be painful. As they get more in touch with their feelings they often feel angry and need to grieve over how their inner life was co-opted by performing for others. Questions should be framed to unearth what Threes believed was expected of them. Ask where they have placed their hope; get to the pain of not feeling accepted for who they truly are. Let them connect with the vulnerable inner child, and not run from it. Accepting their true feelings ultimately allows Threes to love themselves, giving them the freedom to be authentic.

It takes courage to deconstruct an image that American culture has idealized and taught us to value. Threes will need support to resist reverting to old coping mechanisms. Change often occurs in the unfamiliar territory of rejection and loss and Threes need hope that they can be valued for more than performance. Hope is extremely important. Threes need to know that they can be accepted even when they are not dazzling others with their accomplishments.

Be aware of the wing and be familiar with the unhealthy wing descriptions and the path of disintegration.

Support Groups

Support groups have been helpful for many Threes. Their biggest fear is that no one will be there for them if they see their weakness and they will be all alone. Finding a group like a prayer group, where the Three does not have to perform and is accepted for who they are can be a life changing experience. When they get comfortable telling others about their insecurities and experience love and acceptance, they learn that they have value outside of their accomplishments and image, and can be accepted for who they are.

It's not unusual for Threes to be emotionally isolated. It is a good idea to ask the Three if there is anyone in their life they turn to for help. Find out if there is anyone they talk to when they feel sad or experience failure. Because their support system is often weak, a group can offer a safe haven. By taking the focus off the successful image, groups can support a Three's burgeoning effort at honesty, as well as providing a safe environment which allows them to be a person with feelings. It is helpful to get honest feedback from others. Support groups and counseling should provide the Three with a safe place to stop performing and a mirror in which to see their own authenticity. Help them understand they are a human being, not a human doing. Help them learn to value being present to their true experience over their image which they have sold well. When they let go of the need to compete and impress, they find value in their true identity and personal reality.

Final Thoughts

Counseling should provide the Three with a safe place to stop performing and a mirror in which to see their own authenticity. It is actually a relief to them once the counselor sees through the image and recognizes their wounded self. The Three should be valued for being rather than doing. They learn to value being present to their true experience, not to an image sold well. When they release the need to compete and be the best in everyone else's eyes, they find their true individuality and personal truth.

4
THE INDIVIDUALIST

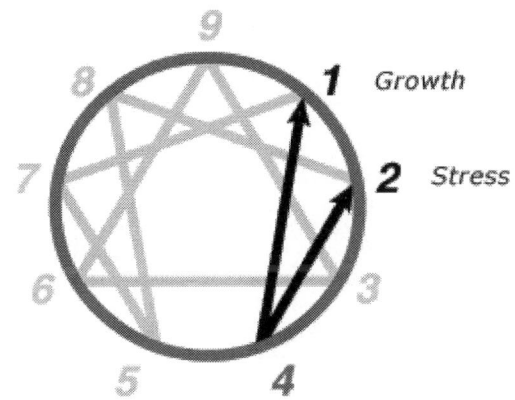

Enneagram Type Four

Fours are self-aware, sensitive, and quiet. They are emotionally honest, very creative, usually personal, but can also be moody and self-conscious. They often withhold themselves from others due to feeling vulnerable and defective. They sometimes feel disdainful and exempt from ordinary ways of living. They typically have problems with melancholy, self-indulgence, and self-pity. *At their Best*: inspired and highly creative, they are able to renew themselves and transform their experiences. Type Four corresponds with the melancholy temperament. I am a Type Six with a Five wing, but due to my melancholy temperament, I share a lot in common with Fours.

Characteristic role: The Individualist
Ego fixation: Melancholy
Holy idea: Origin
Basic Fear: Being commonplace
Basic Desire: To be unique and authentic
Temptation: To beat themselves up and withdraw
Vice/Passion: Envy
Virtue: Equanimity

Key Motivation; Fours desire to express themselves and their individuality. They seek to create and surround themselves with beauty and to maintain certain moods and feelings. They want to withdraw to protect their self-image and they want to take care of their emotional needs before attending to anything else. They want to attract a "rescuer" or a Savior to deliver them.

The Meaning of the Arrows;

Stress/Disintegration point: Two (Disintegrating Fours become dissatisfied like unhealthy Twos)

Security/Integration point: One (Self-actualized Fours are idealistic and progressive like healthy Ones)

Healthy Fours; They become inspired, creative, intuitive and thoughtful. The healthy Four is self aware and self revealing. They are personable, emotionally honest, serious, funny, sensitive and emotionally strong.

Average Fours: Artistic and romantic, they take an aesthetic approach to life, expressing feelings through art, poetry or something beautiful. They become self absorbed, introverted, moody and melancholy. They feel different from others and exempt from living as others do. They get lost in self pity and self indulgence; they have illusions about life and delusions about self. They become dreamers; impractical and unproductive.

Unhealthy Fours: Prone to depression, they become alienated from self and others, self inhibiting and emotionally paralyzed. They are tormented by themselves, self reproaching, self hating and self contemptuous. Despairing, they feel hopeless and turn to self destruction, possibly abusing alcohol or drugs to escape. Emotional breakdown and suicide are very real dangers for the unhealthy Four.

Description

Fours are the sensitive, self absorbed, introspective type. Fours are self-aware and reserved. They are emotionally honest, creative, and personal, but can also be moody, temperamental and self-conscious. Withholding themselves from others due to feeling vulnerable and defective, they can also feel disdainful and exempt from ordinary ways of living. They express themselves through art or something of beauty. They long to be understood and appreciated for their authentic selves, but easily feel misunderstood and unappreciated. They typically have problems with melancholy, self-indulgence, self-pity, and under stress tend to lapse into depression. At their best fours are inspired and highly creative, able to renew themselves and transform their experiences. At their worst they fail to seek practical solutions to their problems, and are prone to fantasize about a savior who will come and rescue them from their unhappiness. They can feel hopeless and turn to alcohol or drugs for an escape from their despair, or worse suffer emotional breakdowns and possibly even attempt suicide.

Recognizing Type Four

Fours are frequently unsatisfied in their relationships, often feeling they are not authentic, profound or satisfying enough. They may be in despair over what seems no big deal to you. Their lives may be structured by tangled relationships. They see things as black/white, either/or, especially relationships. They may take secret pride in their laments, almost bragging about them. They often go through cycles of wanting/getting/rejecting. They may have a present/absent push/pull pattern. They may attach themselves to religion, tradition or a cause for identity reasons. They often seem hypercritical with a disdain for mediocrity. They often present a great deal of dramatic pain.

How you can help

Identify some areas of satisfaction. Help them focus on the good, look on the bright side and see the glass as half full. Recommend a study of

Ecclesiastes. Point out their preoccupation with the absent and unavailable. They want what they can't have, help them appreciate what they do have. This rationality is a good balance for the dramatic unreal emotions they may present. Allow them to ventilate their feelings. Probe for which of their feelings are real. Have them read books by other Fours (Merton, Therese of Lisieux, **The Gospel of John**, Ecclesiastes, Lamentations, Shakespeare, Ann Rice) Let them know what they are really longing for is God. They are longing for a Savior to rescue them, let them know that Savior is Jesus Christ. Help them understand that they can give their worries to Jesus. Art, poetry or writing is helpful, encourage their creative side. Let them know even though God is in control, evil and suffering exist in the world and they are not the only ones who have ever suffered. Prepare them for evil and suffering, help them expect it, be prepared for it and not worry about it but trust God to get them through it. Help them get in touch with their *true* emotions. Explore feelings of shame. Note the flip side of arrogance.

Scripture

Ecc 1:2-4 "Meaningless! Meaningless!" says the Teacher. "Utterly meaningless! Everything is meaningless."
What does man gain from all his labor at which he toils under the sun?
Generations come and generations go, but the earth remains forever.

Feeling

Fours express their feelings in creative ways such as art, poetry, writing, their work or creating something beautiful. They emphasize the subjective nature of feelings in creativity, individualism, introversion, self absorption, self torment and self hatred. They are artists, romantics, and dreamers. They have powerful feelings but feel different from others because they are self aware to a degree that blocks them from getting outside themselves.

The best and worst about Fours is their self awareness. They are in constant conflict between their need to be aware of themselves and their need to move beyond self awareness; between their need to find themselves and their need to escape being trapped in self consciousness. Creativity is the answer to this conflict. In the creative moment when healthy Fours express their emotions without constricting them they produce something beautiful and discover who they are. When inspired they are at the same time most themselves and most liberated from themselves. In the creative moment they are free from the self inhibiting and emotionally paralyzing thoughts that torment them. For a while, the self reproaching, self hating and self contemptuous thoughts give way to the creative expression of who they could be without all the self limiting baggage. This is why all forms of creativity are highly valued by Fours and why inspiration and creativity are so hard to sustain. Fours must transcend themselves to be truly inspired and this is extremely threatening to their self awareness.

Average Fours try to understand themselves by examining their feelings. This introspective search for self leads to such a degree of self consciousness that their subjective emotional states become the dominant reality for them. Though highly emotional, they cannot express their feelings directly. They express their feelings indirectly through the creation of something beautiful.

Fours are internally focused. They feel they are different from most people and they want to know why. They try to find their place in life by withdrawing from it and tracing their emotions. As a result average Fours have difficulty coping with life and Unhealthy Fours have some of the most severe emotional difficulties of all the personality types.

No other personality encompasses both ends of the spectrum to the degree Fours do. They know both the depths to which humans can descend and the heights to which they can climb. In healthy Fours the rich life of the unconscious becomes accessible and is released in all its creative force. Fours sense that they are both spiritual and carnal; they either suffer greatly or become ecstatic over their conflicting nature. Humans exist in a body of flesh but have a spirit that dwells inside and no other type is as keenly aware of the two natures as Fours.

This is why healthy Fours are able to create works of art that others can easily relate to and be moved by. They have been able to unlock the mysteries of human nature by delving deeply into their own.

But alas, like everyone else most Fours do not live at the peak of healthy levels. They turn inward when met with anxiety or stress. They become self conscious, particularly about their conflicting natures and negativity. As an escape, they use their imaginations; they begin to withdraw from ordinary life. They become self absorbed, neglecting people skills and practical applications for management of everyday life. They feel different from others, like outsiders. When unhealthy their negative feelings feed upon themselves. They realize their relentless search for self has led them into a world of useless fantasies and illusions. They hate and torment themselves seeking to destroy what they have become.

Identity Problems

Fours desire to become more conscious of who they really are. But along with their introspection comes more unresolved, contradictory and irrational feelings which they want to sort out before they express themselves. They never feel that their sense of self is strong enough to sustain their identities, particularly if they need to assert themselves. Their sense of identity changes with their feelings. They feel undefined and uncertain of themselves. They can never tell how the next moment will affect them, so it is difficult to count on themselves. Something is missing in themselves, but they can't quite put their fingers on it; they just know they lack SOMETHING.

Average Fours may not know what their feelings are until after they've expressed them. They're afraid they may reveal too much, exposing them to shame or punishment. But by not expressing their feelings, they undermine the possibility of discovering themselves. They are caught in endless self absorption, their consciousness filled with fantasies and memories, ultimately leading to illusions, regrets and a wasted life. Corresponds with the Melancholic Temperament; A person who is a thoughtful ponderer has a *melancholic* disposition. Often very kind and considerate, melancholics can be highly creative – as in poetry and art - and can become occupied with the tragedy and cruelty in the world. A *melancholic* is also often a perfectionist. They are often self-reliant and independent.

Childhood Origins

"Cast all your cares on Him, for you are in His charge." 1Peter 5:7

As children, Fours did not identify with either their mothers or their fathers. They probably had unhappy or isolated childhoods as a result of their parents' relationship, divorce, illness or personality conflicts. Without role models they turned inward and constructed their identities from their feelings and imaginations. They felt alone in life. It seemed to them as though their parents had rejected them for reasons they could not understand. This led them to believe they were somehow defective. Trying to understand themselves became the means by which they hoped to fit into the world. They thought self discovery would help them to not feel so different from others. Their plan backfired though, instead of creating themselves through introspection they became overly self conscious and alienated. They felt vulnerable and helpless to change arousing their aggressions at others, particularly their parents. But because they felt powerless to express their aggression it was turned inward.

Healthy Fours

At their best Fours are profoundly creative, expressing both the personal and the universal, possibly by creating something beautiful. Inspired, self-renewing and regenerating they are able to transform all their experiences into something valuable. Self-aware, self creative, introspective, and on the "search for self," they are aware of feelings and inner impulses. Sensitive and intuitive both to self and others they are gentle, tactful, and compassionate. They are highly personal, individualistic, and "true to self." Self-revealing, emotionally honest, and humane, they have an oxymoronic view of self and life: can be serious and funny, vulnerable and emotionally strong.

Descriptive Terms: Cherishes Beauty, Artistically Expressive, Self-aware, Vulnerable, Inspired, Creative, Intuitive, Refined, Sensitive, Unique, Personal and Revealing, Imaginative

Average Fours

Average Fours take an artistic, romantic orientation to life, creating a beautiful, aesthetic environment to cultivate and prolong personal feelings. They heighten reality through fantasy, passionate feelings, and the imagination. To stay in touch with feelings, they interiorize everything, taking everything personally, but become self-absorbed and introverted, moody and hypersensitive, shy and self-conscious, unable to be spontaneous or to "get out of themselves." They stay withdrawn to protect their self-image and to buy time to sort out feelings. They gradually come to think that they are different from others, and feel that they are exempt from living as others do. They become melancholy dreamers, disdainful, decadent, and sensual, living in a fantasy world. Self-pity and envy of others leads to self-indulgence, and they become increasingly impractical and unproductive.

Descriptive Terms: Self-Absorbed, Feels Different, Enigmatic, Dreamer, Special, Moody, Emotional, Romantic

Unhealthy Fours

When dreams and fantasies fail, they become self-inhibiting and angry at themselves, depressed and alienated, blocked and emotionally paralyzed. They become shamed of self, fatigued and unable to function. They are tormented by delusional self-contempt, self-reproaches, self-hatred, and morbid thoughts: everything is a source of torment. Blaming others, they drive away anyone who tries to help them. Despairing, they feel hopeless and become self-destructive, possibly abusing alcohol or drugs to escape. In the extreme: emotional breakdown or suicide is likely. Generally corresponds to the Avoidant, Depressive, and Narcissistic personality disorders. (See unhealthy type Two description and unhealthy type Three Narcissistic Personality Disorder description)

Descriptive terms: Self-Reproachful, Avoids Ordinariness, Self-pitying, Impractical, Melancholic (see melancholic temperament description), Depressed, Despairing, Alienated, Tormented, Hopeless, Exempt, Fears Success

Subtypes

The Four With A Three Wing

Healthy; The traits of the Four and the Three are somewhat in conflict. Fours are introverted, threes are extroverted. Fours are withdrawn, vulnerable, and self aware. Threes are popular, well defended and lack self awareness. The Fours search for self is in direct contrast to the Threes ability to project an image to others without regard to the real self. The Fours fear of success and fear of exposing themselves is in direct contrast with the Threes charm and extroversion. Nevertheless, both are concerned with self esteem issues; Fours have low self esteem, Threes have high self esteem. This paradox can exist in the same person, although uneasily. Noteworthy examples of this subtype include Tennessee Williams, Paul Simon and Lawrence Olivier.

Because of the Three wing, healthy people of this subtype can be sociable, ambitious and accomplished, often successful in some type of artistic expression. They are in touch with who they are and who they are becoming, but also have an extroverted energy about them. They are usually ambitious, attractive, and popular, having social sensibilities that counterbalances the fours introverted tendencies. They are adaptable, sensitive to others and fun, having a good sense of humor.

Average; Concern for what others think of them helps them out of their self absorption. They project a favorable image, which helps them conceal their real emotional condition more effectively than Fours with a Five wing. They do a good job of concealing their vulnerability and emotional troubles from others. They are competitive and interested in being successful, but they fear failure, self exposure and possible humiliation; they are torn between the need for success and the fear of success.

To the degree that the Three wing is operative, this subtype also has narcissistic tendencies which may serve as partial motives for their behavior. To the degree that their exhibitionistic desires for attention and admiration are unfulfilled in reality, their desires for success can fill their fantasy life and become a focal point for disappointments.

Unhealthy; Since they are still Fours, unhealthy people of this subtype take out their aggressions on themselves. They are self inhibited and alienated from others, depressed and self contemptuous. Depending on the strength of the wing, there will be moments when they act like unhealthy Threes. They can be hostile, malicious and jealous of others. They can be exploitive, opportunistic and duplicitous then feel shame and guilt over these traits. The Threes vindictive malice is rarely acted on by this subtype. If it ever is, neurotic people of this subtype will punish themselves even more severely than they inflict pain on anyone else. Crimes of passion and suicide are possible.

The Four With A Five Wing

Healthy; The traits of the Four and Five reinforce each other. Both are introverted, withdrawn types; Fours to protect their feelings, Fives to protect their security. Very observant of others and their environment. Intellectual but socially insecure. Notable examples include Bob Dylan, Soren Kierkegaard and Hamlet.

Combining intuition with insight, they are the most profoundly creative of the types; having both emotional sensitivity and intellectual comprehension.

Average; Given to introspection, philosophical and religious speculation, their emotional world is their primary focus. They tend to be loners and socialize less than Fours with a three wing, substituting their artistic expressions for themselves. Eccentric, private, independent and unconventional. They are intensely preoccupied with their thoughts. They can be creative in unusual ways. They are usually not interested in trying to communicate with someone who can't understand them. They are interested in expressing their inner vision, no matter how terrifying, bleak or sublime.

Unhealthy; Assailed by self doubt, depression, alienation from others, inhibitions in their work, and self contempt, they resist everything outside the self. If the Five wing is strong, they will resist getting help from anyone, increasing their alienation from others. They tend to project their fears into the environment, resulting in distorted thinking patterns which may include suspicion, paranoia and phobias. Tormented with self hatred, they see very little outside themselves as positive either. They become pessimistic about the meaninglessness of life. This subtype is the most isolated from themselves and from themselves. They are prone to the depressive forms of schizophrenia. Schizophrenia is a mental disorder that makes it difficult to tell the difference between real and unreal experiences, to think logically, to have normal emotional responses, and to behave normally in social situations.

Disintegration; The Four Goes To Two

Neurotic Fours will try to free themselves from their debilitating self hatred in some way, possibly through suicide. They move to Two to escape themselves and become dependent on someone who will provide the love and understanding they have missed.

They are withdrawn for people, but have always wanted and needed people. Their move to Two is an ironic, unintentional acknowledgement of their need for people. They are looking for someone to love them. They believe that if they can find someone who loves them, they can come to love themselves and actualize the good within themselves. Unfortunately neurotic Fours are practically incapable of having a genuine relationship with anyone. They are emotionally disturbed and self contemptuous; they are barely capable of functioning, much less being able to truly love anyone else. They may have some sort of nervous breakdown, indirectly coercing someone to take care of them. Pity substitutes for love. They may also be in financial difficulty and expect to live off someone else. They feel exempt from having any expectations placed on them, even the expectation that they recover.

Ironically, Fours at Two will likely begin to hate the very person they have become dependent upon. Their dependency is a constant reminder of their defects and lack of self esteem. They will alternate between feelings of aggression toward themselves and aggression toward the other. Others will become frustrated with disintegrating Fours because many of their problems were caused or exacerbated by their own actions. They have brought much upon themselves and others will no doubt feel contempt for having to undo what Fours have done to themselves.

They cannot escape the fact that it is futile to attempt to find themselves through someone else since they are filled with self contempt. They will most likely destroy the very relationship they depend on. If deteriorated Fours do not get adequate professional help, they will eventually go insane, create suicide, or both.

Integration: The Four Goes To One

By focusing on something beyond their feelings and imaginations, healthy Fours actualize themselves. They move from subjectivity to objectivity, from self absorption to principled action. They have freed themselves from the cycle of self absorption, no longer controlled by their feelings. Convictions and principles become their motivating forces rather than moods.

They accept that there are values to which it is necessary to submit. They become more disciplined, reaching more of their potential so they can make a difference in the world. By giving up their misguided search for self they find the freedom they have sought through introspection. Ironically, by finally becoming part of the world, they find a context in which to discover themselves.

They no longer think of themselves as different from others. Moving away from self indulgence they submit to reality. They begin to listen to their newfound consciences, willingly putting limits on themselves. Integrating Fours are exceptional teachers, combining objectivity with the riches of the subjective world. Their intuition is reinforced by excellent judgment, personal insight by reason. They are able to use their creative energy to create something (a work of art, an act of kindness, a relationship) from which they can learn the truth about themselves and create genuine self esteem. If their creation is good, then the person who created it must also be good.

Prayers for Type Four

Father, I thank you that you created me and gave me life. Help me to find the purpose you have in mind for me and to live according to your will. I know you created me to bring something good and beautiful into the world. Free me from the damage of my past. Jesus you are the Savior I seek. Rescue me. In Jesus name I ask this, Amen.

Lord, help me to use all of my experiences to grow, to open myself up to people, and to understand that I am not defined by my feelings. Help me to remember that only the feelings I act on express who I am. Amen.

Jesus, please release me from dwelling on the past, wasteful fantasies and romantic longings, wanting to protect myself by withdrawing from others, self doubt, emotional vulnerability, and from all self–indulgence in my emotions and behavior. Forgive me for feeling that people always let me down. Amen.

Lord, release me from the fear that I am unimportant and undesirable, release me from feeling shameful and misunderstood, and from feeling distraught, fatigued, inhibited, inadequate and defective. Free me from self sabotaging thoughts and actions. Free me from all feelings of hopelessness, despair, self contempt, and from turning my anger and aggression against myself. Amen.

Counseling Fours

Some Fours are moody, introspective or quietly reserved; others have a dramatic artistic style. They can present themselves as outsiders. They may be looking for help with depression or unresolved grief. They can have low self esteem and feelings of being flawed. They can be angry, provocative and sometimes intentionally shocking. They are in a deep search for themselves, and the more truth they discover about themselves, the more depressed they become. Their search for self is often their own undoing. They search for the authentic while resisting the ordinary. They may have eating disorders. Be aware of the wings and the path of disintegration. If the Five wing is strong, they will resist getting help from anyone, increasing their alienation from others. Unhealthy Fours with a Three wing take out their aggressions on themselves. They are self inhibited and alienated from others, depressed and self contemptuous. Depending on the strength of the wing, there will be moments when they act like unhealthy Threes.

Fours who abuse substances often have a romanticized self-destructive image of an "artist addict". Attachment to this image can thwart efforts at sobriety. Substance abuse also increases depression and distorts reality, fueling dangerous fantasies and risky behavior.

No other personality type is so keenly aware of both the spiritual and carnal aspects of human nature. They can be attuned to the beauty, creative spirit, depth and paradoxes of existence. At their best they can balance the animal and spiritual parts of life and allow themselves to be both productive and happy. When caught in depression, Fours can be consumed with what is wrong with themselves, even shamefully withdrawing into despair. They can also move in the direction of thinking they are somehow more special than others and not subject to ordinary expectations, over dramatizing their lives as separate from and more difficult than others.

They are often drawn to what is missing. They are tempted to stay with depression and the darker side of life. This can be genuine or can be about image, depending on the individual. They are attracted to what they perceive to be authentic and many have a distinctive, graceful and artistic manner.

The Four persona is idealized in American culture. Cult figures who had successful but tragic lives continue to sell albums, books, movie and promote their own subculture years after their deaths. Elvis Presley, James Dean, Jim Morrison, Kurt Cobaine, Jimmie Hendrix, the list of tragic pop icons goes on. However a task and accomplishment driven culture does not readily value people who search for life's deeper meanings and embrace a poetic aesthetic style.

Fours, especially as adolescents can strongly identify with romantic ideals, yet feel badly for being out of step with cultural norms. While I am a Six, I have a melancholy temperament and identify strongly with the Four. I share many of the same attributes, search for life's deeper meanings, identify with romantic ideals, yet struggle to achieve goals and create a successful life. I have withdrawn into the depths of depression before, and felt that I had special circumstances that exempted me from ordinary expectations. This internal conflict exaggerates a Four's sense of being both special and flawed. It also intensifies their tendency to inhabit exotic fantasies instead of reality.

Childhood Experiences

Fours have a conscious connection to their unconscious minds. This gives them a deep creativity and the ability to recognize the sacred in the ordinary. When healthy, they are capable of creating inspiring works of art that people easily relate to.

As children, Fours often felt abandoned and usually felt a sense of loss. There was at some point the experience of being cherished and then rejected or deserted. This leads them to develop the self image that they are somehow flawed. To compensate for this, they imagine that they are special and unique in ways that no one else can understand. This strategy allows them to separate from the crowd, yet belong to life in a way that others cannot.

This sets up the four for focusing on that which is not. They are never focused on the present. They focus on the future or on what could have been in the past, both of which are unavailable now. They live in a fantasy world, pushing other people away. The efforts of others to connect with them interrupts the pleasure of their private longing and Fours feel vulnerable to more abandonment.

As children Fours are usually sensitive, creative, unique and troubled; either provocative and angry or contained and removed. A Four's envy and longing are supported by the defense mechanism of introjections, the symbolic taking into the self of a loved or hated person or external object – the converse of projection. It is easy to understand how a positive introjection would protect a Four, but introjecting a negative person or object seems paradoxical. The Four would rather focus on the negative though; focus on what they can't have. This is the comfort zone to them. Longing for the unattainable is safer than dealing with reality. Longing for a relationship they cannot have for instance, is safer than having a relationship with a real and available person. Thus the negative introjection gives the Four psychological protection from abandonment. Longing and envy thrive in this environment.

Common Problems For Fours

Because Fours don't fit into the crowd, they often don't feel "normal". This reinforces their sense of being flawed. Their inner experience is often incongruent with what they believe is outwardly normal. Low self esteem results and often brings them to counseling. The hope of being understood and seen as special may draw a Four to counseling. They often want what they can't have. Envy and longing are staples for Fours. Help them appreciate what they do have.

What To Avoid

Just listen to a Four. Don't offer interpretations too quickly, this will leave Fours feeling unseen or judged. Validate their feelings and offer positive feedback before trying to tell them what to do differently. Don't become overly interested in the Four's interesting introspective story line while missing the underlying issues.

Don't be impatient, listen before offering solutions. Don't intervene too quickly, this makes the Four feel even more alienated. Fours would like to have their feelings, perceptions and experiences validated before being told what to do differently. Don't rush in and try for a quick fix, just listen until you are sure you understand. Be careful of criticism. Don't prematurely label them an "alienated outsider".

Counselors can also get caught in helping Fours process their emotions and dramas while forgetting to help the counselee change. Focusing on memories, traumas, and introspective analysis while interesting may feed the counselees false self. Although Fours often court this response, if the counselor falls for it the Four may feel unseen. Look for what is going on beneath their depth and creativity.

Identify some areas of satisfaction and help them focus on the good. Point out their preoccupation with the absent and the unattainable. Because they tend to romanticize and avoid their own shadow, discerning their true feelings is difficult. A counselor could over engage a Four's image or become impatient and prematurely interrupt an important moment of processing. Fours want to be understood, but they also fear being exposed and judged. They may reject any efforts others make to understand them; creating distance by being remote, obscure, or dramatic. While this defense mechanism keeps them from being exposed and judged, it also keeps them from being understood.

This pattern is sometimes acted out in the counseling relationship. A counselor could give a Four well timed honest feedback about what it feels like to be drawn in and then pushed away. The Four may then see their role in creating disappointments in relationships. They may indentify their internal motives and make conscious changes.

They want what they can't have, help them appreciate what they do have. Allow them to ventilate their feelings and probe for which of their feelings are real.

In the transference / counter transference relationship the therapist may feel special, devalued or both. Depressed melancholic Fours can implicitly entreat the therapist to be overly helpful, creating fruitless rescue drama. The real rescuer they seek is God. They are longing for a Savior to rescue them and that savior is Jesus Christ. Help them understand they can give their worries to Jesus,

Fours say when they feel defensive in counseling they may intellectualize, withdraw, be intense emotionally, verbally cutting or project an air of superiority. Talking about feelings can be a way for the Four not to feel them.

What Works For Fours

Fours need to feel safe in counseling. They don't want to be abandoned or judged. They want the counselor to be authentic, acknowledge mistakes and build trust. They value the relationship that develops with the counselor, a sense of trust, lack of judgment, validation of feelings, good boundaries, professionalism, and the elusive chemistry. They need to feel that the counselor really likes them and is genuinely interested in their well being.

They should be slowly and skillfully taken to the depths needed. But they also need to see progress, not repetitiveness. They want to get to the heart of the matter, but they are also terrified that when they do, it will be awful. They need to be able to trust the counselor and not be pushed too hard.

Fours can be intellectual, but they process life through their emotions. Dealing strictly with facts and theories leaves them at a disadvantage because their beliefs stem from their feelings, not their intellect. They hold the feelings of the information they have gathered rather than the factual information. They retain emotional information.

A counselor may need to see past the Four's articulate self insightful persona in order to work with the underlying issues. They can be very capable verbally, while burying the vulnerable interior self. By the time they ask for help, they may sound like they know exactly what their problem is and what they need, but they can't truly get in touch with it.

They have done much introspection and sought to understand themselves, but have been taught not to display their inner self so they need to feel that counselor really hears them on the deepest levels. They need a counselor who can help them put their real feelings into words and help them to understand that it's all right to have those feelings, thereby earning their trust. Being misperceived and being labeled has trained them to conceal their inner self, and they will return to the familiar front they reveal to others when they get uncomfortable being themselves. This false front is a comfortable place, yet presenting it to others makes them feel misunderstood.

For counselors, understanding shame is essential and this is a particularly delicate area for Fours. Don't try to talk them out of their defense in difficult moments, just stay with them through the defense and help them put words to their feelings. Don't try to talk them out of the place their in. Give them time to put their defense in perspective, experience the situation and see things from another point of view. But don't let them wait too long, they will repeatedly replay the situation in their mind. Allow them to ventilate their feelings and probe for which feelings are real.

Counseling should help Fours learn to observe themselves and make conscious choices. Help them to become aware of the critical voice in their head. Empathy is more important than any particular method of therapy.

When Fours engage in cycles of longing, envy and fantasy, it is better to help them get grounded in the present before trying to reach new emotional depths. Shame and pain may overcome Fours at various points, delving into insight alone can actually intensify their defensive longing. Let them know that while it is okay to have the feelings they do, they are not the only ones who have ever suffered. Even though God is in control, evil and suffering exist in the world and they should be prepared for it.

Physical activity such as walking and exercise can help, as well as volunteering and helping others. Serving vulnerable people such as the elderly helps them move beyond themselves and gives them a perspective on their own lives.

Healthy Foundations

When Fours fail to fulfill ordinary life commitments, they damage their relationships, reinforcing their shame. They may have a hatred of tasks, but feel better when they get things done and their life is in order. This is something I share with Fours. When depressed, I hated to do anything and even minor tasks seemed monumental, but getting things done was the best cure for my depression. You should also make Fours aware how others are affected when they don't do ordinary things.

Living in their imaginations and fantasies can seduce Fours away from real life; using intoxicants and mind altering substances can foster their break with reality, choosing to live in the world of what could be or could have been, while ignoring the present reality. They have difficulty finding contentment with the present. They long for more and deeper experiences, keeping them from seeing the good in "now". Help them stay with the mundane, and to see the beauty in the present.

When recovering from addictions, learning to find value in the ordinary is crucial. It is tempting for Fours to retreat into fantasies when painful realities are no longer medicated. Fours are jealous of others who can use substances without problems or serious consequences. The Fours "flaw" complex is especially important to recognize and work with to avoid relapse.

The challenge is always to get the Four grounded in reality, to see the here and now, and to live in the present.

Introjection And Shame

Fours long for a rescuer to come and save them. Show them Christ in this role but make them understand that they have a responsibility to rescue themselves. The Bible teaches both God's sovereignty and man's responsibility. In their fantasies, they are often rescued by someone who sees them as "special".

In addition to learning responsibility, Fours need to learn that comparing themselves to others exaggerates their flawed/special complex. Remind them that we are all flawed and share a common humanity. Revealing personal struggles can help the Four identify with the counselor and feel more normal.

Longing And Envy

Longing is a defense for Fours. They fear that without it, their authentic self will be vulnerable to rejection. When Counseling Fours, listen for how they experience their connection to their own creativity. When they experience music, art, books or movies, what feelings and insights come to them? Through this connection with an external source Fours often feel their most authentic and alive, but they need to learn that the feeling is intuitive and within them and therefore will not abandon them. The counselor can help them accept this insight as their sessions proceed. Help them fight their neurotic belief that they must be lacking something.

Melancholia And Depression

Understanding the difference between melancholia and depression is important when working with Fours. For many Fours grief and sadness are part of their image. Being attracted to the dark side of life is not the same as depression. Fours can find melancholia creatively stimulating but actively avoid depression. As someone who has experienced both, it can be difficult to tell the difference. Melancholia does not require medication, depression sometimes does. Melancholia can feel as troubling as depression and it's hard to distinguish and categorize exactly when I moved from one to the other. I was able to overcome melancholia several times in my life, but depression overtook me and it took medication, therapy, time and most of all Create, Connect, Commit to overcome. Through prayer, research and self discovery, God revealed the Create, Connect, Commit process to me. I recommend that counselors use it with every personality type. It is the only scientifically based complete system of change, and it is the only thing that defeated my depression once and for all. Even the stress of losing my wife of 23 years and going through a divorce while facing major challenges with my job could not sink me into the pit of depression once I learned CCC.

Depression is a state of low mood and aversion to activity. The Diagnostic and Statistical Manual of Mental Disorders defines a depressed person as experiencing feelings of sadness, helplessness and hopelessness. In traditional colloquy, feeling "depressed" is often synonymous with feeling "sad", but both clinical depression and non-clinical depression can also refer to a conglomeration of more than one feeling.

There are some individuals whom may develop mild depression, which may start gradually for no reason. The individual may start to feel tired, restless, lonely and have difficulty sleeping. In many cases, the individual loses interest in sex and wants to be left alone. One may be able to go to work but not have any enjoyment. Mild depression may last a lot longer than slight depression, but can be overcome with changes in lifestyle, psychotherapy and social support.

However, some individuals develop severe depression, which may induce feelings of suicidal ideation as it is common in severe depression. In severe depression, one may feel sad constantly, cry for no apparent reason, have trouble sleeping and focusing , become fatigued, feel worthless, have headaches or even backache . While slight depression has a cause, both mild and severe depression generally are complex disorders, which are not well understood. Mild depression may be related to the environment, such as being unable to cope with a certain job, unemployment, financial problems or loss of a loved one. No one understands why severe depression occurs. Even though many brain imaging studies have been done, the exact neurotransmitters in the brain which play a role in depression are still in question. Most mature Fours have experienced enough depression to suggest ways to lessen or avoid it.

Melancholia (from Greek *μελαγχολία* - *melancholia* "sadness, lit. black bile"), also **lugubriousness**, from the Latin *lugere*, to mourn; **moroseness**, from the Latin *morosus*, self-willed, fastidious habit; **wistfulness**, from old English *wist*: intent, or **saturnine**, in contemporary usage, is a mood disorder of non-specific depression, characterized by low levels of enthusiasm and eagerness for activity.

In a modern context, "melancholy" applies only to the mental or emotional symptoms of depression or despondency; historically, "melancholia" could be physical as well as mental, and melancholic conditions were classified as such by their common cause rather than by their properties.

Similarly, melancholia in ancient usage also encompassed mental disorders which might now be classed as schizophrenias or bipolar disorders. Many Fours relate to melancholia and say that grief and sadness are part of their identity.

While it may be difficult to distinguish between the two, CCC is effective with both depression and melancholia. The combination of introspection through personality typing, reframing, creating new boundaries, setting goals, connecting with other people and committing to progress make CCC the only scientifically based complete system of change and an excellent tool for fighting melancholia and depression. Counselors should learn CCC and help counselees incorporate it into their arsenal of weapons against depression.

Exercise, as little as taking a 30 minute walk, is one of the most effective weapons against depression. Combining exercise with CCC effectively fights depression. You can read more about exercise, diet, and how I overcame depression in "Change Anything; How I Beat Depression and the Process I Used to Create a New Life" available at createconnectcommit.com and at online book distributors.

When Fours avoid feelings they fear will lead to depression, they start to defensively distance themselves from all their feelings and hide behind an image of emotional sensitivity. They have romantic notions about emotionality yet avoid their true emotions. They can cry over a movie but the personal is not so easy for them to know, they are not authentic regarding their own pain. The drama of their emotionality is a paradox, it is a barrier to prevent anyone from getting too close to the Four's true feelings. It stems from trying to be who others want them to be and not being themselves.

Moving On

Accepting that it is time to let go and move on can be especially difficult for Fours. They have been described as "refusing to mourn". Since they can be attached to longing, it's difficult for them to let go. They long for what they have lost, clinging to it and refusing to accept that it is over. Getting them to mourn their loss and move forward presents a challenge for the counselor.

This can be particularly challenging in relationships and when they are going through a divorce. Point them to their future, what will happen if they hang on versus what will happen if they let go. Staying attached to what could have been robs Fours of the experience of what is.

Relationships

Fours unconsciously replicate childhood dynamics in their present relationships, they set themselves up to feel alone and abandoned. Partners and family members are confused by their push-pull approach to intimacy, as well as their emotional intensity. Like Sixes, they have a way of bringing about what they fear. Their fear of abandonment can prompt them to act sarcastic, outrageous and dramatic in ways that shock, ironically bringing about the very thing that they fear. If the counselee acts this way, focus on what he/she intends by the behavior or is feeling underneath it; this can reveal deeper issues and genuine pain. Once their underlying feelings are validated they may feel safe enough to examine their behavior from other people's perspective. They may then see that they create the abandonment which they fear.

Final Notes

Accept Fours for who they are. Listen and understand without judging. Provide enough safety in the counseling relationship and their authentic presence can be exposed when they are ready. Help Fours realize that they have abandoned themselves and the needs they attempt to fill with longing, envy, and seeking a relationship with others can only be met within themselves. Getting Fours connected to their genuine emotions and encouraging/supporting any necessary grieving can free them from dysfunctional longing and envy. When Fours understand that what they really long for is their own essential self, they can become healthy.

5
THE INVESTIGATOR

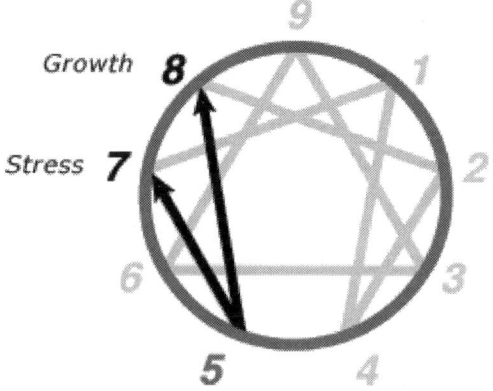

Enneagram Type Five

Fives are alert, insightful, and curious. They are able to concentrate and focus on developing complex ideas, theories and skills. Independent, innovative, and inventive, they can also become preoccupied with their thoughts and imaginary constructs. They may become detached, yet high-strung and intense. They may retreat into their own world, in the safety net of their mind. They typically have problems with eccentricity, nihilism, and isolation. At their Best: visionary pioneers, often ahead of their time, and able to see the world in an entirely new way.

Characteristic role: The Investigator
Ego Fixation: Stinginess
Holy Idea: Omniscience
Basic Fear: Being useless, helpless, or incapable
Basic Desire: To be capable and competent
Temptation: To keep the world at bay
Vice/Passion: Avarice
Virtue: Detachment

Key Motivation: Fives want to possess knowledge, to understand the world, to have everything figured out as a way of defending themselves against threats from the world. Five is my wing and I must say I do have this tendency.

The Meaning of the Arrows:

Stress/Disintegration point: Seven (Detached Fives suddenly become hyperactive and scattered like Sevens)

Security/Integration point: Eight (When they master the real world and not simply their own minds, Fives become more self-confident and decisive like healthy Eights)

Healthy Fives; Become visionaries, understanding the world profoundly, making new discoveries, possibly a genius. Observing, knowledgeable, an expert, innovative, produces exciting and valuable ideas.

Average Fives; Intellectual, analytical, specialized, a scientist into thorough research and scholarship. Detatched, enjoys creating complex theories and complicated interpretations of reality. Eccentric, extremist, iconoclastic.

Unhealthy Fives; Reclusive and isolated from reality. Cynical, obsessed with strange ideas, paranoid. Insanity with schizophrenic tendencies common.

Description

Fives are the intense cerebral type. They are perceptive, secretive, and isolated. Fives are alert, insightful, and curious. They are able to concentrate and focus on developing complex ideas and skills. Independent, innovative, and inventive, they can also become preoccupied with their thoughts and imaginary constructs. They become detached, yet high-strung and intense. Fives essentially fear that they don't have enough inner strength to face life, so they tend to withdraw, to retreat into the safety and security of the mind where they can mentally prepare for their emergence into the world. They typically have problems with nihilism, and isolation. Fives are often a bit eccentric; they feel little need to alter their beliefs to accommodate majority opinion, and they refuse to compromise their freedom to think just as they please. At their best they are geniuses, visionary pioneers, often ahead of their time, and able to see the world in an entirely new way, observing everything with extraordinary insight. At their worst they don't feel adequately defended against the world. To compensate they adopt an attitude of careless indifference or intellectual arrogance, which has the unfortunate consequence of creating distance between themselves and others. They can become reclusive and isolated from reality. They often retain their fears that life is somehow going to demand more of them than they can deliver. They can become paranoid and susceptible to gross distortions and phobias. Type Five is the Wing of my personality.

Recognizing Type Five

Despite high intelligence, they may be inarticulate, at least until they think carefully about what they want to say. They may be threatened by new information if it clashes with their belief system. Try to link new information to what you think they already believe. Their world may be their own mental, private one, their own version of reality they retreat to and feel safe in. They may not be introspective or in touch with their feelings, even though they might talk "about" them. Conformity may be a way of maintaining privacy. As they mature, locked up feelings may erupt. They may complain that commitment feels like a loss. They may feel that privacy is both safety and a prison. They may have lots of pious practices as a defense. They may avoid any strong feelings.

How you can help

Help them enlarge their range of emotions, activities, and interests. Help them articulate their inner world. Help them put their experiences into words. Remind them: involvement in activity isn't the same as involvement with people who are participating in the activity. Help them socialize and interact. Help them see that behind their desire for knowledge is the desire for love. Maturity is found in developing relationships with the external world. Reframe commitment as a gain instead of a loss. Fortress/home/prison can become interchangeable. Untangle their different feelings. Bodywork is often quite helpful, it releases pent up stress. Intimate relationships can be a means to reach out to the external world.

Scripture

Ecc 1:13-18 I devoted myself to study and to explore by wisdom all that is done under heaven. What a heavy burden God has laid on men!
 I have seen all the things that are done under the sun; all of them are meaningless, a chasing after the wind.
 What is twisted cannot be straightened; what is lacking cannot be counted.
 I thought to myself, "Look, I have grown and increased in wisdom more than anyone who has ruled over Jerusalem before me; I have experienced much of wisdom and knowledge."
 Then I applied myself to the understanding of wisdom, and also of madness and folly, but I learned that this, too, is a chasing after the wind.
 For with much wisdom comes much sorrow; the more knowledge, the more grief.

Doing

Fives are in the doing triad. They emphasize thinking over doing. They emphasize thinking so much that they retreat into their mental world, becoming intensely involved with their thoughts. They are more at home in their minds abstractly analyzing the world than they are living in it.

Fives, Sixes and Sevens focus their attention on the world outside themselves. This statement may seem like a contradiction, as Fives and Sixes are introspective and Fives are constantly engrossed in their thoughts. The area of focus of their thoughts comes through their sense perceptions, which they can never be completely sure of because they are uncertain about what lies outside of themselves. Their thoughts are the only things they know with certainty. They have an inward need to find out how their perceptions of the world match up with reality, hence they are outwardly focused, though deeply cerebral.

They correspond to Jung's introverted thinking type;

"Introverted thinking is primarily oriented by the subjective factor…it does not lead from concrete experience back again to the object, but always to the subjective content. External facts are not the aim and the origin of this thinking, though the introvert would often like to make his thinking appear so. It begins with the subject and leads back to the subject, far though it may range into the realm of actual reality….Facts are collected as evidence for a theory, never for their own sake. (C.G. Jung, Psychological Types, 380)

Security and Anxiety

Average Fives have problems with security because they fear that the environment is unpredictable and potentially threatening. Fives protect themselves by being extremely observant; anticipating problems before they happen, particularly with other people. Who they are stems from their attempts to defend themselves from real or imagined dangers; their curiosity, insight, need to make sense of their perceptions and eventually their paranoia all stem from their fear of their environment.

When Fives are healthy they become realist, able to observe reality as it is and comprehend the complex at a glance. Their search for security skews their perception of reality however. They jump to conclusions by projecting faulty interpretations on their environment. They want to be able to defend themselves by having everything figured out. When they become unhealthy, they take their eccentric ideas to absurd extremes. They become obsessed with completely distorted notions, ultimately becoming paranoid, utterly terrified by the threatening visions which they have created in their minds.

Their trouble perceiving reality objectively leads to anxiety. They are afraid of letting anyone or anything influence them or their faults. They fear being controlled. They are willing to be possessed by an idea, as long as it originated in their minds. But they are uncertain whether or not their perceptions of the environment are valid. They do not know what is real and what is the product of their own minds.

Origins

Fives had ambivalent relationships with both parents. For whatever reason, their parents were not dependable sources of love and reassurance. They may have been nurtured erratically or had parents who were emotionally disturbed, caught in a loveless marriage, divorced, alcoholic or who had some other dysfunction.

They became ambivalent toward both parents and toward the world. They lived in a state of constant alertness; they feared being controlled by others so they trained themselves to make observations about their parents and their environment, to anticipate events and take protective measures accordingly.

They need to understand their environment and at the same time defend themselves against it. They develop the same love-hate relationship with their environment that they have with their parents. They want to identify with the world, but at the same time feel detached form it. They resolve their ambivalence by not indentifying with anything other than their thoughts about the world outside themselves. Their thoughts are "good" while outside reality is "bad" so it must be vigilantly observed.

They find their parents, the world, other people and outside reality fascinating, they feel they must keep it all at a distance to avoid being controlled. Because of this dualistic thinking, Fives envision everything as being split into two fundamental areas; the inner world and the outer world. They group things; subjects and objects, the known and the unknown, the dangerous and the safe, etc..Seeing themselves as subjects and others as objects sets the stage for how they deal with reality throughout their lives.

Healthy Fives

At their best, they become visionaries, broadly comprehending the world while penetrating it profoundly. Open-minded, they take things in their true context. They make pioneering discoveries and find entirely new ways of doing and perceiving things. They observe everything with extraordinary perceptiveness and insight. Mentally alert, curious, searching intelligence: nothing escapes their notice. They have foresight and the ability to predict. Able to concentrate: they become engrossed in whatever has caught their attention. Excited by knowledge: they often become experts in some field. Innovative and inventive, producing extremely valuable, original works. They are highly independent, idiosyncratic, and whimsical. They have the wisdom to put their knowledge to work.

Descriptive Terms; Knowledgeable, Observant, Perceptive, Thoughtful, Insightful, Profound, Thorough, Wise, Gentle, Theorist, Speculative, Original, Innovative, Keeps Confidences

Average Fives

Average Fives fear that they do not know enough to make their theories or discoveries public. They feel that more research and experimentation is needed and they have to involve themselves even more deeply with their subject. (The more they know, the more they realize how little they know.) They become highly analytic and specialized. Healthy Fives have wisdom; they know what to do with their knowledge. In contrast, average Fives are in pursuit of knowledge for knowledge's sake. They analyze everything in great detail, dissecting things mentally to find out how they work. They attempt to be objective but end up taking things out of context. They can't see the forest for the trees. They make a science out of whatever they are interested in. They become intensely involved theorist. In time the complexities they create in their minds cause new and more complicated problems for them. Nothing is clear or certain and anxiety increases. They begin to force their conclusions; their minds seek order. They move from "What If?" to "It Is So." They read more into things than is actually there.

Still they are smart enough that they're not usually totally off the mark. They're too smart not to have something interesting to say. Their problem is not knowing which of their ideas are valuable and which are not.

Descriptive Terms; Understanding, Researcher, Concentrated, Non-threatening, Self-Reliant, Interprets, Detached, Intense, Private, Distant

Unhealthy Fives

Unhealthy Fives become extremely antagonistic toward anyone who disagrees with them. Their aggressions are aroused when people question their ideas, or worse if their ideas are ridiculed or dismissed it really grabs their ire. Their ideas are wedded to their self images. Their thoughts are who they are. To maintain their identities they go on the offensive; those who disagree with them must be discredited, their ideas proven worthless, there solutions shown to be false, their world exposed as an illusion. Thus unhealthy Fives unwittingly provoke others into rejecting them, then become antagonistic and nihilistic about the value of all relationships. They become isolated and cynical. Their need to reject the beliefs of others is so strong they take pleasure in debunking everything positive in life. Human relationships are impossible, and human nature is rotten to the core. Unhealthy Fives take delight in deflating the values others live by and consider themselves wise for not having fallen for these "false" beliefs. Their "great intellectual honesty" keeps them from falling prey to the "false" beliefs others are deceived by. Cynical, they throw out the baby with the bathwater. There may be some truth to their theories about the flawed beliefs of others, but they dismiss the ideas of others completely; with no regard for the truth except their version of it. They live in the world "according to them." Objectivity is not their forte. Faith, love, kindness, and friendship are all extremely difficult for them to believe in because of their fear of involvement with others.

Unhealthy Fives aggressive impulses fueled by the intensity of their minds, repel everything that might influence them. They stew in their feelings of contempt for everything. They become delusional and paranoid. Paranoid delusions of persecution may alternate with compensating delusions of grandeur. They may begin to believe they are being watched by someone important; God or extraterrestrials maybe, providing neurotic Fives with a sense of importance. Paranoid elements may be mixed with grandiose delusions. Their thoughts take on a life of their own. The thoughts become uncontrollable, scaring them when they don't want to be scared. They cannot escape their fears because they originate in themselves, fueled by their racing minds. Life becomes unbearable; they see too much, the blinders have been removed. Like Rowdy Roddy Piper in the cult classic "They Live" they have found the sunglasses that allow them to see the un-seeable. The truth is that it is their minds that are devouring them. The world is filled with horrors because their minds are filled with horrors. Seeking oblivion, they may commit suicide or have a psychotic break with reality. Deranged, explosively self-destructive, with schizophrenic overtones. Generally corresponds to the Schizoid Avoidant and Schizotypal personality disorders.

Descriptive Terms; Determined, Antagonistic, Eccentric, Reclusive, Cynical, Self-Absorbed, Fearful, Uncertain, Alienated, Nihilistic, Distorts Ideas, Compartmentalizes, Isolated From Reality

Subtypes

The Five With A Four Wing

The personality traits of the Five and the Four are somewhat in conflict with each other. Fives are intellectuals, they operate more on theory than experience; Fours internalize everything to intensify their feelings. The combination of the two types makes one of the richest subtypes, combining artistic and intellectual achievement. Noteworthy examples include Albert Einstein, Emily Dickinson and Stanley Kubrick.

Healthy; Intuition and knowledge, sensitivity and insight, artistic creativity and intellectualism all exist in this subtype. They see beauty in formulas and theories. To this subtype, the beauty of something is an indication of its truthfulness; beauty is the confirmation of the objective rightness of an idea. This subtype has a strong sense of intuition. They are more humanistic, artistic, personal and emotional than Fives with a Six wing.

Average; Introverted and emotionally self absorbed, detached from the environment and involved in their thoughts. They use their analytic abilities more to keep people at a distance than to understand them. They are moody and hypersensitive to criticism. They are intensely focused on their work and their ideas, but the Four wing makes them emotionally vulnerable, hindering their work. Alcohol, drugs or sex may serve as an escape.

Unhealthy; May fall prey to depression or be disturbed by aggressive impulses. Jealous and contemptuous of others, they regret that they must isolate themselves from the world so they envy the success of others in it. Their emotions and intellect are in conflict. If they become neurotic, they are one of the most alienated of all types. They become hopeless, nihilistic, self inhibiting, isolated, and self defeating. Suicide is a possibility.

The Five With A Six Wing

The traits of the Five and the Six reinforce each other. This is one of the most difficult types to contact intimately or sustain a relationship with. They have problems trusting others because they are Fives and the Six wing reinforces anxiety. This makes any kind of risk taking in relationships difficult. So their interpersonal relationships end up being erratic and are not generally an important part of their lives. Notable examples are Sigmund Freud, Charles Darwin and Stephen Hawking.

Healthy; Loyal and committed to their families and beliefs, extraordinarily hard workers, caring little for their own comfort and much more for the fulfillment of their duties and their work. They possess an intellectual playfulness and a good sense of humor as well as other attractive, lovable qualities. People of this subtype do have a deep capacity for friendship and commitment once they have tested others and allowed them to come close. There can be an endearing element in their desire to be accepted by others.

Average: Generally have problems with relationships. They don't know what to do with their feelings or how to express them. They have no awareness about how they communicate themselves to others. They are insensitive to their own feelings and emotions as well as those of others.

They are the intellectual, nerdy type; completely wrapped up with intellectual pursuits. They live in their minds, immersing themselves in their work to the exclusion of everything else. When interpersonal conflicts arise they bury themselves even deeper in their intellectual work. They avoid resolving problems with passive-aggressive techniques, putting people and problems off rather than dealing with them directly.

Unhealthy; Have a tendency to be suspicious of others and extremely fearful of intimacy of any sort. The isolation and paranoia of the unhealthy Five are reinforced by the Six's suspicion and fear of being persecuted. They also have the Six's tendency to overreact, thus acting in masochistic, self defeating ways.

Disintegration; The Five Goes To Seven

The main problem Fives have is not being able to move from thinking to doing. They must find a source of security within themselves to allow them to act with some degree of confidence. Neurotic Fives need to reestablish contact with reality, but are completely incapable of doing so. When they disintegrate they act impulsively and hysterically. They act out anxiety like a manic depressive, characteristic of an unhealthy Seven.

They go from an isolated paranoid state in which there fears keep them inactive to a state of wildly manic activity. They leap into mindless actions by which they succeed only in getting themselves in deeper trouble. Since they are still neurotic shifting into activity cannot satisfy their real needs; they are incapable of learning from their newfound energy and activity. They are irrational and make decisions with extremely poor judgment. They still don't identify with anyone or anything so they cannot make any useful contact with the environment. They go totally out of control.

They may create self-fulfilling prophecies as their erratic and irresponsible behavior brings about some of the terrible things they have feared. They may end up being killed for example, not because of some vast conspiracy they have created in their minds, but rather due to their reckless behavior. Fearing that they have reached some sort of horrible dead end in their lives they may impulsively do permanent harm to themselves or someone else. As their anxiety peaks they may do something irrevocable such as murder or suicide.

Integration; The Five Goes To Eight

Fives typically feel that there is always more to know before they act. They will always feel insecure until they have mastered the real world and not just their own minds. Their aggressions and other impulses tend to overpower their minds; their egos are too weak for their ids.

Healthy, integrating Fives incorporate their perceptions of the world into themselves. They identify with their environment rather than just observing it. They overcome their fear of the environment and learn to trust it. Thus their self confidence grows, in the manner of healthy Eights.

When they go to Eight, Fives also realize that, as little as they think they know, it is still more than almost anyone else. They no longer feel they must know absolutely everything before they act. They learn more as they do more, they will be able to solve new problems as they arise. They lose the illusion of absolute certitude.

Integrating Fives act from the actualization of their own genuine intelligence. While they don't know everything, they know enough to lead others with confidence. The value of their ideas has been confirmed by reality and they no longer fear acting. They develop the courage it takes to put their and themselves to the test. They come to the realization that they have something valuable to contribute to the world. Their thoughts are finally given expression in action and very possibly in leadership as they move to Eight. Integrating Fives put their theories into action and show others how to do what only they know how to do.

Prayers for Type Five

Lord, help me to support others from the fullness of my heart, to find serenity in being compassionate toward others, and to reach out to others confidently as an equal. Amen

Jesus, I have faith and confidence in you. Reveal the meaning of my struggles and help me understand that life with you as Lord is both meaningful and rewarding. Help me accept uncertainty about the future and teach me to trust in you. I am now secure and grounded in your strength Lord, thank you for your protection. Amen.

Jesus, forgive me for avoiding my life by escaping into my mind. Release me from feeling that I always need to know more before I act. Teach me how to Plan-Do-Study-Act. I accept that I cannot "get it right the first time." I know how to plan, give me the confidence to act on my plans even if they are imperfect, then to study the outcome and make adjustments. I thank you for the sense of confidence that comes as a born again child of God. Amen.

Lord, release me from the agitation and restlessness of my mind and from feeling that I am a misfit. I do not have to know "everything". Forgive me for being secretive and hiding from people. Help me to take care of my health and to stop postponing my emotional needs. Amen.

When unhealthy :Father, forgive me for desiring to antagonize others and ruin their peace of mind, for being cynical and for feeling contempt for the normalcy of others. Release me from the fear that others will exploit me, from my dark and destructive fantasies and from isolating myself by rejecting others. Help me to depend on others. Release me from my fears of the world around me and from the fear of being violated and overwhelmed by others. Amen

Counseling Fives

Fives may be shy and guarded, appearing flat. They may offer brief responses, or intellectual pondering. They may have difficulty communicating, thinking carefully before speaking. They may act superior, over intellectualize and avoid feelings. They may come to counseling out of loneliness, or just to understand how emotional and social systems function. They may be brought in by a spouse seeking better communication. They may seem anxious, scanning for danger, somewhat paranoid, afraid of exposure or intrusion. Be aware of the wings and the path of disintegration.

Some Fives seem unaware of social conventions and openly answer questions concerning areas which are normally loaded with social secrecy; eating disorders, substance abuse, sexual or other compulsions. They can abuse substances to relieve anxiety, using alcohol or drugs to numb and quiet their fears.

At their best they are engaged in their own life through their relationships and work. When they are able to do what they feel passionate about, they are willing to give of their time, knowledge and emotions. They are visionary and able to see the world in new ways, often ahead of their times.

When Fives are unhealthy, they get trapped in loneliness. They avoid having to give to others and hoard their belongings. They retreat into their own world, their attention is focused on maintaining privacy and observing the external world. They spend a lot of time gathering information, which seems to provide them safety by allowing them to know more than others.

The introspective lifestyle of the Five is out of touch with the aggressive, busy, forward thinking aspects of American culture. The Five's mental acuity can set them apart socially, making their other gifts overlooked and undervalued. This is reflected in the growing trend of diagnosing naturally introverted types with "Social Anxiety Disorder". The marketing of SAD by the pharmaceutical industry encourages clinicians to diagnose normal children who have the characteristics of Fives and give them medication to become more extroverted.

Childhood Experiences

Fives have an intuitive intelligence and wisdom that is not intellectual. They also have an ability to be fully present without being attached to outcome. As children, Fives can experience the world as overwhelming, intrusive or unreliable. They are sensitive to other people's emotional states and often come to believe that others will not meet their needs without wanting too much in return. So they learn to depend on themselves, to need less from others as a defense, minimizing the risk that nothing will be available from others. They guard their privacy and gather and hoard information. (I have a five wing and share many of the characteristics of the Five, but I have a need to share what I have learned. I do however hoard books, tapes and information. I am not keen on sharing books, as they often are not returned, and I never know when I will need the information for a sermon or book I am working on.)

Some Fives remember childhoods in which they felt intruded upon, perhaps because of a crowded family environment or because of needy or demanding parents. Other fives were starved for attention and recall an atmosphere of emotional scarcity. Either experience prompts the child to hold on to what little they have. Most Fives remember feeling comforted by time alone, when they often read books, watched movies, or played with computers or video games to mentally escape. The arcade was one of my favorite places growing up, and I could never get enough of the escape playing video games provided. Lifting weights alone, in a shed in my backyard provided a similar escape. I retreated into my own little world.

Social rules were often a source of confusion and loneliness, further prompting the Five child to withdraw. Doing their own thing becomes a source of relief for the Five, out of choice or out of need. It is safer not to deal with intimate relationships. In my case, this was born out of necessity, and I suppose is why Five is my wing and not my primary type.

On the surface Fives may appear self contained and undemanding; even as children they may not seem to need much. As a result unintentional neglect can materialize. They reduce their needs to avoid disappointment and the appearance of independence can lead to neglect.

Avarice applies to Fives in as much as they hoard information and protect their private world. They are torn between the need to relate to others and the need to pull back and protect their private holdings. Their defense mechanism of isolation leads them to unconsciously compartmentalize; they minimize the possibility of being overwhelmed by anything they have not already mentally anticipated and maintain a sense of privacy and control while with others. They also stay remote from their own emotional truth. They rationalize it away. A Five's internal emotional isolation mirrors their external reactions to others.

What Brings Fives To Counseling

Fives are attracted to psychology and the Enneagram. I suppose it was my Five wing that attracted me to both. At 46, setting out to get a PhD in psychology was not a feasible plan. I already had a degree in Biblical Studies, so I chose Christian counseling and studied the Enneagram on my own. I was surprised to find so much information on the Enneagram when I had never heard of it before I took a personality test at Similarminds.com.

Both the Enneagram and psychology provide valuable understanding about interpersonal realms. Both can potentially make Fives even better observers. The detached observer role comes easy to them, but they often feel lonely and have a genuine desire to have satisfying intimate relationships. Counselors need to understand that Fives are subtly dissatisfied with their lives. Underneath the intellectual front, the power of human interaction is missing. This can lead to becoming sour, critical and despairing. It is the missing element of connection with others that usually brings Fives to counseling. Help them connect with others. Behind their desire for knowledge is a desire for love and acceptance. Help them learn to socialize and interact.

What To Expect

You never know what you will get with a Five. They may be quiet with a "poker face" offering no nonverbal clues or they may talk your ears off. They may try to impress you with their intelligence, they are good at intellectualizing and they can also be competitive. Don't get caught in an intellectual battle with them. They tend to withdraw when they get too close. When defensive, they can shut down and become totally unavailable for open hearted discussion. They may feel vulnerable, but still feel they are smarter than you. They avoid exposure and minimize risk in relationships. Once a problem is exposed, Fives weigh whether going to counseling is worth it. Counseling takes time and Fives want to know what they'll get in return for their investment. They are curious about the deeper meaning of life, and they want to be understood, so this may help them stay with counseling.

What Works For Fives

Trust is the main issue if anything is going to be gained from counseling. They need to know that they can trust the counselor and having clearly defined boundaries helps. They will probably lean towards keeping the sessions on an intellectual level; however this will not create change. But if forced into their feelings too quickly, they will become defensive.

Fives can be very insightful, but insight may not be what they need most. They want you to be impressed with their intelligence and insight, when what they need most is to open their heart. But getting to the heart of the matter will feel threatening for them. Be aware of that need and the fear of going there. Go slow. Work with their intellectual defense gently and persistently. Help them access their feelings and emotions. They need to be drawn to an emotional state rather than a thinking state. Mirroring and empathizing with the Five's emotions are helpful. Identify and acknowledge their basic feelings. Understand that it is difficult for the Five to be in this vulnerable situation, show compassion and acceptance.

Don't discount their intelligence. It is important to Fives that counselors recognize that their intellectual strengths are an important resource. Knowledge creates power in counseling. It is important to establish the sense that what they bring intellectually is valuable, especially as they integrate feelings and emotions with intellect. Acknowledging what is already there makes the new territory less threatening. Let them know they do not have to leave the safety of their mind in order to experience their emotions. It is about integrating, not abandoning one for the other. The counseling process should establish for the Five that both the counselee and counselor have something to bring to the table. The counselor is there to get the Five in touch with their heart and their mind is a valuable tool to aid in the process.

At different times in their lives, Fives might have different goals in counseling. They follow a developmental path from ideas to emotions, from acquiring psychological knowledge to integrating their feelings. In an early phase, they may seek a therapist or counselor with an intellectual reputation. They are most interested in the intellectual aspects of psychology, psychotherapy or counseling at this stage. The Christian counselor may find themselves in conversations more about theology and psychology than actual counseling. In later stages, the Five will be more concerned with the counselor's relationship skills.

Make the Five feel comfortable and safe when learning the language of feelings and interpersonal communication. Even a little anxiety can be overwhelming for Fives in the early stages of counseling. The counselor needs to provide a lot of safety.

Be careful with questions about feelings. You can inadvertently humiliate Fives by asking questions they can't completely answer. Questions about emotions can be confusing. They may not know how they feel. It is better to begin with physical feelings. Ask about bodily feelings, dry mouth, butterflies in stomach, etc.. Help them connect physical sensations to emotions.

Remember that the mind is the safe place for Fives and they will retreat there when threatened. The safer they feel in the relationship with the counselor, the more confident they will be about taking emotional risks. Being in the reflective atmosphere of counseling awakens the Five's capacity to self observe and promotes change.

Help them understand what they are avoiding, what they are trying not to feel. When they take their defenses down they can hear the inner voice they have tried to avoid by hiding in their intellectual defense.

Some Fives are difficult to read, they can display a poker face and hide nonverbal clues, making kinesic interview techniques ineffective. Getting feedback to determine if therapy is on track presents a challenge. In this case, the best thing to do is ask them if they are comfortable with the direction counseling is taking. The counselor can ease their own tension and get honest feedback by asking non-pointed questions, just ask the Five to rate how they think you are doing as a counselor. Ask for suggestions. Ask what is helping and what is not. Let them know that it is important for you to know how they are doing. This is important for Fives, who often feel overlooked. At Wellspring, one of the psychologists told me another had said I had a poker face and was difficult to read. Letting me know this helped me offer feedback, and let me know they were trying to read me. It helped me for them to be honest and ask for feedback. (Five is my wing).

Learn the timing of the Five. Some of them take a long time to answer a question or share a thought. It is necessary to be patient. They are usually focused on replying honestly, accurately and authentically. Don't rattle them with more questions while they are thinking. They will take this as being pushy. Don't expect a lot of emotions from Fives either.

Interpret carefully with Fives. Interpreting too quickly can feel overwhelming and unsafe for the Five. Give Fives a chance to examine your interpretations. Presenting them in a "take it or leave it" fashion is helpful for Fives and feels safer to them, allowing them a choice.

Helping the Five learn more about relationships should be a goal of counseling, depending on the individual and the reason they came into counseling in the first place. Behind their quest for knowledge is a quest for love. Growth is found in developing relationships with the external world.

Avoid sounding judgmental with Fives. Make sure the counselee actually hears what you are trying to say, as they can be paranoid. If troubling thoughts can be identified and dealt with before they harden into conclusions, counseling will stay on track.

Fives often talk of feeling isolated and overlooked, both as a source of safety and sadness. They are prone to act in ways that unconsciously invite being overlooked. In counseling, this may result in Fives not offering information unless it is specifically asked for. Being heard and taken seriously by the counselor is one effective treatment for the Five's feeling overlooked. Keeping a rhythm helps. If counselors demonstrate that they are paying attention and are aware of issues in an ongoing way Fives will feel more confident. Respond genuinely and briefly to whatever the counselee says. Begin new sessions by reviewing what you talked about the previous week. Maintaining continuity is important to the analytical mind of the Five.

Fives need to have a sense of exchange with the counselor. The relationship can cause anxiety because of its imbalance. Being asked to share while getting nothing back makes the Five uncomfortable. They do not like the feeling of being studied. It helps to take a sharing approach, sharing some of your own experiences and treating them as an equal, not a project.

The safety of counseling can help Fives learn to get more of what they want in a relationship. Their inner voice is often self condemning and causes them to withdraw because they feel pressure to perform perfectly even in casual social situations. Sharing your own imperfections and struggles with a Five will help them find common threads to build upon, and open them to a more trusting relationship. Discovering that we all say things that are not quite what we mean can help Fives risk sharing what they think and feel. Their social experiences can be reviewed in counseling. Brainstorm new possibilities and practice communication. The counselor can provide feedback as to how the Five is most likely perceived in social situations. The security of being accepted by the counselor may ultimately lead to security in other relationships as the Five becomes more comfortable. Successful counseling will help the Five lessen their social isolation and reduce the gap between their thoughts and emotions. Fives often seem to give up without trying in relationships and generally need to communicate what they feel and need. They need to learn to listen to how others feel and respond in turn.

When there is sufficient trust in the relationship, the counselor can help link the current issue to childhood origins if that is indicated. Encouraging Fives to keep a journal of feelings, relationships, notes from counseling and personal reflection can be useful and takes advantage of the Five's inclination to privately reflect on their experiences. Having them write about childhood experiences and linking those to current issues can be helpful as well.

Final Thoughts

Counseling should create a safe environment that helps Fives experience their feelings. Open them up to relationships. The Fives significant intelligence is no substitute for relationships which require access to emotions, expose them to vulnerability and are sometimes spontaneous. Having Fives acknowledge that others are emotionally important to them and they actually gain by sharing themselves are goals of counseling. Help them enlarge their range of emotions, activities and interests.

Non-attachment is the gift of the Five. It means being fully involved in your experience and yet being able to let go. Counseling can help by providing a relationship in which the Five can deepen their capacity to be connected to themselves and others. Healthy Fives become visionaries, understanding the world profoundly and making new discoveries.

6
THE LOYALIST

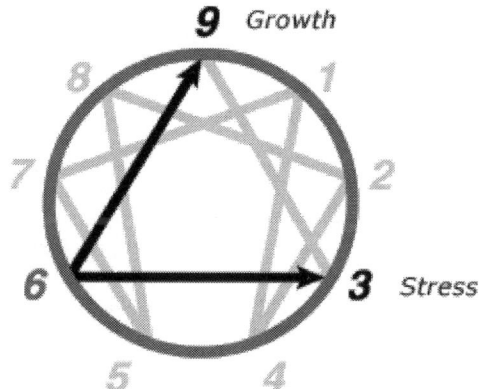

Enneagram Type Six

The committed, security-oriented type. Sixes are reliable, hard-working, responsible, and trustworthy. Excellent "troubleshooters," they tend to foresee everything that can go wrong and this can become a problem. They foster cooperation, but can also become defensive, evasive, and anxious—running on stress while complaining about it. They may be cautious and indecisive, but also reactive, defiant and rebellious. Whatever you say about them the opposite is also true. They typically have problems with self-doubt and suspicion. Sixes have the most complex relationship with authority of all the types. *At their Best*: internally stable and self-reliant, courageously championing themselves and others.

Characteristic role: The Loyalist
Ego fixation: Cowardice
Holy idea: Faith
Basic Fear: To be without a support system in an unforgiving world
Basic Desire: To feel safe
Temptation: To question the intentions of everyone around them
Vice/Passion: Fear
Virtue: Courage

Key Motivation; Want to have security, to feel supported by others, to have certitude and reassurance, to test the attitudes of others toward them, to fight against anxiety and insecurity.

The Meaning of the Arrows;

Stress/Disintegration point: Three (Paranoid, anxious Sixes try to win over others, like unhealthy Threes, to cover up their anxiety)

Security/Integration point: Nine (Positive-thinking Sixes become more peaceful, open and receptive like healthy Nines)

Healthy: Trusting of self and others, self affirming, independent yet interdependent and cooperative, treating others as an equal. Loveable, endearing and popular, able to elicit strong emotions from others. Committed, loyal, reliable, responsible and trustworthy. Capable of great acts of courage, creative, likeable, a loyal friend.

Average: Seeks a trusted authority to be loyal to, religion, political party, organization etc. Has an oxymoronic relationship with authority. Dutiful but suspicious, tends to react against authority. Ambivalent, passive aggressive, indecisive, evasive, cautious, authoritarian, partisan, scapegoating and blaming others to compensate for their fears. Avoids assuming too much responsibility due to a fear of failure.

Unhealthy: Insecure, clinging, dependent, self disparaging, anxious, anxiety prone. Acts irrationally bringing about what they most fear. Self defeating masochistic tendencies. Addictions for Sixes can include dietary rigidity, working excessively, and misuse of caffeine, amphetamines, and depressants. Sixes are susceptible to alcoholism. Can become so anxious and insecure that they cannot function.

Description

Types Sixes are sometimes referred to as Skeptics or Questioners. Sixes need to be safe and secure, to fit in and to belong. They want to have certainty and security, putting their faith in a trusted authority, belief system or tradition. Yet at the same time they are skeptical and question authority. They are faithful, friendly, conservative and/or cautious. They consider themselves loyal, dedicated and reliable. They seek the sense of accomplishment that comes from doing a job well and they have a strong sense of duty.

A walking contradiction, they can be wary and cautious one minute and/or rebellious and courageous the next. They tend to fear making important decisions; although at the same time, they resist having anyone else make decisions for them. They want to avoid being controlled, but are also afraid of taking on responsibility.

They are highly reactive and often take the position of the devil's advocate. Depending on the situation, they can be friendly and outgoing or reserved and skeptical. A dedicated employee they prefer the role of buddy, loyal family member or trusted employee. They are reluctant to take on an authority position because they fear the responsibility that comes with it. They have a fear of failure which makes decision making difficult for them. They tend to foresee everything that could possibly go wrong, often worrying about the future and predicting every possible outcome. They are attracted to people who are strong, protective and/or have prestige. They seek trusted, reliable authorities and allies.

At their best their greatest strengths are their abilities to test for the truth and to recognize and challenge a bad authority. Loyal and dedicated, they understand the value of making sacrifices for a cause they believe in and are willing to enforce society's rules to ensure safety and security for all. They believe that if everyone followed the rules and cooperated with one another, the world would be a better place. They are capable of great acts of loyalty and courage.

At their worst they focus on feelings of fear and doubt and scan for danger, hidden motives or agendas. They have a tendency to focus on the worst-case scenario. Their fears and doubts can keep them from taking action and lead to self doubt and mistrust of others. They are often depressed and anxious and can become paranoid, anxiety ridden, and so insecure that they cannot function. This actually happened to me, and I am thankful for the Enneagram system helping me to understand what happened.

Recognizing Type Six

They may be ambivalent about many things, having a love/hate relationship with those closest to them. They may accept a rational position, but not act on it. Fear kicks in easily. They often have trouble taking action. Worry replaces doing and the fear of failure causes procrastination. They may imagine the worst case scenario; "What if." They have a knack for seeing everything that could possibly go wrong, like the melancholy temperament, only worse. They may feel most anxious at the time of success. They may constantly scan the environment for danger. They often practice their words in advance and prepare for possible future conversations, never wanting to be caught off guard. They often second guess themselves to the point of taking no action at all. They may provoke you just to find out what you think. They may be groupies. They may distrust your information, your sources, etc. They may be taut, unable to relax often.

How you can help

Create an atmosphere of trust. Nothing else happens until trust is established. Physical relaxation helps take the focus off obsessive thinking, ironically, so does physical activity. You may have to repeat yourself, Sixes minds are constantly working and they're not always the best listeners. Physical activity such as walking and lifting weights does the mind good and improves mood, encourage it. Start a walking or fitness program with them.

It helps them feel they are accomplishing something and taking action and is good for both the psychological and physiological benefits. Teach them to doubt their doubting process. Ask "What if you're wrong?" Exaggerate to the absurd. "And if we're lucky, we'll die first." "If we're fortunate the world will end, we'd be better off." Call them on their habit of projection. Don't let them blame others for where they are. Bring fears into reality. They fear most what is in their imagination. Show them most of their fears have never happened and that if they made it this far, surely they can survive whatever happens. Help them choose a larger role in the community. Guided imagery is excellent prayer for them. Massage and all bodywork are helpful. For Christians, angels are helpful. Remind them they have a Guardian Angel. Remind them of the importance of prayer. (Consistent message: "fear not.")

Scripture

▫Mat 6:25 -34 "So I tell you, don't worry about everyday life--whether you have enough food, drink, and clothes. Doesn't life consist of more than food and clothing?
 Look at the birds. They don't need to plant or harvest or put food in barns because your heavenly Father feeds them. And you are far more valuable to him than they are.
 Can all your worries add a single moment to your life? Of course not.
 "And why worry about your clothes? Look at the lilies and how they grow. They don't work or make their clothing,
 yet Solomon in all his glory was not dressed as beautifully as they are.
 And if God cares so wonderfully for flowers that are here today and gone tomorrow, won't he more surely care for you? You have so little faith!
 "So don't worry about having enough food or drink or clothing.
 Why be like the pagans who are so deeply concerned about these things? Your heavenly Father already knows all your needs,
 and he will give you all you need from day to day if you live for him and

make the Kingdom of God your primary concern.

"So don't worry about tomorrow, for tomorrow will bring its own worries. Today's trouble is enough for today.

Doing

Sixes are the primary personality type in the Doing Triad. They are the most out of touch with the ability to make decisions and act on their own. They need reassurance, almost as if they seek permission to act. Their spouses are usually people whom they can depend on to make the tough decisions. They will seek reference from an authority figure, institution or belief system before acting. What Sixes want most from life is security, and what they fear most is losing that security. They look to an authority figure to tell them what they can and cannot do.

Sixes are full of contradictions. Whatever you say about them the opposite can also be true. They are emotionally dependent yet unrevealing. They want to be close to others, but maintain their distance until they feel safe. They are fearful of aggression yet sometimes highly aggressive themselves. They seek security yet feel insecure. They can be likeable and endearing or unfriendly and mean spirited. They try to escape hardship yet inadvertently bring hardships on themselves. Sixes are reactive, fluctuating from one state to another rapidly because they are subject to anxiety. In response to anxiety, they look to an authority figure to put it to rest. Sixes are ambivalent. They fluctuate between aggressiveness and dependency. They feel strong and weak, dependent and independent, passive and aggressive. It is difficult to predict the state Sixes will be in from moment to moment. Their personality changes with their mood, and their mood changes with circumstances. Incidents and events that mean little to anyone else can seem like major tragedies to Sixes. Don't overreact when they overreact. Give them time;

healthy to average Sixes will come to their senses and see they are overreacting to trivial incidents when given time to reflect.

Sixes are not only ambivalent toward others, they are ambivalent toward themselves. They like themselves, then they hate themselves. They have confidence, then seem helpless, as if they couldn't do anything without help from someone else. They feel cowardly at times, and at other times are capable of great acts of courage. A double set of dependent and aggressive impulses operate within them because Sixes are also ambivalent to their own internal authority, their superego.

The result is a person who fluctuates from one emotional state to another. They have no stability and thus no security, the one thing they desire most in the world. Their actions are often indecisive and circuitous. Second guessing themselves, they often undermine their own actions. This is why they are the personality type most out of touch with "Doing".

Maintaining their sense of self requires that both sides of their psyches interact with each other. They cannot embrace one side of themselves and ignore the other, they must accept who they are. Suppressing their dependant nature will not make them independent. For better or for worse, they are both sides of the coin. When they are healthy both sides work hand in hand with each other. When tension between the two sides increases so does anxiety and therein lies the problem.

Security and Anxiety

Sixes are the type most conscious of their anxiety. Other personality types displace their anxiety or can be unaware of it. Sixes own theirs, they are anxious that they are anxious. Sometimes they are able to resist it and sometimes they succumb to it. They may not show how anxious they really are. At times they may be angry, aggressive and belligerent. Nevertheless it is anxiety that is the underlying cause. Aggression is either a reaction to or an expression of their anxiety. Because they are ambivalent they may also feel insecure. They don't know how they feel about other people and don't know how they feel about themselves. Sixes want other people to like them, but they are suspicious of others and question their true feelings and motivations. They test others before trusting them, always looking for signs of approval or disapproval. If average Sixes travel the path of disintegration (stress) and deteriorate into neurosis, they become so suspicious of others they become paranoid, anxiety ridden and so insecure that they cannot function. I've experienced this firsthand. Sixes correspond to Jung's introverted thinking type;

"It is extremely difficult to give an intellectual account of the introverted feeling process, or even an approximate description of it, although the peculiar nature of this kind of feeling is very noticeable once one has become aware of it." (C.G. Jung, Psychological Types, 387)

Sixes are a walking contradiction and even Jung had a difficult time describing this personality type. The psyche of Sixes continually changes, they are a mixture of introvert and extravert. They react to whatever they have done by doing the opposite, especially when feeling anxiety. This sets off a domino effect, as they react to this new state and then to the next, and then to the next. They second guess themselves to the point of being paranoid. For example they may be affectionate, then fearing they will be taken advantage of become cold, suspicious and distant. Then, becoming anxious about their suspicions, they seek reassurance that the relationship is still okay. Then when they receive reassurance, they become suspicious of the other person's motives and they overcompensate by becoming defensive, acting as if they do not need the other person, and on the cycle goes.

If you have trouble understanding someone who is a bundle of contradictions, you are probably dealing with a Six. For instance Sixes are emotional, but they do not show their emotions directly. They give mixed signals because they are ambivalent about themselves and others. Sixes react to their feelings and communicate their reactions more than their feelings. Unless they are healthy, others can rarely tell what's on their minds.

When they are compliant, they feel weak. If they seek independence, they feel they will alienate those who provide them with security and be punished in some terrible way. Their key to becoming healthy is to find balance between their conflicting sides. They must allow both sides to exist. Suppressing one at the expense of the other will not solve their problems.

Origins

Sixes identify positively with a father figure. As children, they wanted the security of being approved of by their father figure and felt anxious if they didn't receive it. As they grew up, this need of approval from a father figure shifted; to other individuals, a teacher, a mentor, a supervisor, a boss or a spouse. It also shifted to more abstract father figures such as civil authorities or belief systems from which they could obtain security.

As children, Sixes learned to feel secure by trying to please their fathers. My father died when I was 17. I now realize I spent the rest of my life seeking the approval I felt was lacking. I felt that I never measured up to his expectations, and at high points in my careers, often wished that he was there to see me.

As children, Sixes learned to follow the follow the rules and become responsible members of society by being obedient. For me, this took place in school. (I was a straight A student, until the sixth grade, when problems with bullying and racial tensions brought on bigger things to contend with. Up until then I always tried to please the teacher.)

In learning to seek approval by being obedient, they were conditioned to believe that value exists outside of themselves, in the authority who will reward them if they do what they are told. Sixes fear retribution from the authority and what they have internalized of it (their superego) for disobedience. While they seek to please authority, they are also somewhat distrusting of authority, and this brings us back to the walking contradictions that Sixes are. They may even rebel against authority, but the pattern of orienting themselves to life by obtaining the approval of others is ingrained in Sixes and remains consistent in one form or another.

Sixes can be the most engaging, lovable people of all the types when they are healthy. They are playful, childlike and unpredictable. They want to be liked and can be especially endearing. Once they trust you, you cannot have a more faithful friend. They will fight for a friend more than for themselves.

Average Sixes are often too dependent on the authority figure, while at the same time fighting their dependent nature with passive-aggressive ambivalence. Depending on which side gets the upper hand, average Sixes can be the most petty and mean spirited of people, prejudiced and authoritarian, not at all loving or endearing as they are when healthy.

Unhealthy Sixes feel painfully insecure. They are extremely anxious, overreacting to everything; their wildly fluctuating emotions controlling their unpredictable actions. If they cannot resolve their anxieties and conflicts, Sixes become self punishing, inadvertently bringing about the very consequences they fear.

Healthy Sixes

At their best Sixes become self-affirming, trusting of self and others, independent yet interdependent and cooperative with others as equals. Belief in self leads to true courage, positive thinking, leadership, and rich self-expression. They are able to elicit strong emotional responses from others: very appealing, endearing, lovable, and affectionate. Trust is important in bonding with others, forming permanent relationships and alliances. They are dedicated to individuals and movements in which they deeply believe. They become community builders: responsible, reliable, trustworthy. Hard-working and persevering, sacrificing for others, they create stability and security in their world, bringing a cooperative spirit to all they do.

Descriptive Terms; Upholds Authority, Warm-Hearted, Responsible, Cooperative, Trustworthy, Committed, Likable, Engaging, Loyal, Practical, Appealing, Endearing

Average Sixes

Average Sixes start investing their time and energy into things they believe will be bring safety and stability. Organizing and structuring, they look to authorities for a sense of security. Constantly vigilant, anticipating problems, they seek a trusted authority figure they can trust and obey. To resist having more demands made on them, they react against others passive-aggressively. They become evasive, indecisive, cautious, procrastinating, and ambivalent. They can be highly reactive, anxious, and negative, giving contradictory, "mixed signals." Internal confusion makes them react unpredictably. You never know what to expect when dealing with a Six. They change with their internal feelings, second guess themselves and shift from one extreme to the other continually. They may be confident one moment then insecure the next. Extraverted then introverted. Friendly then withdrawn. To compensate for insecurities, they become sarcastic and belligerent, blaming others for their problems, taking a tough stance toward "outsiders." Highly reactive and defensive, dividing people into friends and enemies, while looking for threats to their own security. They are authoritarian while fearful of authority, fearful of aggression yet capable of acting aggressively, highly suspicious, yet, conspiratorial, and fear-instilling to silence their own fears.

Descriptive Terms; Interdependent, Seeks Permission , Rule Follower, Ambivalent, Minimizer, Cautious, Worrier, Obedient. True Friend, Faithful

Unhealthy Sixes

Fearing that they have ruined their security, they become panicky, volatile, and self-disparaging with acute inferiority feelings They fear they have offended their authority figure and will be punished. It could be God, a religion, an organization or the law they are at odds with, fearing they have done something to bring on the wrath of God. Seeing themselves as defenseless, they seek out a stronger authority or belief to resolve all problems, yet are distrustful of the authority and if they continue in disintegration (stress) eventually believe they have offended their authority figure and fear retribution. This becomes a self fulfilling prophecy; they inadvertently bring about the very consequences they fear. This was my own experience as I deteriorated into neurosis and my paranoia actually brought about the very things I feared.

Unhealthy Sixes become highly divisive, disparaging and berating others . Feeling persecuted, that others are "out to get them," they lash-out and act irrationally, bringing about what they fear. Fanatical, violence is possible. Hysterical, and seeking to escape punishment, they become self-destructive and suicidal. Murder is more likely than suicide. Alcoholism, drug overdoses, "skid row," self-abasing behavior likely. Generally corresponds to the Passive-Aggressive and Paranoid personality disorders.

Paranoid personality disorder is a psychiatric diagnosis characterized by paranoia and a pervasive, long-standing suspiciousness and generalized mistrust of others.

Those with the condition are hypersensitive, are easily slighted, and habitually relate to the world by vigilant scanning of the environment for clues or suggestions to validate their prejudicial ideas or biases. They tend to be guarded and suspicious and have quite constricted emotional lives. Their incapacity for meaningful emotional involvement and the general pattern of isolated withdrawal often lend a quality of schizoid isolation to their life experience.

Descriptive Terms; Overly Dependent yet Overly Independent, Contradictory, Focused on Authority yet fears Authority, Indecisive, Rebellious, Projects Blame, Extremely Paranoid, Neurotic, Insomniac, Schizophrenic, Evasive

Subtypes

The Six With A Five Wing

The personality traits of the Six and Five are somewhat in conflict with each other. Sixes are oriented towards dependency on others while Fives are oriented towards detachment from people in order to avoid be influenced by anyone. Notable examples of this subtype include Paul Newman, Billy Graham and myself. Understanding my personality type has helped me grow, overcome depression, conquer my fears and improve my weaknesses.

Healthy; Healthy people of this subtype are endearing and interesting. They may have a strong intellectual streak, depending on the strength of the Five wing. They frequently have keen insights, are observers of people, and can usually predict how others will react. Their perceptions are more original than those of Sixes with Seven wings, but because Six is the primary type they come across not as intellectuals but as extremely competent, knowledgeable individuals.

Average; The anxiety Sixes are prone to causes people of this subtype to be more intense than Sixes with a Seven wing. Cynical, negative and contentious, they are usually constricted in the expression of their emotions. This subtype is often found in the business and legal fields. They see the world as a threatening place, are often suspicious, private, fanatical and involved in some organization that offers mutual protection. They also tend to be the most attractive of the Six subtypes. Arrogance and brashness may be overcompensation for feelings of inferiority and insecurity.

Unhealthy; Extremely suspicious leaning toward paranoia. They may abuse alcohol or drugs as a way of dealing with anxiety and paranoid delusions or to suppress their feelings of inferiority. They may become self destructive, the extent and nature of will be hidden from others because of their reclusive nature. They can also be violent. Intense stress will likely lead to outbreaks of rage and destructive behavior accompanied by breaks with reality. Murder is more likely than suicide.

The Six With A Seven Wing

The personality traits of the Six and the Seven reinforce each other. People of this subtype are more extroverted, fun, interested in having a good time, more sociable and less focused on their environment and themselves than Sixes with a Five wing. Notable examples are Johnny Carson and Andy Rooney.

Healthy; Healthy people of this subtype want to feel accepted and secure with others. Happiness is important to them, and they want material things. They are extremely likeable and sociable, not taking things too seriously. They may be accomplished in many areas and like fields that bring them into contact with other people. They are usually playful and funny, coping with life and its tensions with a good sense of humor.

Average; Average people of this subtype do not handle anxiety, tension or pressure well. They use passive-aggressive means to get out of unpleasant situations and deflect with their sense of humor. They easily sour on people who have brought them displeasure however they do more blustering than real damage. They are less prone to be destructive of others and more apt to be self destructive.

Unhealthy; When unhealthy they are more disposed to becoming dependent on others, and make no attempt to disguise the depth of their emotional needs. Feelings of inferiority combine with the desire to escape themselves.

They have few means of dealing with anxiety, and as it worsens they become increasingly emotionally erratic. Their flight from anxiety often leads to mania. They act out their subconscious fears, overreacting more readily than the other subtype. They are subject to debilitating panic attacks and suicide attempts as a way of eliciting help are likely.

Disintegration; The Six Goes To Three

Sixes who go to Three no longer turn their aggression against themselves, rather they turn it against others to see them suffer. Aggression towards others has been suppressed to elicit love and protection from others. But when they go to Three the inner restraints on their aggression has been removed and it surfaces in its pure, undiluted form. Sixes become as psychopathic as unhealthy Threes. Deteriorated Sixes strike out at others violently to overcome their feelings of inferiority once and for all. They vindictively hurt others, even though their victims may not have been the ones at fault.

Sixes who go to Three manifest all the traits of unhealthy Threes. They are consumed with hatred and the desire to destroy those who do not love them. Like unhealthy Threes they become pathological liars. They are still Sixes though, so they are ambivalent about those they hate. Their still divided psyche wants to elicit love from the very person they may be violent toward.

 I went through all the stages of the unhealthy Six and deteriorated into neurosis before recovering. I had a hard time accepting the theory of further disintegration to Three. But when I examined my actions I saw that I did take on characteristics of the Three in my recovery from unhealthy Six. I didn't fully disintegrate into an unhealthy Three however. I sank into atypical depression, and when I recovered from that became a healthy Six. I still struggle with the Six's issues. Seeing the path of disintegration in my own life was startling. It is amazing that the Enneagram system can so accurately predict human behavior. There is however something psychology and the Enneagram do not consider; the power of God and His plan in the life of believers. God had a purpose and a plan for me and when I put my life back in His hands I no longer traveled the path of disintegration.

Integration; The Six Goes To Nine

Sixes need to resolve their biggest issues; ambivalence, anxiety and insecurity. This is precisely what happens when they go to Nine. Sixes at Nine are much more emotionally open, receptive and sympathetic toward people; as a result they broaden their emotional spectrums. They become emotionally stable, peaceful and self possessed. They overcome their dependent tendencies and become autonomous and independent. Others can rely on them. They are able to reassure and support others rather than seeking reassurance and support for themselves.

Sixes at Nine are quite different from even healthy Sixes, a revolutionary change for the better has taken place; they become independent yet paradoxically closer to others than ever before. Ironically, integrating Sixes develop a greater number of friends than they had when they looked to others for security. No longer reactive to people, they are able to form stable unions with people. Others seek them out because they are so balanced, mature and well disposed to people. They still have the playfullness and sense of humor of the healthy Six, with added benefit of the Nines' sunny disposition, optimism and kindheartedness, traits not normally associated with type Six.

Integrating Sixes finally attain security and the ability to trust others, traits that have always eluded them. Once they've learned that they can trust themselves, they learn to trust others. It is my goal to become an integrating Six.

Prayers for Type Six

Father, I find true authority in you. I yield to you and submit my life to you. Help me to act courageously in all circumstances. I give my fear and worry to you, take them far from me. In Jesus name, Amen

Help me to be understanding and generous to all who need me. I affirm the kinship I have with every believer. Amen

Lord, I am secure in you and able to make the best of whatever comes my way. I meet difficulties with calmness and confidence. I have faith in you, and faith in the gifts you have given me. Amen.

Lord thank you that I can keep my own identity in groups and relationships and that I am independent and capable. Thank you for the confidence and security you give me. I rest in your strength. In Jesus name, Amen.

Lord, release me from looking to others to make me feel secure, I find true security in your strength. Release me from my fear of taking responsibility for my mistakes. Release me from being negative and complaining. Release me from being evasive and defensive with those who need me. Give me the strength and desire to help my brothers in need. In Jesus name, Amen.

Father, release me from blaming others for my own mistakes and problems; I own my life and I accept responsibility for my actions. I am responsible for the choices I have made. Guide me in all that I do, in Jesus name, Amen.

Jesus, release me from my fear and dislike of those who are different from me. Release me from acting tough to disguise my insecurities. Release me from acting cowardly and unsure of myself, from feeling incapable of functioning on my own and of being suspicious of others and thinking the worst of them, Amen.

Lord Jesus, please release me from taking out my fears and anxieties on others, from overreacting and exaggerating my problems, and from feeling trapped and desperate. I find my strength in the shadow of your wings. I abide in you and trust you wholly. Thank you for the peace that comes with accepting you as Lord. I rest in your strength, safe in your mighty arms. My faith and confidence is in you, Amen.

Lord, release me from my fear of being abandoned and alone, from my self-defeating, self-punishing tendencies and from all feelings of dread about the future. Help me accept uncertainty about the future and teach me to trust in you. I am now secure and grounded in your strength. In Jesus name, Amen.

Counseling Sixes

Phobic Sixes may be obviously anxious and scan their environment for danger. Counter phobic Sixes may be confrontational and aggressive. They may be questioning, mistrustful or suspicious. They are likely to talk about worst case scenarios and often perceive themselves as victims. Last minute cancellations are likely. Be aware of the wings and the path of disintegration.

When healthy, Sixes are highly perceptive. They have excellent intuitions about people and their environment. They are excellent problem solvers and can be visionary.

When unhealthy, they chronically perceive the motivations of others to be malevolent. They can withdraw into paranoia, become accusatory and not follow through on their commitments.

Sixes constantly scan for danger. They are also loyal, have an offbeat sense of humor and are aware of things that others overlook. Prone to doubt, they often read too much into things, overreact and second guess themselves. They question authority, yet seek a competent authority to believe in. They manage fear in two seemingly contradictory ways; by being phobic and avoiding what scares them or by becoming counter phobic and challenging their fears. Most Sixes live on a continuum between the two extremes.

The American news media feed the Six's sense of fear and worrying. But positive thinking is more of our idealized image of mental health. Popular psychology also promotes the idea that negative thoughts are unhealthy and being optimistic is healthy. Sixes are well aware of how their personality style conflicts with the cultural norm. The pressure to think positively directly opposes the Six's core strategy. Imaging the worst case scenario and preparing to deal with it can be a useful strategy. The worst rarely happens, and if one is prepared to deal with the worst, anything less is easier to handle.

Childhood Experiences

Sixes have the most complicated relationship with authority of all the personality types. As children, they often experienced people in authority and positions of trust as unpredictable, deceptive or even dangerous in varying degrees. Most Sixes remember that their basic sense of safety and trust was damaged. For me, it was in a school system that failed to protect me. I was picked on, beaten and abused by older students and groups of students my age. The teachers and principals did nothing about it. When I learned to fight back, I was punished, even though those who had abused me were never punished. I learned to distrust authority and constantly scan the environment for danger. My mistrust of authority was confirmed later in life when I fought corruption in the Sheriff's Department that I worked for.

Sixes learn to avoid surprises by anticipating future harm. This may be helpful in recognizing actual danger, but it causes them to lose touch with the present and cling to inaccurate and fearful assumptions. As children they learned to be hyper-vigilant and doubting as defense mechanisms.

Sixes protect themselves with the defense mechanism of projection. **Psychological projection** or **projection bias** (including **Freudian Projection**) is the unconscious act of denial of a person's own attributes, thoughts, and emotions, which are then ascribed to the outside world, such as to the weather, the government, a tool, or to other people. Thus, it involves imagining or *projecting* that others have those feelings.

Projection is considered one of the most profound and subtle of human psychological processes, and extremely difficult to work with, because by its nature it is hidden. It is the fundamental mechanism by which we keep ourselves uninformed about ourselves. Humor has great value in any attempt to work with projection, because humor presents a forgiving posture and thereby removes the threatening nature of any inquiry into the truth.

Paleo-anthropologically speaking, this faculty probably had survival value as a self-defense mechanism when homo sapiens' intellectual capacity to detect deception in others improved to the point that the only sure hope to deceive was for deceivers to be self-deceived and therefore behave as if they were being truthful.

In classical psychology, projection is always seen as a defense mechanism that occurs when a person's own unacceptable or threatening feelings are repressed and then attributed to someone else.

An example of this behavior might be blaming another for self failure. The mind may avoid the discomfort of consciously admitting personal faults by keeping those feelings unconscious, and redirect their libidinal satisfaction by attaching, or "projecting," those same faults onto another.

Sixes attribute to other people or objects their own unacceptable thoughts, feelings, motives or desires. When in the defensive mode they see their internal issues as belonging to external forces. Projection can be negative or positive, but others are perceived as larger and more powerful than themselves by Sixes. They avoid responsibility by attributing authority, power or their own unwanted feelings to others. This protects their self image of someone powerless and innocent in the face of conflict or difficulty. It also leaves them with an anxious feeling of impending doom.

Common Problems For Sixes

Sixes are troubled by anxiety more than any other type. Chronic anxiety, confusion about relationships and losses may bring Sixes to counseling. They may also be seeking guidance from a competent authority figure. When Sixes arrive at a calm period in their lives, a rewarding career or a stable, loving relationship, their stormy mental life becomes inconsistent with the facts. They may seek counseling to prevent their anxiety from spoiling a good thing.

If Sixes enter high profile careers without being grounded in solid values, it can precipitate a crisis. They may begin to doubt their competence. They may feel like victims of their own success. The pressure of what would happen if they aren't able to sustain their success can be overwhelming.

Sixes have difficulty in relationships. Divorce can be devastating and Sixes will try everything to hold on to a relationship long after they should let go. Security is the main issue for Sixes and the thought of losing it is the source of their anxiety. Self doubt cycled with overcompensating confidence often leads to confusion and anxiety.

What To Avoid

Sixes may perceive counselors as failed authority figures. Avoid labeling them or committing to unquestioned processes. If a counselor respond's to a Sixes doubt and questioning by trying to pin the Six down, it can make things worse. Don't come across as being the authority with Sixes, let them know you're on their side. Their conflicted nature will result in provocative insights that are often contradictory. Help validate their perceptions and gain their trust gradually before being critical. Sixes need an interpersonal relationship with the counselor. Offering too much information without being personal is a mistake with Sixes. They need the ideas to be offered in the context of a relationship. They need to understand the context also. Remember you will also have characteristics of the Five or Seven to deal with depending on the wing. Five wings are more reclusive while Seven wings make no attempt to disguise the depth of their emotional needs.

Trying to argue them out of their worst case scenarios is another mistake to avoid. Instead, work on having them prepare to deal with it, and plan for it. The worst rarely happens and if they can deal with the worst, they can deal with anything less. Trying to convince a Six that things are not so bad generally increases the Six's anxiety and sense of alienation. They could feel the counselor doesn't listen well or grasp the complexity of their situation.

Don't push Sixes to accept your solutions. This will lead them to believe that you are not listening, but simply imposing what you think will help. Listen to their objections and "yes but" answers. Sixes will be ambivalent toward your advice and will often need to go through the questioning, back and forth process before putting any plan into action.

In transference, Sixes may project their own authority onto a counselor by either idealizing or devaluing them. Be careful how you handle this. Playing along with the Six's authority projection, acting paternal and reassuring could be temporarily comforting, but ultimately could lead to the counselee feeling that the counselor had become inauthentic, which would be the case thus confirming their sense of distrust.

Some Sixes express their anxiety and doubt by cancelling sessions at the last minute, keeping the option of counseling open while struggling with their ambivalence. Sixes say when they feel defensive in counseling they may become ambivalent and phobic, aggressive and disagreeable or intellectual and theoretical. Decision making becomes an arduous task. They switch from yes to no and look to others for answers. They may project and blame others for their feelings, overreacting and lashing out with a degree of anger that's disproportionate to the situation. They may withdraw and become overly emotional. They almost always feel misunderstood. Try not to be judgmental, and be respectful if you disagree with them.

What Works For Sixes

For Sixes, what the counselor does is more important than what the counselor says. Being on time, having a sincere and caring attitude, and respecting the counselee are critical for the Six. Many Sixes expressed anxiety over being asked if they wanted to schedule another appointment. This created self doubt and wondering, they didn't know if this was a signal counseling should be done or exactly how to take it. Sixes have difficulty making decisions so the counselor should be specific about what the counselee needs as far as future appointments.

Sixes search for a trustworthy authority so counselors should be ready to be scrutinized closely. Trust needs to be established each session with Sixes. Don't assume because they trusted you in the past it is automatic now. Obviously some trust does carry over but if a Six has a moment of panic or fear a therapist should not assume too much continuity. Check for skewed interpretations, comparing what you say with how the counselee interprets it.

Sixes may attribute omnipotence to counselors and expect them to protect the Six from any possible discomfort. Sixes pose some challenging problems. To what degree should the counselor anticipate and cater to the Six's needs? When does the counselor confront the Six's unrealistic expectations of perfect re-parenting from an infallible authority.

Counselors need to be cautious with Sixes but trying to avoid any situation in which they might feel anxious is not possible or helpful. In fact, it may be helpful to identify and expose the Six's demand that others provide them with more safety than is reasonable, exposing the basic dependency which keeps them stuck. They can take back their projections and claim more of their own responsibility and thus their own power over their lives. Working directly with this dynamic as it occurs in the counseling relationship can be a golden opportunity for a corrective experience.

The combination of worst case scenario thinking and projection often leads Sixes to feel they are at the mercy of forces beyond their control. Counselors should initially sympathize with their helpless feelings. Ask them how they feel or what they say to themselves when they experience "bad luck". Build from that though, "It sounds like you have been wronged, what can you do now though? What have you done in the past that was productive when bad things like this happened?" "What would you say to yourself in this situation?" The idea is to evoke the Six's observing ego and inner authority rather than having the counselor offer advice and opinions. The answers to such questions may help the Six connect to the actual events from which a neurotic reaction sprang. They need to come to recognize reality even if they don't understand why they overreact to it. Work to help them recognize their own power. Have them take responsibility for their lives rather than projecting and feeling that they are victims of circumstance, misfortune and bad luck. Do it in a sympathetic manner however. Teach them that taking responsibility brings empowerment. Owning their lives and accepting that they are ultimately responsible for where they are in life will lead to a sense of ownership and empowerment. They may have subconsciously set themselves up for failure in the past. Look for this pattern and expose it, it is common in Sixes. It must be recognized and avoided.

I believe the self sabotaging behavior of Sixes sometimes takes place at the subconscious level. As I was writing this section, I became aware of a situation in my life in which I was setting myself up for disaster. I had already set it in motion and began to worry that there were going to be ramifications. I then realized that I had control. I took control of the situation and prevented the fall out that would have occurred with my original plans. I could see that I was about to sabotage myself. I was subconsciously setting myself up for punishment, which I would have blamed on others. I would have been responsible for my own undoing. The ability to recognize and prevent such behavior is crucial for Sixes to be able to move into and stay in the healthy range.

Many Sixes already have the solutions to their problems. The counselor just needs to remind them of what they already know, which removes their confusion and distorted thinking.

When their current reactions remain overwhelming and unchanged by counseling, search for the influence of past trauma. Revisiting past trauma and understanding how it was interpreted may be helpful. Correcting distorted self blame for the past empowers the Six to trust what they know in the present. An atmosphere of trust, safety and honesty is essential.

Fear And Anger

When in their fearful state, Sixes build cases against others which sometimes lead to angry outbursts that leave others feeling blindsided. Then Sixes may retreat. This unpredictable behavior impacts relationships, causing others to walk on eggshells or just avoid the Six. Sixes are often unassertive, not expressing feelings, they have a fear of what will happen if they express a need. The feelings build and this leads to projecting their intent onto others. They need to learn to pay attention to these feelings.

Have them look for physical signs of anger, ask what it feels like when their anger starts. It helps them to learn to identify and communicate their feelings before they intensify. When working with fear and anger, it helps Sixes to identify the physical signs before the pressure builds up too high and they explode. They need to learn to express something when it is small, instead of letting it build to anger.

Sixes can get suddenly accusatory and angry during counseling, especially in couples counseling. They may then get caught in their own reaction. Regret and guilt set in after the outburst and it is difficult for the Six to recover. Their accusing self tells them they have done a bad thing.

Sixes need to hear your observations, possibly deny them, wrestle with them, then have time to let them sink in. Recognize the signs that anger has set in and get them to talk about it. Ask, "What are you angry about right at this moment?" "What do you feel about what was said?" "Do you agree or disagree?" "Does what was said make you angry?" "Tell me what you are thinking and feeling right now." Sixes tend to see themselves as weak and others as strong. Immediately disowning the impact of their own aggression protects their self image as the vulnerable one. Showing them their aggression contradicts the powerlessness they like to maintain.

Sixes are loyal and stay in bad relationships, despite feeling angry and resentful. Understand that while they may seem loyal to a fault, they are actually looking for security. Explore how their relationships are serving them.

Projection

Depressed people can sometimes be helped by supportive comments. They soak up everything that comes their way. But anxious people wear a suit of armor when it comes to supportive comments. Nothing seems to get through. Depressed people tend to feel guilty and inadequate, so they know they need to change. Anxious people also feel guilty and inadequate, but feel that something else has to change. They objectify what depressed people personalize.

Sixes are anxious, they own their anxiety. They are anxious about being anxious. Work on moving their locus of control from external to internal. Projection is the Six's armor. It keeps the responsibility on others while the

Six waits for others or something else to change. This defense mechanism of projection protects them psychologically, but it makes them feel that they are not the problem and makes change difficult.

Counselors need to identify with Sixes. What is going on in their heads is more real to them than what is actually taking place. Learning to recognize projection is especially useful to Sixes. Guide them to see their projections in a gentle way. Don't expect them to see it, they need help in this area because over time maintaining their projections has created self-fulfilling prophecies and they can find a lot of evidence to support their cases for blaming bad luck, circumstances and others for their problems. When the Six learns to take responsibility, it is painful realizing that they are responsible for where they are in life. But it is also empowering. They must learn that they are not just pinballs forced through life with someone else controlling the flippers and that they actually have control over their lives.

Projection blocks intimacy since Sixes stop seeing others accurately. Being able to see that others are actually vulnerable human beings doing the best they can is something Sixes only accept when they recognize their own power. Seeing that others are equally vulnerable also makes more satisfying relationships possible. Help them integrate their own power as well as empathize with the vulnerability of others. Help them to walk in the other person's shoes and realize they often exhibit the same behavior that rouses their anger when others engage in it. Help them accept more responsibility and deal with the complexities of life.

Their powerless self image has actually been a source of protection for Sixes, it is part of their ego defense. Making excuses and blaming others shifts the responsibility from themselves. Situations in which they have more power than others are stressful. Sixes often fear success because they are afraid of the responsibility that comes along with it. Help them to see the areas they have already been successful in and accept and use the power they possess.

Projection can make Sixes become paralyzed by their fears and overcomplicate courses of action. Help them break their problems down and make them simple, putting the course of action in small, doable steps. Do the same thing with goals, take big goals and break them down into manageable steps. Doing the small steps and celebrating small successes is empowering to Sixes.

Feelings

It may be helpful to have Sixes shift their attention from their heads to their bodies. They have a tendency to stay in their heads and intellectualize everything. They're not always aware of their feelings. Gently make them aware of their body sensations, gut reactions, feelings and what is going on in their heart. They need to learn to experience their bodies and relaxation techniques are good. When they are feeling anger, help them locate the response in their bodies. One of the difficult things for me was learning to recognize the signs and not act on them or speak immediately. Anger often leads me to say or do things I quickly realize where a mistake. If I can take a moment, recognize the anger, then calm myself before I react, it eliminates a lot of problems I would otherwise cause for myself. I can easily take something someone says the wrong way and my instinct is to react immediately, which leads me to say something I later regret. If I can recognize how someone's statement has made me feel and take a moment to reflect I can control my response. Learning not to react comes from recognizing the signs in your body. The tenseness, the anger, the desire to immediately become defensive must be recognized and controlled. Sixes are often labeled as moody, because a reaction to words taken the wrong way can swing them into defensive mode.

Sixes have found such practices as weight training and martial arts helpful for maintaining their connection with their bodies, increasing self confidence and decreasing fear. Massage and other physically relaxing techniques are also helpful.

A calm, grounded attitude and occasional silence can also be helpful. Remind Sixes to slow down, be in their own body and stop worrying. Help them let go of their fear of the worst case scenario. Remind them of past experiences and how they have gotten through them. Tie feelings to memories and let them experience those feelings. Sometimes there are no words to offer for what they are experiencing and just being there for them and offering your understanding and support is important to them.

Letting go of their mental defenses long enough to experience their feelings requires courage. They may fear losing some of their mental sharpness. But recognizing feelings will help them learn to have more control, and learn to act, not react. It also helps for counselors to encourage Sixes to be honest about what they want, and work with any fears that this admission may produce. Sometimes it may be helpful for Sixes to imagine various scenarios and their outcomes and recognize the body signs that go along with how these situations make them feel. Explore what it would be like if the Six went after what he/she really wants in life.

Final Thoughts

Sixes need to be liberated from their dependency. Doing so is extremely empowering. There will always be some anxiety and the lingering uncertainty beneath the surface. Sixes must learn to feel the fear and do it anyway. It takes courage for Sixes to live in the present when their minds are busy warning them about future disasters. Counseling should be a safe place where Sixes can reflect and assess their fears and worries. They may be fixated on their negative imaginations about the future. The counselor will need to help them open up to all possibilities including their true desires. Knowing what it is that they truly want may be one of the biggest challenges for Sixes. Their lives have controlled them instead of them being in control of their lives. Help them to see that they have the steering wheel, then map out a coarse and put them on the right path.

7
THE ENTHUSIAST

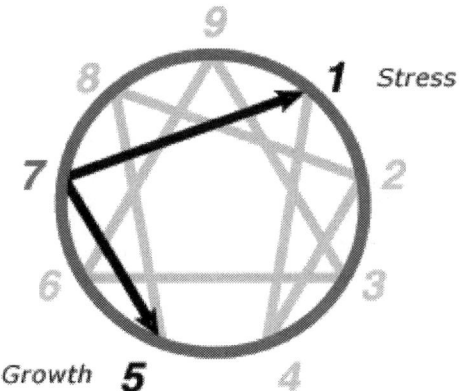

Enneagram Type Seven

Sevens are outgoing, versatile, and spontaneous. Playful, optimistic extraverts they are high-spirited, and practical. They can also misapply their many talents and become over- extended, scattered, and undisciplined. They constantly seek new and exciting experiences. They can become distracted and exhausted by staying on the go. They typically have problems with impatience and impulsiveness. *At their Best*: they focus their talents on worthwhile goals, becoming appreciative, joyous, and satisfied.

Characteristic role: The Enthusiast
Ego fixation: Planning
Holy idea: Work
Basic Fear: Boredom
Basic Desire: To experience as much of the world as possible
Temptation: Moving too fast
Vice/Passion: Gluttony
Virtue: Sobriety

Key Motivation; Want to maintain their freedom and happiness, to avoid missing out on worthwhile experiences, to keep themselves excited and occupied, to avoid and discharge pain.

The Meaning of the Arrows;

Stress/Disintegration point: One (When forced to stand still, Sevens become irritable and impatient like unhealthy Ones. They throw all their energy into some plan by which they hope to regain control.)

Security/Integration point: Five (Confident, experienced Sevens bring a sense of calm to hectic situations like healthy Fives.)

Healthy Sevens; Grateful, appreciative, joyous, ecstatic, responsive, enthusiastic, vivacious and lively. Awed by the wonders of life. Productive, does many different things well. Multitalented, high achiever.

Average Sevens: Sophisticated and worldly. Constantly seeks new experiences. Extraverted, uninhibited, hyperactive, materialistic. Into conspicuous consumption, greedy, demanding and excessive.

Unhealthy Sevens: Rude, offensive and insensitive to the needs of others. Strictly interested in what they want. Impulsive, infantile, obnoxious, out of control, acts out instead of dealing with anxiety. Addictive, compulsive, manic depressive.

Description

Sevens are the busy, variety seeking type. They are extroverted, optimistic, versatile, and spontaneous. Playful, high-spirited, and practical, they can also misapply their many talents, becoming over-extended, scattered, and undisciplined. They are essentially concerned that their lives be an exciting adventure. They are quick thinkers who have a great deal of energy and who make lots of plans. They constantly seek new and exciting experiences, but can become distracted and exhausted by staying on the go. They typically have problems with impatience and impulsiveness. They tend to be extroverted, multi-talented, creative and open minded. They are enthusiasts who enjoy the pleasures of the senses and who don't believe in any form of self-denial. Sevens are practical people who have multiple skills. They know how to network and to promote themselves and their interests. At their best they focus their talents on worthwhile goals, becoming appreciative, joyous, and satisfied. At their worst they are prone to addictions of all sorts, whether it is to shopping, gambling, drugs, sex or alcohol.

Recognizing Type Seven

They often lack motivation unless they're in trouble. They may appear charming and in control when they're actually afraid. They may replace feeling with thinking, usually about the future. They consider trivial things unduly important. They find it difficult to focus. They look much happier than they are. They may reframe pain into learning or redemption too quickly. They may have trouble staying in the present. They often have trouble acknowledging guilt. They may run away as an escape in any number of ways.

How You Can Help

Bring the Seven to the present time and place. Point out avoidance patterns. Remind them of their inner life. Decide on a form of prayer or meditation and stick to it. Keep spiritual exercises simple and uncomplicated.

Distinguish between inner authority and a faked superiority. Where is the order in their life? Symbolic order helps at times. Bodywork is helpful, make sure they sustain it. Encourage introspection (this will be a challenge.) Search for real feelings, don't buy quick thoughts and quick fixes. Direct them to social involvement. Avoid glamour.

Scripture

Mathew 6:33 "But seek first the kingdom of God and His righteousness, and all these things shall be added to you."

Doing

The problem with doing for the Seven is that they overdo. They overdo everything in a search for happiness. They love their environment and respond strongly to stimuli, throwing themselves into everything they do. Whatever they do leads to more doing. They are guided by experience and they want to experience everything. Their self esteem is fed by obtaining a steady stream of sensations among the tastes, colors, sounds, aromas and textures of the material world. Everything desirable exists outside of themselves in the world of material things and experiences. They have little interest in what they cannot immediately sense. Neither introspective nor people oriented, they are experience oriented. They are extroverted, pragmatic and materialistic. The world exists for pleasure and it is their purpose to get what they want for themselves.

Sevens correspond to Jung's extroverted sensing type;

"As sensation is chiefly conditioned by the object, those objects that excite the strongest sensations will be decisive for the individual's psychology. The result is a strong sensuous tie to the object….Objects are valued in so far as they excite sensations, and, so far as lies within the power of sensation, they are fully accepted into consciousness whether they are compatible with rational judgments or not. The sole criterion of their value is the intensity of the sensation produced by their objective qualities…

No other human type can equal the extraverted sensation type in realism. His sense for objective facts is extraordinarily developed. His life is an accumulation of actual experiences of concrete objects....What he experiences serves at most as a guide to fresh sensations....Sensation for him is a concrete expression of life – it is simply real life lived to the full. His whole aim is concrete enjoyment, and his morality is oriented accordingly. (C.G. Jung "Psychological Types" 362-363)

Security and Anxiety

As enjoyment decreases average Sevens feel anxious and insecure, leading them to overdo their activities even more. As they become hyperactive, they enjoy what they do less. They become more anxious and insecure and are tempted to dissipate themselves even further. It is a vicious cycle, as if they could cure their anxiety by piling on more activity. They become addicted to staying in motion.

Sevens are completely intolerant of anxiety. Introspection makes them anxious so they avoid it. They are drawn to extraversion, repressing their anxiety with activity. They lose themselves in ever increasing activities to avoid anxiety and unhappiness. The problem is they get diminishing results; the more they do the less satisfaction their experiences provide. They try to fix this by adding more activity, but soon discover that nothing makes them happy. They cannot be satisfied by what they do. Terrified and enraged at their predicament, they feel that life has played a cruel joke on them and deprived them of happiness.

Origins

As children, Sevens had a negative orientation to their mother figures. They feel frustrated by their mothers, who did not make them feel secure. Deprivation, unfortunate circumstances, a long illness, being orphaned or some other experience may have shaken their expectation that the good things in life would be given to them. The fear of deprivation becomes their fundamental motivation. They demand that all their desires be satisfied.

Possessing all they think will make them happy becomes a substitute for their mother's love.

Healthy Sevens

At their best, they assimilate experiences in depth, making them deeply grateful and appreciative for what they have. They become awed by the simple wonders of life: joyous and ecstatic. They see the boundless goodness of life. They are highly responsive, excitable, enthusiastic about sensation and experience. They are the most extroverted type: stimuli bring immediate responses—they find everything invigorating. Lively, vivacious, eager, spontaneous, resilient, cheerful. They easily become accomplished achievers, generalists who do many different things well: multi-talented. Practical, productive, usually prolific, many areas of interest.

Descriptive Terms; Spontaneous, Multi-Talented, Enthusiastic, Extroverted, Versatile, Exuberant, Full of Delight, Joyful, Futuristic, Amusing, Networker, Playful, Free, Fun

Average Sevens

As restlessness increases, they want to have more options and choices available to them. They become adventurous and worldly but less focused, constantly seeking new things and experiences: the sophisticate, connoisseur, and consumer. Money, variety, image, keeping up with the latest trends important.

Unable to discern what they really need, they become hyperactive, unable to say "no" to themselves, throwing themselves into constant activity. They become uninhibited, doing and saying whatever comes to mind. They fear being bored: in perpetual motion, but doing too many things—many ideas but little follow through.

They get into conspicuous consumption and all forms of excess. Self-centered, materialistic, and greedy, they never feel that they have enough.

Demanding and pushy, yet unsatisfied and jaded, they are addictive, hardened, and insensitive.

Descriptive Terms; Appreciator, Experiential, Gregarious, Humorous, Planner, Loves Variety, Options Open, Lively

Unhealthy Sevens

Desperate to quell their anxieties, can be impulsive and infantile: do not know when to stop. Addictions and excess take their toll: debauched, depraved, dissipated escapists, offensive and abusive.

In flight from self, acting out impulses rather than dealing with anxiety or frustrations: go out of control, into erratic mood swings, and compulsive actions (manias).

Finally, their energy and health is completely spent: become claustrophobic and panic-stricken. Often give up on themselves and life: deep depression and despair, self-destructive overdoses, impulsive suicide. Generally corresponds to the Bipolar disorder and Histrionic personality disorder.
Histrionic personality disorder (HPD) is defined by the American Psychiatriic Association as a personality disorder characterized by a pattern of excessive emotionality and attention-seeking, including an excessive need for approval and inappropriate seductiveness, usually beginning in early adulthood. These individuals are lively, dramatic, enthusiastic, and flirtatious.

They may be inappropriately sexually provocative, express strong emotions with an impressionistic style, and be easily influenced by others. Associated features may include egocentrism, self-indulgence, continuous longing for appreciation, feelings that are easily hurt, and persistent manipulative behavior to achieve their own needs.

Descriptive Terms; Materialistic, Hyperactive, Impulsive, Excessive, Acts out anxiety , Escapist, Superficial, Rebellious, Fears Depth, More is Better , Seeks Immediate gratification , Runs from here to there

Subtypes

Seven With A Six Wing

The traits of the Seven and the Six are in a certain amount of conflict with each other. Sixes are people oriented, Sevens are oriented toward things. Sevens value experiences and are quite capable of fulfilling their own needs themselves. Sixes depend on finding approval and security from others, while Sevens depend on the environment to make them happy. People of this subtype will attempt to find fulfillment for themselves, while looking to other people as additional sources of enrichment and happiness. Notable examples include Mickey Rooney and John F. Kennedy.

Healthy; Healthy people of this subtype are lighthearted, playful, have a good sense of humor and are lovable and endearing. Even though their main personality type is aggressive, they also want others to like and accept them. They tend to be generous to others, giving socialites whose warmth and wit make them popular. They tend to have many contrasting traits which makes them likeable and interesting.

Average; Average people of this subtype are defensive and impulsive. They seek approval and fear being anxious or alone. They desire to be loved and fall in love easily. They just as easily fall out of love as soon as the romance has worn off. Average people of this subtype enjoy having strong sensations and falling in love is one of them. They have a sense of humor and can be quite funny but their underlying anxiousness is closer to the surface than in healthy people of this subtype. They are gregarious but insecure about what others think of them; impulsive but anxious about their decisions; materialistic yet anxious about money. As their anxieties surface they tend to become increasingly insensitive about others without realizing it. They tend to get self-centered, demanding that others help them through bouts of anxiety. While the Six wing softens the Seven's aggressive nature, It also reinforces its anxiety.

Unhealthy; Unhealthy people of this subtype tend to be insecure. They seek the approval and affection of others. They are susceptible to problems with inferiority and anxiousness, which are problems for Sixes and Sevens. They may tearfully yet arrogantly demand that others solve their problems for them. If this doesn't work they become hysterical and helpless; driving others away and then trying to bring them back. They are highly prone to self-destructive behaviors and dramatic, masochistic episodes such as suicide attempts.

Seven With An Eight Wing

The traits of the Seven and Eight reinforce each other and produce a combination which is very aggressive. They are aggressive in two ways; they make demands on their environment and use the strength of their egos to enforce those demands. Notable examples include Joan Collins and Lauren Bacall.

Healthy; Exuberant and enthusiastic, since they are primarily Sevens. The Eight wing adds elements of self-confidence, will power and self assertion. This helps them overcome obstacles and endure whatever hardships might be in their way. They have a strong capacity for leadership. They are known for their quick minds and sharpness. They are typically extremely accomplished, since the Eight's self confidence enables Sevens to engage in many different activities. Their strong egos allow them to persevere until they succeed.

Average; Average people of this subtype are more practical and worldly than Sevens with a Six wing. They pursue their own desires with little regard for others, law or morality. The Eight wing makes them more forceful and egocentric in everything they do. They are greedy for money and do whatever it takes to get it. They are not concerned with avoiding conflicts; they find confrontations stimulating and thrive on the excitement. They are more selfish and hedonistic than Sevens with a Six wing.

Unhealthy; An unhealthy mix of the manic traits of the Seven and the antisocial, violent traits of the Eight make these people completely ruthless, especially if someone has something they want. Unhealthy Sevens often fly out of control and unhealthy Eights overestimate their power, so people of this subtype are extremely reckless and dangerous. They may become destructive when they act out and can be devastating to others.

Disintegration; The Seven Goes To One

Neurotic Sevens are in a panic, recklessly out of control. In desperation, they throw all their energy into some direction or plan in order to regain a sense of control and in so doing go to One. Self control is what they need most, and going to One seems to offer it. They are looking to center themselves and find emotional stability. All the energy that went into their pursuit of happiness implodes into hatred for those who have frustrated them. They suddenly streamline their existence and their interest in a person or thing becomes an obsession. Obsession is a subconscious way of dealing with anxiety which was formerly served by mania. The manic defense becomes an obsessive defense by which neurotic Sevens hope to regain control over themselves and repress their anxiety. They sadistically punish anyone who does not give them what they want. Punitive impulses and condemnation of others are all part of going to one.

Going to One does not work however. The connecting point around which neurotic Sevens hope to find their salvation is entirely outside themselves, ironically serving as a kind of psychological fly paper for their destructive impulses to stick to. The person who they look to for their salvation becomes instead the focus of their hatred. Rather than suppressing their destructive impulses or dealing with them constructively they turn them on the very person they are looking to to save them. They become the focus of all the hatred Sevens have for those who have frustrated their desires in the past.

Deteriorated Sevens are impulsive, violent and their thinking is disturbed. They are dangerous and in a fit of hysterical passion or a moment of temporary insanity they may hurt the very persons they turn to. Even if not homicidal, deteriorated Sevens may become violently abusive to their children or spouses. If they succeed in harming others, their manic defense may finally give way to severe depression with suicide the ultimate result.

Integration; The Seven Goes To Five

Integrating Sevens no longer fear that they will be deprived of happiness. They have already attained psychological balance. By going to Five they become involved with things in depth. Integrating Sevens create the foundation they need to find stability and security in their lives by internalizing their experiences.

Integrating Sevens want to know more about what has made them so content because they feel genuine gratitude for their extraordinary happiness. They want to know more about the world, not just experience it. Their focus of attention has shifted from themselves to the world around them. They no longer see the world as existing only for their own personal gratification. They are contemplators and not just consumers. Their thankfulness blossoms into a feeling of wonder and curiosity about creation.

Sevens at Five have progressed far from their tendency to be escapists. They concentrate on their experiences and are rewarded for their efforts, gaining vastly in the satisfactions they receive. They allow reality to penetrate them and bring the full force of their considerable skills and talents to bear on their experiences. They maintain their healthy enthusiasm and productivity, and may end up contributing something original to the world.

Prayers for Type Seven

Lord, release me from my reckless and destructive impulses, all compulsions and addictions and from feeling that I will be overwhelmed by anxiety. Forgive me for insulting or abusing others to vent my frustrations and for running away from the consequences of my actions. Free me from the habit of burning myself out by trying to satisfy all of my desires. Amen.

Lord, don't let my insecurities drive me into dangerous situations and behavior. Help me not to sacrifice my health for instant gratification. Free me from being demanding and impatient with others. Amen.

Free me from feeling that there will not be enough for me. Release me from always feeling that I need more. Free me from wanting every moment to be exciting and dramatic. Amen.

Jesus, forgive me for believing that external things will make me happy. Release me from the habit of escaping from myself through distractions and constant activity. Help me stop letting my lack of self discipline ruin my opportunities and help me break the habit of overextending myself with more than I can do well. Amen.

Lord, I am happiest when I am calm and you are at the center of my life. Help me to say no to myself without feeling deprived. I know with you as Lord, there will be enough of whatever I need for me. I trust you to meet my needs. Amen.

Jesus, help me to be resilient in the face of setbacks, to find satisfaction in ordinary things and to stay with projects until I complete them. Help me to care deeply about people and be committed to their happiness. Reinforce the spiritual dimension to my life. Thank you for all you've given me, I am profoundly grateful to be alive. Amen.

Counseling Sevens

Sevens can appear curious and interested, often minimizing their own problems. They can positively spin their pain and difficulty. They may be charming and self-referencing. They can project an air of superiority about their lives. They may use excessive, overly positive words like fabulous, fantastic, wonderful, etc. Many Sevens initially come to counseling as part of a couple or family. They can mentally understand their problem but find some way to avoid real change. Painful relationship patterns or childhood trauma may come up. They can be critical and confrontational if they feel limited or pinned down by a line of questioning. Substance abuse may develop if their need for unlimited positive options is frustrated by pain and difficulty. They can be aggressive when rationalizing their addictions; reframing other people's concern as their problem.

Healthy Sevens are joyful and enthusiastic about life. They are attracted to beauty and have an expansive sense of possibility. They value others and are accepting and tolerant.

Unhealthy Sevens are self doubting, anxious and manage their fears by obsessing over their own pleasures and plans for the future. They see others as tools for themselves, either as companions or audiences. If others get in the way or otherwise limit Sevens they become a source of irritation. Sevens fixate on positive futures. They have a swift mental energy that helps them integrate ideas and see the big picture. They easily engage others with their relational style. They are active, charming and entertaining.

American culture embraces the persona of the Seven with images of youth, fun, adventure and denying limits. Pop culture rationalizes addiction and encourages people to medicate their pain. Addictive behavior is portrayed as being patriotic by the advertising media.

Childhood Experiences

Sevens have an inherently joyful nature. They live in the moment, whatever the moment may be; pleasant or unpleasant. As children, they were afraid that they couldn't depend on others to give them the attention they needed. They learned early on to compensate for any environmental limits by using their creative energy to imagine the world they wanted, having adventures and concocting a pleasant way to see life.

They also learned to disconnect from pain. They looked forward to future plans to avoid the discomfort of the present situation. This can manifest in relationships. Sevens often distance themselves and disconnect in advance of the relationship actually ending. This helps them to avoid pain that comes when the disconnection hits full force. They look forward to what relationship will be next and imagine how nice it will be. The habit of keeping future pleasures in mind is an expression of what many books on the Enneagram call "gluttony", a way that Sevens escape their pain through mental and physical appetite. Early on Sevens sensed that their needs were not being met by others and they decided to meet them for themselves. In order to avoid pain they kept their energy and attention on pleasant possibilities, keeping their options open. They were often the fun leaders in their groups and families, in charge of keeping others pepped up and happy. They may later replicate this in adult life.

The Seven's defense mechanism is rationalization. Rationalization protects their preoccupation with unlimited options and allows them to ascribe acceptable or worthwhile motives to thoughts, feelings or behavior which really have other unrecognized motives. To rationalize is to unconsciously justify. They may do it in a variety of ways. When they talk about their childhood experience, they often minimize the impact that authority and difficulty had on them. They can also reframe difficult memories as positive. They will minimize the negative impact events had on them and spin it into something positive; rationalizing that something good came out of it. Remember, Sevens are fearful people who don't sound fearful.

Common Problems For Sevens

Sevens will rarely seek counseling. They may come in with a spouse for couples counseling and sometimes stay on individually, but the counselor will have to convince them that he/she is competent and that counseling can make life better. They generally do not admit that they have problems. They rationalize problems into something positive, putting the best spin on it. They approach counseling with an attitude of detached curiosity. Counseling is a place to express parts of themselves that don't fit their sunny image. They want to avoid pain, but have a hard time admitting that. They will have to become deeply uncomfortable before penetrating their own denial.

Get Sevens to focus on the here and now, they shut out their unpleasant reality by focusing on their options and a future they think they can create. They live in the future. While this is a helpful strategy in some ways, they need to deal with reality. There are problems and they are pretending they don't exist, rationalizing them, and living in the possibility of the future. Point out their patterns of avoidance. Distinguish between reality and a faked superiority. Getting them to be introspective will be a challenge, but they need to face reality. Introspection makes them feel anxious so they avoid it. Spiritual exercises should be simple and uncomplicated for Sevens.

Excessive activity is a common problem for Sevens. When they lack enjoyment, they feel anxious and insecure, so they pile on activity, becoming hyperactive and enjoying what they do even less. The more they do the less enjoyment their activity provides. They fear being bored so they throw themselves into perpetual motion, doing too many things.

This is where you may be able to capitalize on their focus on the future. Get them to set goals for 1 year, 5 years and 10 years. Focus on what is truly important. Then break it down and show them they need to limit their activity to only the areas that are most important, and that added activity is not the solution. Show them they need to deal with the underlying cause of their lack of pleasure. Point out that by avoiding dealing with their issues, the same underlying unhappiness will still be there in a year, 5 years and 10 years even if they reach their goals.

Sevens are good at cheering people up, but when they go to others to be cheered up they are often let down. There is a lot of pressure for them to be happy, they may feel that it's their job to be "up." Counseling should provide a safe place to relieve that burden.

What To Avoid

The defenses of a Seven can effectively keep counselors from seeing their underlying pain and difficulties. Sevens can emanate their belief that others unnecessarily dwell on the negative. They can be angry and shocked at unpleasant feedback. They prefer good news. Spouses and counselors may unconsciously avoid getting on the wrong side of Sevens by offering only positive feedback which they readily accept.

When Sevens feel counselors don't understand their real issues they can adopt a stance of intellectual superiority. This attitude may cause the counselor to distance the counselee and such transference/counter-transference can lead to failure.

When a counselor starts feeling entertained by a Seven's charming personality, it is wise to be suspicious. Sevens can lie and play games to impress the counselor. Don't be taken in. It is a challenge to get down to reality with Sevens. When their charm fails, they can get angry about being misunderstood. They feel to challenge their positive self image is to misunderstand them.

On the other hand, it can be counterproductive for counselors to pursue Sevens' feelings too aggressively. When Sevens allow themselves to have feelings, fear and pain feel like they will never end. Stripping away their defenses is not a good strategy.

Any approach perceived as authoritarian, absolute or too directive is also guaranteed to fail. Sevens don't like being told what to do. Counselors will have to be careful how they approach Sevens.

When Sevens say everything is great, it may be the view they wish to believe rather than the way they really feel. Having an idealized self image feeds their conflict avoidance. Sevens likely have no idea how they feel. They need help getting in touch with their true feelings. They like to stay in the big picture and not get down to things like feelings. Let them keep control in the counseling session, but name and define what needs to change.

When confronting the Seven's defense avoid making them feel trapped. Backing them into a corner can instigate a counterproductive reaction. Sevens resist what they perceive as being dragged down into the mundane world.

Sevens may idealize counselors and the boundaries can get blurry. The Seven feels more comfortable being an equal with the counselor. Although the Seven needs their defense respected, good therapeutic boundaries are still recommended.

What Works For Sevens

When the conditions are right, it can be easy to get past a Seven's defenses. Recognize that they are masking, keep them in the truth and give them information. Sevens need to be released from reckless and destructive impulses, compulsions addictions and feeling that they will be overwhelmed by anxiety if they slow down and allow themselves to feel. They need to work on being demanding and impatient with others. They often overextend themselves with more than they can do. Help them focus on the truly important things and break the habit of being busy to be busy. Help them to focus and stay with a project until they complete it. Unhealthy Sevens are escapists; help them deal with their reality not just escape it.

Reframing

Sevens use *reframing* to avoid difficulty as well as to face it. Reframe back. Remind them that they are missing out on many of life's interesting experiences by avoiding their own depths and feelings. Other people can go into their negative feelings and find great value. Have them look for any patterns in their history that have led to accumulated losses. Take an inventory of their relationship history. Ask them what losses have resulted from their narrow focus on the positive.

When counseling becomes emotionally difficult, Sevens' commitment may wane. They may rationalize or argue against the value of staying with the difficult material. They tend to dismiss serious issues and stay positively focused to avoid dealing with pain. A Seven could tell a story that positively reframes their role in a problem or even reframe their reframing. Reframing is both a curse and a blessing. It is an effective form of denial. This defense mechanism works, but is also most likely the root cause of relationship problems. Help Sevens recognize when and what they are avoiding. Point out discrepancies in what they are saying; confront their spin on things. Ask about their immediate motivation and feelings.

Having flexibility and choices is extremely important to Sevens. Counseling can provide an opportunity to edge near their fear of being limited. Ask them what will happen if they are limited, how it makes them feel, and if they have felt this way before. Deeper issue like grief may come up. It is helpful to emphasize equality and teamwork in the relationship. Make the Seven feel that you are working together. Treat it like a game you are playing together, like solving a mystery or putting a puzzle together.

Charm And Fear

Being in counseling can cause anxiety so remember that Seven is a fear type, since they mask their fear with charm. Charm is usually their first defense, and is used as a diversion. Point out that there is a choice of directions when a diversion comes up. Which direction leads away from pain and which direction leads towards pain? Underscore that it is a choice. If they choose the direction that leads to pain, ask them what it would be like to stay there. When they use the charm defense, acknowledge it without criticizing and gently lead them back into sadder feelings. Acknowledge all the pieces of the Seven so they can learn to accept themselves.

Sevens can look like they know what they want, but fear and anxiety may drive this appearance. They always want to look like they are handling things. They are in conflict between their head and their heart. Understand that their underlying fear can come out as anger. If anger surfaces, probe for fear. Help them see the positive side of dealing with fear. Speak to the part of them that needs and wants to grow. Let them know this their chance to be heard, to get to know parts of themselves that are unique and valuable, but that facing difficulty and pain is their choice and that it's survivable.

Emotions

A Seven's emotional state can change quickly as they shift in and out of their pain. The thing they fear most is emotion. They will try to stay in their heads and away from emotions. They quickly come out of pain, they have developed extensive defense mechanisms, and will move from pain to cheerfulness. If you observe this, ask what got them to recover so quickly. Ask if they are sure they are not covering up their pain, and if they need to stay with it a little longer.

They may try to stay "up" for their counselor's sake. If you move from pain to happy too quickly they may pick up the cue that you want them to feel better, making them think they have to feel better. They may feel they are taking care of the counselor by being happy. They expect themselves to be happy and believe everyone else expects the same. These mood shifts are usually automatic for Sevens. Give feedback to help the Seven be aware of the behavior and understand their motivation.

It is helpful for Sevens to get in touch with their bodies, especially when their minds are over-active. They need to allow themselves to get in touch with their own feelings and to trust those feelings as valid and important signals about life. The Seven needs to learn to listen to his/her heart and feelings, not just his/her head. They are in the habit of cutting off their feelings, get them to stay with them, even if they are uncomfortable. They need to get to the other side of their feelings.

Sevens tend to be distracted by visual stimulation, which can keep them in their minds. Have them close their eyes and shut out all distractions. Get them to listen to their bodies, and experience their feelings.

It's important to listen and not move into problem solving too quickly. The counselor needs to let the Seven know there is meaning and value in staying with feelings. Let them know they will get something out of their pain. Use humor with direct and gentle answers.

Sevens may find they have a lot in common with Fours when they find value in staying with their pain and grief. When they deconstruct their egos, they find value in their feelings.

Final Thoughts

Counseling can help deconstruct a Seven's defensive charm and idealized self and help him/her to tolerate the truth of their feelings. They need to see through their happy image and yet appreciate how it kept them safe in the past. When Sevens stop denying the present, they open up to a wider range of life. When they have access to all their feelings they expand the boundaries of who they are. Aware, awake and present, they find the joy of knowing themselves.

8
THE CHALLENGER

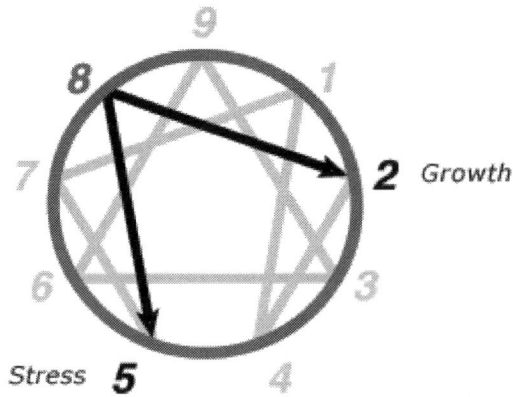

Enneagram Type Eight

Eights are self-confident, strong, and assertive. They are protective, resourceful, straight forward, and decisive. They can be ego-centric and domineering. Eights feel they must control their environment, especially people, sometimes becoming confrontational and intimidating. Eights typically have problems with their tempers and with allowing themselves to be vulnerable. *At their Best*: self-mastering, they use their strength to improve others' lives, becoming heroic, magnanimous, and inspiring.

Characteristic role: The Challenger
Ego fixation: Vengeance
Holy idea: Truth
Basic Fear: Of being harmed or controlled by others, of violation
Basic Desire: To protect themselves, to determine their own course in life
Temptation: To be too self-sufficient
Vice/Passion: Lust
Virtue: Magnanimity

Key Motivation; Eights want to be self-reliant, to prove their strength and resist weakness, to be important in their world, to dominate everyone and everything, and to stay in control of their situation.

The Meaning of the Arrows;

Stress/Disintegration point: Five (Eights become withdrawn and isolated like unhealthy Fives in their pursuit of control)

Security/Integration point: Two (Proactive, forward-thinking Eights learn to become helpful and cooperative like healthy Twos)

Healthy Eights: Magnamimous, courageous, heroic, great. Assertive, confident, srong, natural leaders, easily inspires others. Decisive authoritative, commanding, protective and honorable.

Average Eights: Enterprising, individualists, often entrepreneurs. Forceful, aggressive, domineering, willful, combative, confrontational, intimidating, belligerent, adversarial.

Unhealthy Eights: Relentlessly aggressive and ruthless, dictatorial, a tyrant. Develops delusional grandiose self image. Megalomaniacs, vengeful, violent, barbaric and murderous.

Description

Eights are the powerful domineering type. They are unwilling to be controlled, either by others or by their circumstances; they fully intend to be masters of their fate. They are self-confident, strong, and assertive. Protective, resourceful, straight-talking, and decisive, but can also be egocentric and domineering. Eights feel they must control their environment, they are confrontational and intimidating. Eights typically have problems with their tempers and with allowing themselves to be vulnerable. They generally have powerful instincts and strong physical appetites which they indulge without feelings of shame or guilt. They want a lot out of life and feel fully prepared to go out and get it. They need to be financially independent and often have a hard time working for anyone else. This leads some eights to opt out of the system and become outlaws. They want to be in the top position and have a difficult time functioning anywhere else on the ladder. Eights have a hard time lowering their defenses in intimate relationships. Intimacy involves emotional vulnerability and such vulnerability is one of the Eight's deepest fears. Betrayal of any sort is absolutely intolerable and can provoke a powerful response on the part of the violated Eight. Control issues dominate their relationships. At their best they are self-mastering, they use their strength to improve others' lives, becoming heroic, magnanimous, and inspiring. At their worst they are prone to anger, unbalanced and their bouts of anger can turn into fits of rage. Unhealthy Eights are frankly aggressive and when pushed, easily resort to violence. Such Eights enjoy intimidating others whom they see as "weak" and feel little compunction about walking over anyone who stands in their way. They can be crude, brutal and dangerous. Wayne Thatcher is an unhealthy Eight. The law enforcement officer he was paying off was an average to unhealthy eight, he dealt more in intimidation than violence, but accomplished the same end.

Recognizing Type Eight

They fill up the room with focused energy. They may test you frequently before they trust you. They define themselves by what they're against. Power is their central issue. They have black and white either/or thinking. They may operate out of mere surface impressions. They are often oblivious to their inner processes. They have trouble admitting their needs. They have difficulty acknowledging vulnerability.

How You Can Help

Bodywork like massage is helpful. Determine "whose" justice they are seeking. Introduce complexity and nuance. Point out their tightly focused attention. Distinguish between authority and control. Try to broaden the discussion and area of focus. Direct their anger at legitimate targets. Help them admit their needs. Help them claim inner values. Have them argue the opposing position to break focus.

Scripture

Proverbs 3:31, 32 "Do not envy a man of violence and do not choose any of his ways, for the LORD detests a perverse man but takes the upright into his confidence"

Relating

Eights correspond to Jung's extroverted intuitive type;

"The extraverted intuitive….has a keen nose for anything new and in the making. Because he is always seeking out new possibilities, stable conditions suffocate him….Neither reason nor feeling can restrain him or frighten him away from a new possibility, even though it goes against all of his previous convictions.

Consideration for the welfare of others is weak. Their psychic well being counts as little with him as does his own. He has equally little regard for their convictions and way of life, and on this account he is often put down as an immoral and unscrupulous adventurer. Since his intuition is concerned with externals and with ferreting out their possibilities, he readily turns to professions in which he can exploit these capacities to the full. Many business tycoons, entrepreneurs, speculators, stockbrokers, politicians, etc., belong to this type….

It goes without saying that such a type is uncommonly important both economically and culturally. If his intentions are good, i.e., if his attitude is not too egocentric, he can render exceptional service as the initiator or promoter of new enterprises. He is the natural champion of all minorities with a future. Because he is able, when oriented more to people than things, to make an intuitive diagnoses of their abilities and potentialities, he can also "make" men. His capacity to inspire courage or to kindle enthusiasm for anything new is unrivaled, although he may already have dropped it by the morrow. The stronger his intuition, the more his ego becomes fused with all the possibilities he envisions. He brings his vision to life, he presents it convincingly and with dramatic fire, he embodies it, so to speak. But this is not play acting, it is a kind of fate." (C.G. Jung, *Psychological Types,* 368-369)

Eights are confident they can assert themselves until they reach their goals and if they are not too egocentric, their personal goals will be beneficial to others. Eights are the natural leaders among the personality types. They may achieve some level of greatness and accomplish goals that while being a personal expression will also greatly benefit society.

They tend to become egocentric though, carried away by the momentum of their egos. They pit themselves against others in a struggle for power. They feel others must fall in line with them for the greater good; the accomplishment of their goals.

If they become unhealthy, they are dangerous. Ruthlessly aggressive in the pursuit of their goals, the rights and needs of others will be sacrificed in the relentless pursuit of their goals. When healthy, they have a great capacity for exerting a positive influence on many people. When unhealthy, no other type can so completely abuse power and become so totally destructive.

Aggression and Repression

Types in the Relating Triad have problems with a lack of self-development as a result of repression. Each of these types has aggressive impulses which are totally repressed (Nine) sublimated into their work (One) or forcefully expressed (Eight). None of theses three types feels that anything is wrong with them and they all repress some aspect of the self which affects their personalities. They believe that all problems exist outside of themselves, in the world. They attempt to dominate their environments (Eight), Find union with their environments (Nine) or improve their environments (One).

Repression enables them to go about their lives unencumbered by self doubt or anxiety. They feel no anxiety over the consequences of their actions; if it went wrong it was someone else's fault. While such a disposition is pleasant for these types, it makes life difficult for others.

Eights often have a fundamental imbalance in their psyche due to repression. Something is missing in them. They are one dimensional, their consciences are underdeveloped. Their egos and ids dominate their superegos. They lack the ability to identify with others and recognize the rights and needs of others. Only very healthy Eights have the capacity for empathy; most feel that they alone have rights. Getting their way takes precedent over right and wrong; their own needs and desires are the only ones that matter. Everyone and everything are merely pawns to be used to accomplish their goals- looking out for their own self interest, extending their power and ensuring their survival.

Because of their inflated ids, average to unhealthy Eights lack the ability to put limits on themselves, they are lustful, confrontational, aggressive, and assertive constantly stretching their limits. They fear submitting, so dominating everyone is essential lest they fail to prevail and be forced to submit to someone else. They fear that would mean being treated as badly as they have treated others. Ironically, Eights would not have to fear others if they did not treat others so badly.

Origins

As children, Eights became ambivalent to their mother figures. They had to assert themselves aggressively to get their mothers to respond to their needs. Dominating their mothers created the belief that they, though mere children, were stronger than an adult. They learned that asserting themselves was the way to get what they wanted. They got comfortable dominating others without fear of retribution or guilt. They repressed feelings of fear and doubt, defying them the same way they defied their mothers. They refused to be weak or seek forgiveness from anyone. Defying fear and guilt prepared them for future acts of defiance allowing their feelings to remain suppressed.

Because they relate to others through their own identities, they think everyone else is like them; that others enjoy confrontation and conflict as much as they do. Average Eights see everything in terms of power; they take advantage of whatever weakness they sense in others. Their aggressive stance in life is bound to have negative consequences for others and will eventually be disastrous for themselves. The more unethical, immoral, illegal and barbaric their actions become the more their own survival comes into question.

Healthy Eights

Become self-restrained and magnanimous, merciful and forbearing, mastering self through their self-surrender to a higher authority. Courageous, willing to put self in serious jeopardy to achieve their vision and have a lasting influence. May achieve true heroism and historical greatness.

Self-assertive, self-confident, and strong: have learned to stand up for what they need and want. A resourceful, "can do" attitude and passionate inner drive.

Decisive, authoritative, and commanding: the natural leader others look up to. Take initiative, make things happen: champion people, provider, protective, and honorable, carrying others with their strength.

Descriptive Terms; Confident, Charismatic, Inspiring, Protective, Powerful, Decisive, Strong, Builder, Leader, Determined, Magnanimous, Constructive

Average Eights

Self-sufficient and financially independent, they become enterprising, pragmatic, "rugged individualists,". Risk-taking, hardworking, denying own emotional needs they begin to dominate their environment, including others: they want to feel that others are behind them, supporting their efforts. Swaggering, boastful, forceful, and expansive: they want to be the "boss" whose word is law. Proud and egocentric, they want to impose their will and vision on everything, not seeing others as equals or treating them with respect. They become highly combative and intimidating to get their way: confrontational, belligerent, creating adversarial relationships. Everything becomes a test of wills, and they will not back down. They use threats and intimidation to keep others off balance and insecure. However, unjust treatment makes others fear and resent them, and possibly unite together against them.

Descriptive Terms; Takes Charge, Expansive, Struggles, Fights for Fairness, Forthright, Forceful, Adversarial, Dominant

Unhealthy Eights

Defying any attempt to control them, they become completely ruthless and dictatorial, "might makes right." The criminal and outlaw, renegade, and con-artist, they are hard-hearted, immoral and potentially violent.

They develop delusional ideas about their power, invincibility, and ability to prevail: megalomania, feeling omnipotent and invulnerable they recklessly over-extending themselves. If they get in danger, they may brutally destroy everything that has not conformed to their will rather than surrender to anyone else. Vengeful, barbaric and murderous they have sociopathic tendencies. Generally corresponds to the Antisocial Personality Disorder. **Antisocial personality disorder (ASPD or APD)** is defined by the American Psychiatric Association's *Diagnostic and Statistical Manual* as "...a pervasive pattern of disregard for, and violation of, the rights of others that begins in childhood or early adolescence and continues into adulthood."

Descriptive Terms; Power Broker, Confrontational, Intimidating, Impulsive, Grandiose, Controlling, Blunt, Defiant, Destructive, Vengeful, Explosive, Rageful

Subtypes

Eight With A Seven Wing

The traits of the Eight and the Seven reinforce each other and produce a very aggressive subtype. Eights seek power and Sevens seek experiences and possessions. They are the least other related and most egocentric of all the subtypes, making them the most difficult for others to get along with easily. Notable examples include Henry Kissinger and Frank Sinatra.

Healthy; Highly extroverted, action oriented and extremely energetic. They take the initiative all the time with great gusto and confidence of success. The healthy Eight's charisma combines with the healthy Seven's ability to enjoy life producing an extraordinarily outgoing personality. Their Inner strength and vitality may be so outstanding that they have a public and possibly historic impact.

Average: Very interested in power and money. These two goals reinforce each other. Average people of this subtype have a strong business sense, are highly extroverted and have tremendous drive. They invest an enourmous amount of energy into their work, interests and adventures. They easily dominate their environment, especially other people. They are robust, earthy and materialistic people who are firmly grounded. They pursue what they want aggressively, like a predator after prey. They can be egocentric and selfish. They manipulate others, treating people as objects, are pawns in their power games. They have no compassion for others and seem to have no conscience. They are overcompensating for insecurity about money and power; they can never have enough of either to make them feel secure in life.

Unhealthy; ruthless and impulsive; they do things which will later be regarded as brilliant or totally ignorant. They are offensive and tyrannical, verbally and physically brutal, lashing out anyone who has frustrated them or got in their way. They have explosively violent tempers and quickly fly into a rage. Their manic tendencies reinforce their delusions of omnipotence; they may blow their money feeding their inflated notions of themselves.

They lose control when they are anxious or threatened. They defend themselves from anxiety by acting out; striking first, attempting to destroy before being destroyed.

Eight With A Nine Wing

The traits of the Eight and the Nine are somewhat in conflict with each other. Depending on the strength of the wing, people of this subtype are more people oriented than Eights with a Seven wing. They are less self assertive, possessing a quiet strength and power held in reserve. They are less aggressive than the other subtype but can still be aggressive when necessary. Notable examples include Johnny Cash and Pablo Picasso.

Healthy; At ease with themselves and others. They don't feel they must assert themselves at all times. They are open to concerns beyond their own self interest, particularly those of family. Strong willed but mild mannered, they have deeper feelings than the other subtype. They are able to forge strong bonds with others. They may be involved with the arts, nature and children.

Average; Begins to show a definite split between the two sides; the aggressive, competitive side they show in public and the passive people oriented side they show to spouses and family. Their expansive forcefulness is grounded in some impenetrable fortress of imperturbable strength which others are not allowed to breach. This part of them is undisturbed and at peace, but not visited as much as it should be. It remains an idea. This subtype dominates other, but with a delicate touch. They can be intimidating and belligerent, then accommodating and kind hearted, especially to those who are close to them.

Unhealthy; Can be destructive without remorse, combining ruthlessness with indifference, immune from anxiety. They can become robotic, machine like, acting in a depersonalized way, swatting people aside, crushing them without any personal feelings. They are less violent than the other subtype, but can get into a strangely dissociated state of mind, personally regretting the suffering they cause yet not feeling any empathy or having any real appreciation for the gravity of what they do. There is a trade off for the lesser degree of violence they wreak on others; they live longer thus possibly doing more damage in the long run to those who live with them.

Disintegration; The Eight Goes To Five

Unhealthy Eights have abused their power so much that they have made enemies of everyone. They go to Five as a tactical retreat from belligerent action to the safety of thought. They try to maintain their power by being shrewder and more premeditated; the union of absolute power and perfect safety, a seemingly unbeatable combination. They will act less recklessly and attempt to act with more foresight, being more secretive, enabling them to strike without warning and hide from their enemies until they are ready to destroy them.

This, however, is not what actually happens. When neurotic Eights go to Five, they become extremely paranoid about their continued survival. By going to Five and isolating themselves, they can no longer act effectively in defending or asserting themselves. Their power swiftly disintegrates, giving cause for their paranoid fears.

As paranoia increases, so does their isolation and their isolation feeds their paranoia, a vicious cycle. For the first time in their lives, Eights become extremely anxious because their defense mechanisms, especially counterphobia and denial, no longer protect them. They become terrified of being punished for their crimes. Paranoia may drive them to break with reality and lose whatever ability they have to defend themselves. Schizophrenia is a real possibility.

If their enemies have not been able to defeat them before, they will certainly have the opportunity now. Disintegration leaves the Eight in an extremely vulnerable condition. The person who was once mighty now lives in abject terror, not only by the fear of the vengeance of others but by the anxiety which floods their minds.

Integration: The Eight Goes To Two

Growth for Eights lies in the direction of opening themselves up to others rather than dominating them. When healthy Eights go to Two, they learn to use their power to nurture others. Healthy Eights can be heroic and magnanimous, but principally to groups of people from whom they stand apart. But when they integrate to Two they put aside their lofty position and relate to others as individuals and as equals.

They begin to identify with others rather than against them. They develop empathy and compassion. They become nurturing, generous, helpful and genuinely concerned for the welfare and aspirations of others. They care about the needs of others as if they were their own. They learn to care about others rather than caring only about power and this crowns their leadership capacities.

They also learn a secret that Dale Carnegie taught. The way to be successful is to become genuinely interested in others. By using their power for others, they learn that they are not diminished or in jeopardy. They create something truly new, extending themselves in the world by that most powerful force, love itself.

Eights can learn the higher lessons of love at Two, ultimately seeing themselves as the servants of others. Putting themselves in this humble yet exalted position is actually an act of heroism, especially for those whose orientation has been to take pride in self sufficiency.

Prayers for Type Eight

Father, release all anger, rage and violence from my life. Release me from dehumanizing myself by violating others in any way and from being verbally or physically abusive. Help me to see that taking vengeance will not free me from my own pain. Release me from my secret fear of being vulnerable or weak. Forgive me for hardening my heart against suffering. Amen.

Jesus, release me from believing that I do not need others and that I must bully people to get my way. Release me from my fear that others will control me. Forgive me for feeling that I must only take care of myself. Release me from my fear of losing to anyone. Help me to understand that it is okay to be afraid sometimes. Amen.

Lord, free me from attempting to control everything in my life. Forgive me for denying my need for affection. I no longer feel that anyone who does not agree with me is against me. Release me from allowing my pride and ego to ruin my health and relationships. Amen.

Help me to care about other people and to let others share the glory. Help me to be big hearted, honorable and worthy of respect. I am most fulfilled by championing others. I have tender feelings and good impulses, help me to be gentle without being afraid. There is no greater authority than you Lord. Help me to master my passions, love others and ask for their love in return. Amen.

Counseling Eights

Eights have high energy and a noticeable intensity. They are usually forthright and direct. They may be confrontational and demanding readily shifting into anger and blame. They positively spin their own behavior. In relationships they can be controlling and sometimes overwhelming. They may forget their own past behavior and at other times be ruthlessly hard on themselves. They can be nurturing and protective parents. Substance abuse may evolve from excessively enjoying sensory pleasure combined with their need to deny their underlying pain and vulnerability.

Healthy Eights are magnanimous, sharing their power and energy in a community spirit. Natural leaders, they want the best for everyone and have high moral standards. They are less guarded that average Eights and able to share the tender side of their hearts.

Unhealthy Eights can be overpowering and insensitive to others. Aggressively taking what they impulsively desire. They ignore the impact of their aggressive behavior even as they deny their own vulnerability.

Pop culture has a love affair with the energy of Eights. Americans love heroes like Clint Eastwood, playing roles of protective vengeance. The culture rewards aggressiveness and supports their strong persona. Female Eights feel more pressure to temper their aggression with feminine qualities. It is more common for female Eights to integrate to Two, being more people oriented that male Eights.

Childhood Experiences

As children Eights observed a world where the weak were often victimized and the most powerful made the rules. Those who had power, parents, teachers, authority figures seemed to misuse it and couldn't be trusted for protection. Eights have an instinctual sense of truth and the inherent ability to relate to others without prejudice. They protected themselves by intensifying their instinctual life force. This made their energy available, abundant and pleasurable. They often cared for and defended others. They may have felt it was their duty to protect others.

The parent's of Eights often find it difficult to manage the child's aggressive energy and many Eights remember not being held or nurtured. Some parents respond to the child's power with mixed signals, punishing their aggression yet admiring it.

Some Eights put their abundant energy to use being good students and community leaders. Others choose to live on the edge of social approval; fighting, being an outsider, seeing established authority as the enemy. They may have a tough time in their careers because the idea of someone being their boss seems absurd to them.

Some Eights saw themselves as being insecure and shy, but this was probably not how others saw them. Even when conditions forced them to suppress their energy, the importance of being strong and protecting others was constant.

Eights protect their egos with the defense mechanism of denial, unconsciously disavowing their thoughts, feelings, wishes, needs or any external facts that are consciously unacceptable. The core neurotic impulse of Eights is lust. This can be sexual in nature but also includes lust for whatever the Eight desires, especially power.

Lust drives Eights to be powerful and act on their most pressing desires which makes them feel omnipotent. They then deny their weaker feelings and the negative impact of their actions. By acting swiftly and impulsively, Eights avoid reflecting on their own behavior, maintaining a momentum that prevents them from recognizing the harm they cause to others. This denial keeps them from feeling their own vulnerability and doubt as well.

Common Problems for Eights

Only a major problem would bring Eights to counseling. Their capacity to handle pain without acknowledging it and the reinforcement they get from others for being strong steers them away from self reflection. The most likely reason for an Eight to seek counseling is the threat of loss of significant others. Someone important to the Eight is usually about to leave them if they show up for counseling. When they've hurt someone who they don't want to lose it challenges their belief that it is okay to hurt people.

When the neurotic importance of being in complete control conflicts with relationships Eights can be caught off guard by the feelings that surface.

What To Avoid

You need to see through the Eights defenses and be honest with them. While they need you to be strong, acting tough will not work. They see through acting and role playing. Watch for quick answers. If you ask questions that are emotional or thought provoking the Eight may clam up or give a quick answer that is all bull. Counselors who accept the bull lose the Eights attention and trust.

Formulaic approaches that allow Eights to stay on the surface or require them to play a role usually don't work for Eights; like cognitive therapy. Eights feel it is just too safe and allows them to look good without getting to their vulnerable place. It encourages them to stay the same.

Eights may perceive counselors with a reflective style as too passive or weak. An anxious style doesn't work well for them either. If they think the counselor is not strong enough, they may start protecting them by concealing their own needs.

Defensive Eights can test and challenge counselors with an impatient, contentious presentation. Some counselors may be intimidated and contract while others could be tempted to adopt a false toughness. Eights will read the counselor quickly and give up in disgust if it doesn't look promising. For counseling to work, the counselor will have to know how to read the Eight's defenses and the fear it covers.

When Eights feel defensive in counseling, they say they test and challenge to see if the counselor is willing to be there with them, they need to know. They assume that the counselor will not get them and often come in with a chip on their shoulder. They want counseling to be fast, effective and efficient. They want help more than they will indicate. They may be suspicious and filled with angry denial. If the counselor can't stand up and fight, they will go elsewhere.

What Works For Eights

Eights want the foundations of counseling set as quickly as possible. They need a counselor to be strong, honest and smart so they feel safe enough to be vulnerable. Counselors need to know how hard it is for Eights to establish trust. A forthright approach is good. A fast, hard hitting approach that sends the message you have something to offer seems to work well for Eights. You need to effectively meet the Eight's energy, be very direct and offer a solid dose of reality. Tell them the truth. Eights want us to be honest, to speak from the most authentic intelligence of our body, mind and heart.

During various developmental stages and life crises, having a safe nurturing relationship can be critical for Eights. Eights may have fond memories of teachers and mentors who took an interest in them. Bring the memories of such people into your sessions as allies in the current work. Talk therapy can be helpful too. For some Eights, just having a safe place to to talk and tell the truth to someone they can trust is helpful.

Many female Eights report relationships where they have felt controlled. Despite being tough on the surface, many have also been victims of physical and verbal abuse. The Eight's strong persona can attract dependent-aggressive men and some Eights equate fighting with intimacy.

Female Eights can also feel guilty about their own aggression and try to suppress it. They can benefit when counselors help them identify appropriate boundaries and teach them ways to avoid getting caught in their own aggression. Some may fail to protect themselves from present abusive behavior because they haven't forgiven themselves for past relationship failures.

There may be some gender identification issues for female Eights. Finding a healthy, powerful feminine identity can be a heroine's journey for Eight women. They need to know their own feminine power.

Eights need more protection in counseling than is readily obvious. The tendency in couple's counseling is to expect the Eight to change. Counselors may push unfairly against the Eight's energy because they seem strong enough to take it. Understand and decode the Eight's strong reactions, they often feel misunderstood.

The abundant energy of Eights allows them to mask the side effects of substance abuse and high risk behavior. Counselors may need to look below the Eight's surface assurances that everything is fine and consider these dangers even if the Eight won't. Eights can use drugs and still be high functioning individuals. The truth is they are lonely at the core level. They can't express it because they can't admit it. The drugs numb the pain.

Eights say they often neglect themselves and believe they can't depend on anyone else. They often feel they are un-needful and undeserving of compassion. They feel they need no one's caring. They can also mask their need for protection with surface toughness toward the counselor. They don't want to admit it but secretly need protection. They overcompensate for this need with toughness and aggressive behavior. Expressing the need would make them vulnerable and they can't allow that.

Working with an Eight's childhood history depends on the counselor's style as well as the Eight's interest, need and readiness. Eights can be hyper sensitive to perceived manipulation and a counselor who acts too caring may be suspected of being phony. Responding too emotionally can seem manipulative. A counselor's caring may remind Eights of painful buried parts of their history, something they may not be ready to endure. They could also reframe empathy as weakness, concluding that the counselor is not strong enough to help them.

Denial

An Eight's first impulse is to deny their own capacity to hurt others. Finding buried remorse over damage the Eight has done will take some digging. When Eights begin to face the damage they have caused they can get depressed. Both their anger and their passion for life then may be absent.

Eights are self-forgetting, which predisposes them to act impulsively in ways they may later regret. It may be helpful to teach them to visualize their anger rather than acting on it. Mental pictures breaking down what happens when they are angry may prove to be helpful.

When Eights are impatient and judgmental it often means that their vulnerability is close to their conscious awareness. Anger is a way to shut the door on their vulnerability. On this edge, Eights are out of touch with all their feelings except anger. They are wrapped in denial and afraid. When a threatening moment comes, along with it comes the danger of being exposed and the weak self being uncovered. The defense is to shut down the process and just get angry, denying the moment that had just loomed close and threatening.

Counseling can give Eights a context for examining their denial of the guilt and regret they feel about any damage they have caused. It can also help them identify their most authentic intentions which are often masked by their aggressive reactions.

Eights' competitive nature and discomfort with vulnerability sometimes translates into picking on others or vengeance. Some Eights believe whatever makes them feel both strong and justified. This can lead to hurting others and a lack of integrity.

Some Eights harshly judge others, hold themselves exempt and act vengeful. When they are ready to face their behavior, helping them deconstruct their assumptions is useful. Ask what they think about others and where they are. Have them think about the judgments they make about others. Ask why they make such judgments and how they know they are right. This will be difficult at first, they tend to see questioning themselves as weakness.

Be aware that vengeful thoughts are gatekeepers for deeper feelings that will surface when the Eight's thought patterns are interrupted. When they interrupt their lustful, vengeful energy, they may feel unmasked and childlike. They can especially benefit from tools that help them heal the innocent child within. Learning to be truthful while staying compassionate is the goal at this point. Meditations that focus on the heart can be especially helpful.

Closing Thoughts

You should meet an Eight's tough defense with honesty and authentic strength. Offer solid information delivered with compassion and competency. The Eight's denial needs to be skillfully confronted. As they recognize the damage done by the momentum of their aggression, stay truthful but also help them alter, understand and forgive their own behavior. You may also have to offer a protective quality when an Eight's vulnerable self, no longer masked by denial, begins to emerge. The path of growth for Eights is to remember their quality of innocence and integrate it as a rightful aspect of their true strength.

9
THE PEACEMAKER

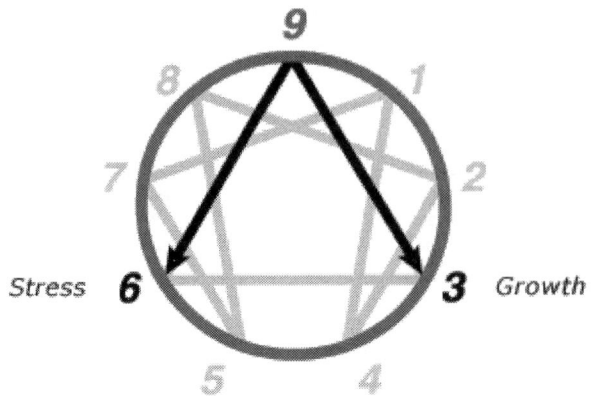

Enneagram Type Nine

Nines are the easygoing self-effacing type. Nines essentially feel a need for peace and harmony. They tend to avoid conflict at all costs, whether it is internal or interpersonal. Their desire to avoid conflict generally results in some degree of withdrawal from life, and many Nines are, in fact, introverted. They are accepting, trusting, and stable. They are usually creative, optimistic, and supportive, but can also be too willing to go along with others to keep the peace. They want everything to go smoothly and be without conflict, but they can also tend to be complacent, simplifying problems and minimizing anything upsetting.

Nines tend to adopt an optimistic approach to life; they are trusting people who see the best in others; they commonly have a deep seated faith that things will somehow work out for the best. They typically have problems with inertia and stubbornness. The Nine's desire to avoid conflict sometimes translates into an overall conservative approach to change. Change can provoke unpleasant feelings and disrupt the Nine's desire for comfort. Less healthy Nines seem incapable of motivating themselves to move into action and bring about effective change. When change does come however, Nines find that they are usually well able to adapt. They tend to be more resilient than they give themselves credit for. At their best they are indomitable and all-embracing, they are able to bring people together and heal conflicts. At their worst Nines tend not to give themselves enough credit in general, and their self-effacing attitude often seems to invite others to take them for granted. This can cause anger to build beneath the surface inside the Nine's psyche, which can erupt into consciousness in occasional fits of temper which quickly blow over. Their anger more often manifests itself in passive aggressive foot-dragging. Being overlooked is often a source of a deep sadness in Nines, a sadness that they scarcely ever give voice to.

Stress/Disintegration point: Six (Nines get more anxious, suspicious, and negative like unhealthy Sixes and may exhibit more aggressiveness)

Security/Integration point: Three (Nines begin to work at developing themselves and their potential and move into greater action in the world, like healthier Threes)

Healthy Nines; Self possessed, autonomous, fulfilled and content. Receptive, emotionally stable, peaceful, optimistic, reassuring, supportive, patient, good natured, unpretentious and genuinely nice.

Average Nines: Self effacing, goes along to get along, accommodates others too much, too easy going, gets lost in activity as an escape. Disengaged, passive, complacent, minimizes problems to appease others. Becomes fatalistic and resigned, believes nothing can be done to change their situation.

Unhealthy Nines; Repressed, underdeveloped, ineffectual, neglectful, refuses to see problems. Runs from conflict, eventually cannot function. Multiple personalities possible. Becomes depersonalized, disoriented and catatonic.

Description

Nines are the easygoing self-effacing type. Nines essentially feel a need for peace and harmony. They tend to avoid conflict at all costs, whether it is internal or interpersonal. Their desire to avoid conflict generally results in some degree of withdrawal from life, and many Nines are, in fact, introverted. They are accepting, trusting, and stable. They are usually creative, optimistic, and supportive, but can also be too willing to go along with others to keep the peace. They want everything to go smoothly and be without conflict, but they can also tend to be complacent, simplifying problems and minimizing anything upsetting.

Nines tend to adopt an optimistic approach to life; they are trusting people who see the best in others; they commonly have a deep seated faith that things will somehow work out for the best. They typically have problems with inertia and stubbornness. The Nine's desire to avoid conflict sometimes translates into an overall conservative approach to change. Change can provoke unpleasant feelings and disrupt the Nine's desire for comfort. Less healthy Nines seem incapable of motivating themselves to move into action and bring about effective change. When change does come however, Nines find that they are usually well able to adapt. They tend to be more resilient than they give themselves credit for. At their best they are indomitable and all-embracing, they are able to bring people together and heal conflicts. At their worst Nines tend not to give themselves enough credit in general, and their self-effacing attitude often seems to invite others to take them for granted. This can cause anger to build beneath the surface inside the Nine's psyche, which can erupt into consciousness in occasional fits of temper which quickly blow over. Their anger more often manifests itself in passive aggressive foot-dragging. Being overlooked is often a source of a deep sadness in Nines, a sadness that they scarcely ever give voice to.

Recognizing Type Nine

They may appear to be without any hard edges and still be angry. They may drift off in conversation. They may not know how to get on with their lives.

They may have a tough time making decisions. They may merge with any group/idea/cause they contact. They may have lots of time and no energy. They may have lots of energy for the wrong things. They may seek comfort through accommodation. They may try to hand over their life to you. They may go through the motions seemingly unconscious through repetitive behavior.

How You Can Help

Ask for priorities. Point out their wandering attention. Keep asking, "Why are you doing this?" Note black/white either/or judgments, they are made mindlessly. Help them distinguish thoughts from feelings. You may at times have to make them uncomfortable. Notice when high energy is a way of staying unconscious, just doing repetitive motion, it's a diversion. Support them when they discover they don't know what they want. Give them structure for prayer and reflection.

Scripture

Mathew 5:9 "Blessed are the peacemakers, for they will be called sons of God."

Relating

Nines are the primary type in the Relating Triad and the most out of touch with their ability to relate to the world as an individual. They tend to relate by identifying with another. Unless they are very healthy, they lack self awareness and have a naïve view of the world around them.

They generally subordinate themselves to others. They have a difficult time becoming independent and developing their own identities. Relationships allow them to merge with others, and having a union maintains their emotional stability. Preserving their inner peace through a relationship becomes more important than developing their own potential. They relate to the world through others.

Only the healthiest among them achieve self awareness. Average Nines have a passive orientation to life. Although they cannot see it, their lack of self development hinders their attempts to truly love others. To "love thy neighbor as thyself" one must first love themselves. This doesn't really matter to them though as personal growth, individualism, and self development are not as important to them as peace and accommodation are.

Repression and Aggression

In the Relating Triad, along with Eights and Ones, Nines have a problem with repression of some part of their psyches. These three types compensate in one area for underdevelopment in another. Nines have repressed the self in order to accommodate others. Eventually, their sense of self can become so repressed they live in a fantasy world or live totally through someone else. By living in a world of illusions they become so disengaged from other people and the world that nothing can bother them; at peace but removed.

Their quest for peace leads them to go too far, avoiding all conflict, going along to get along until they have no identity of their own.

Nines repress their aggression. They equate assertiveness with aggression if it threatens their relationships. In effect they repress their assertive impulses so well that are not aware they exist. They are still affected by these impulses however.

They ignore these impulses out of existence. When they do act aggressively, they deny that it happened. Their peace is somewhat of an illusion a willful blindness. They do not realize that they have sacrificed their identity to maintain their peace. Their denial, disengagement and disassociation are all negative forms of aggression; passive aggression. They are far more aggressive than they realize and their repressed emotions can eventually be detrimental. Corresponds to Jung's introverted sensing type;

"He may be conspicuous for his calmness and passivity, or for his rational self control. This peculiarity, which often leads a superficial judgment astray, is really due to his unrelatedness to objects. Normally the object is not consciously devalued in the least, but its stimulus is removed from it and immediately replaced by a subjective reaction no longer related to the reality of the object. This naturally has the same effect as devaluation. Such a type can easily make one question why one should exist at all…

Seen from the outside, it looks as though the effect of the object did not penetrate into the subject at all. This impression is correct inasmuch as a subjective content does, in fact, intervene from the unconscious and intercept the effect of the object. The intervention may be so abrupt that the individual appears to be shielding himself directly from all objective influences…if the object is a person, he feels completely devalued, while the subject has an illusory conception of reality, which in pathological cases goes so far that he is no longer able to distinguish between the real object and the subjective perception….Such action has an illusory character unrelated to objective reality and is extremely disconcerting. It instantly reveals the reality alienating subjectivity of this type. But when the influence of the object does not break through completely, it is met with well intentioned neutrality, disclosing little sympathy yet constantly striving to soothe and adjust. The too low is raised a little, the too high is lowered, enthusiasm is damped down, extravagance restrained, and anything out of the ordinary reduced to the right formula – all this in order to keep the influence of the object within the necessary bounds. In this way the type becomes a menace to his environment because his total innocuousness is not altogether above suspicion. In that case he easily becomes a victim of the aggressiveness and domineeringness of others. Such men allow themselves to be abused and then take revenge on the most unsuitable occasions with redoubled obtuseness and stubbornness. (C.G.Jung, *Psychological Types,* 396-397)

Origins

As children, Nines identified with both parents. They didn't need to distinguish themselves from their parents because their emotional needs were thoroughly satisfied by positive identification with both parents. They enjoyed having all their eggs in one basket and usually had their way. Easy going, obedient and happy, they generally required only minimal discipline. They were eager to please.

They had happy, stable childhoods during their developmental years when their personalities were formed. They recall their childhoods with a nostalgic fondness. They may have had a time in later childhood when difficulty shattered their early carefree existence, but their personalities had already formed.

Because they identified positively with both parents, they learned to maintain their sense of self by identifying deeply with other people. They seek union with others and peace. They fear separation from those they have identified with. They will subordinate themselves to others in order to preserve the peace.

Healthy Nines

Become self-possessed, feeling autonomous and fulfilled. They have great equanimity and contentment. Paradoxically, at one with self, and thus able to form more profound relationships. Intensely alive, they are fully connected to self and others. They become deeply receptive, accepting, emotionally stable and serene; trusting of self and others, at ease with self and life, innocent and simple. Healthy Nines are patient, unpretentious, good-natured, genuinely nice people.

Optimistic, reassuring and supportive, bringing people together: a good mediator, synthesizer, and communicator.

Descriptive Terms: Not-self-conscious, Unpretentious, Good Natured, Reassuring, Easygoing, Self-effacing, Supportive, Patient, Accepting, Receptive, Gracious

Average Nines

Fear conflicts them, so they become self-effacing and accommodating, idealizing others and "going along" with their wishes, saying "yes" to things they do not really want to do; going along to get along. They fall into conventional roles and expectations. They use philosophies and stock sayings to deflect others.

They are active, yet disengaged, unreflective, and inattentive; losing themselves in their routines. They do not want to be affected, so they become unresponsive and complacent, walking away from problems, and "sweeping them under the rug." Their thinking becomes hazy and ruminative, mostly comforting fantasies, as they begin to "tune out" reality, becoming oblivious. Emotionally indolent, they are unwilling to exert self or to focus on problems: indifferent.

They minimalize problems, to appease others and to have "peace at any price." Stubborn, fatalistic, and resigned, as if nothing could be done to change anything. They lose themselves in wishful thinking, and magical solutions. Others become frustrated and angry by their procrastination and unresponsiveness.

Descriptive Terms; Accommodating, Appreciative, Comfortable, Complacent, Minimizer, Content, Protective, Peaceful, Resigned, Unifying

Unhealthy Nines

They can be highly repressed, undeveloped, and ineffectual. They feel incapable of facing problems: become obstinate, dissociating self from all conflicts. Neglectful and dangerous to others. Wanting to block out of awareness anything that could affect, them, they dissociate so much that they eventually cannot function: numb, depersonalized. They finally become severely disoriented and catatonic, abandoning themselves, turning into shattered shells. Multiple personalities possible. Generally corresponds to the Schizoid and Dependent personality disorders.

Schizoid personality disorder (SPD) is a personality disorder characterized by a lack of interest in social relationships, a tendency towards a solitary lifestyle, secretiveness, and emotional coldness. There is increased prevalence of the disorder in families with schizophrenia. SPD is not the same as schizophrenia, although they share some similar characteristics such as detachment or blunted affect. **Dependent personality disorder** (DPD), formerly known as *asthenic personality disorder*, is a personality disorder that is characterized by a pervasive psychological dependence on other people.

Descriptive Terms; Non-responsive, Self-Deprecating, Passive-Aggressive, Disengaged, Repressed, Resigned, Fatalistic, Stubborn, Obstinate, Oblivious, Punitive, Lazy

Subtypes

Nine With An Eight Wing

The traits of the Nine and the Eight conflict with each other; Nines are passive and desire harmony with others, while Eights are aggressive, asserting themselves and following their self interests. People of this subtype tend to be oriented to others, receptive, unselfconscious, passive and so forth, while some part of them asserts itself strongly, at times anyway.

This is one of the most complicated subtypes because the component types diametrically oppose each other. Notable examples include Gerald Ford and Walter Cronkite.

Healthy; The Eight wing adds an element of inner strength and will power. Despite their unselfconsciousness, healthy people of this subtype are able to assert themselves effectively, yet they have an expansive passionate quality about themselves. Despite their graciousness and concern for others, they can be strong and forceful. Despite their ability to put others first and work toward common goals, they can be courageously independent. Despite an easy going manner, they can have formidable tempers. They give the impression of strength, good nature, sensuality and power.

Average; Tend to compartmentalize their emotions. While their self image is one of peacefulness, they may occasionally be quite aggressive without realizing the extent of it. They can be complacent about achieving success in some areas of their lives while being extremely competitive in others. Because neither the Eight or Nine is a particularly intellectual or thinking type, they may seem slow witted, though good natured.

They have strong drives for psychological and sexual union. Their self interest is bound up with material comfort. When their defenses are aroused, they do not wish to hurt others so much as to protect themselves and their property. They can become belligerent and confrontational, but with little long lasting personal animosity. They are protective of their families, beliefs and way of life and their greatest ire is raised against those who attack these areas. But once the crisis is past they are generally peace loving and do not hold a grudge for long.

Unhealthy; Capable of violence with little concern about the consequences. Aggressions and id impulses are strong in people of this subtype and there is little superego or conscience to regulate these forces. They are particularly jealous of their spouses. Separation from a loved one through the alienation of affections is devastating to the Nine's sense of self and inflames the Eight's rage out of wounded pride. As a result, Nines with an Eight wing can be physically dangerous and highly reactive, striking out impulsively. They may retaliate against those with whom they have come into conflict while dissociating themselves emotionally from the harm they inflict.

Nine With A One Wing

The traits of the Nine and the One tend to reinforce each other. Nines repress their emotions to maintain their peace, while Ones do it to maintain self control. This subtype tends to be more emotionally controlled and calmer than the other subtype, although they may at times display anger and moral indignation. Notable examples include Ronald Reagan, Henry Fonda and Jimmy Stewart.

Healthy; Possess enormous integrity and are extremely principled. They have great common sense which helps them be wise in their judgments, particularly about others. They have a strong sense of fairness when called on to judge situations and act objectively. The One wing adds a thinking component to this subtype balancing the Nine's unselfconsciousness. They are interested in sharing what they know and appreciate the ideas of others. They enjoy teaching and may be moral leaders, leading by example. The Nine's openness is combined with the One's objectivity resulting in a simplicity and peacefulness toward others and moderation toward themselves.

Average; May be crusaders of some type because they want to improve the world in whatever way they can. They usually have fixed conservative ideas about everything and are confident of their opinions. They tend to be orderly and self controlled. They are more emotionally controlled and less openly passionate than the other subtype. They can also be quite busy planning and organizing the environment while maintaining the emotional disconnectedness of average Nines. Usually complacent and disengaged wanting to avoid conflict yet can be easily moved to anger since they are edgy. They may rationalize, moralize or appeal to political, class or religious ideologies to bolster their arguments. They can be surprisingly impersonal and callous, disregarding others. They abstract from the real world a great deal in favor of their idealistic notions.

Unhealthy; Can be punitive toward others. They can become extremely angry, although in a highly compartmentalized way, acting impulsively in the spur of the moment. They are more resentful than the other subtype, stewing over wrongs and injustices. If they act they can be quite arbitrary, contradicting their more ordinary behavior. OCD tendencies are among their neurotic traits; they may become obsessive about their apparent problems yet dissociate themselves from their compulsive actions and real trouble. Defense mechanism are not as well developed as in the other subtype, neurotics here will tend to feel their conflicts more and will therefore be more likely to have severe emotional problems or breakdowns if they become very unhealthy.

Disintegration; The Nine Goes To Six

When unhealthy Nines go to Six, anxiety finally breaks through their massive repression. All the feelings and realizations they have denied come crashing down upon them. The once easygoing person now becomes an overreacting hysteric, anxiety ridden, fearful, agitated, apprehensive, tearful and panicked. They may become abjectly self abasing and self destruct so that others will have to care for them.

They may well do something self-defeating and humiliating, putting themselves in worse positions than ever before. They seek self punishment to assuage the guilt they feel for letting others down and making them suffer and self abasement to repair the separation from others by drawing people back to them.

These psychological tactics will not work however. Besides anxiety Nines have also subconsciously let loose aggression toward themselves and others. They become self punishing and full of self hatred. They also lash out at anyone who increases their hostility rather than immediately relieving it.

Deteriorated Nines have no defenses with which to handle anxiety or aggression. They can no longer deny the anxiety of being rejected by those they care about. They will likely turn to alcohol and drugs to control their hysteria. Suicide is possible.

If something pushes them over the edge neurotic Nines may very well split into multiple personalities. They disintegrate into the most extreme state of dissociation from who they are. They have escaped from self awareness and now breaking into parts they flee from themselves. To abandon themselves as persons and live as one of their separate selves is a solution of sorts. It is not really they who live but someone else who they can live through.

Integration: The Nine Goes To Three

When healthy Nines integrate to Three, they become self confident and interested in developing themselves and their talents to the fullest extent possible. They move from self possession to making something more of themselves. They are healthy and balanced. They can no longer live through someone else nor do they need to conform to conventional roles as sources of self esteem and identity. They become who they are by asserting themselves properly, entirely capable of dealing with reality as persons in their own right. They get in touch with the id, the aggressive and instinctual side of themselves. They no longer fear their aggressive impulses.

Their sense of peace becomes more solid as they discover that they can assert themselves without being aggressive toward others. Being themselves does not endanger their relationships as they feared. Their relationships actually become more mature and satisfying. They no longer feel they have to be self effacing. By becoming themselves they attract others who find them more interesting and desirable than ever before.

Prayers for Type Nine

Lord, I actively embrace all that life brings and I am excited about my future. Thank you that I can look deeply into myself without fear. Help me to be steadfast and dependable in difficult times. Thank you for the unique abilities you have given me. My confidence is in you. Amen.

Lord, thanks to you I am confident, strong and independent. Thank you for helping me think things through. Forgive me for living through others and not developing myself. Free me from inattentiveness and forgetfulness. Release me from feeling that most things are just too much trouble. Amen

Jesus, help me not to overdo my habit of losing myself in comfortable habits and routines. Release me from feeling threatened by significant changes in my life. Release me from seeking quick easy solutions to my problems. Amen.

Lord, release me from neglecting myself and my needs. Release me from wishful thinking and giving up too soon. Release me from dependency and the fear of being on my own. Release me from ignoring problems until they become overwhelming. Amen.

Lord, help me to see my own aggressions. Forgive me for being numb and emotionally unavailable. Free me from my feeling that there is nothing I can do to improve this life. Give me the strength to change the things I can, and the wisdom to do everything I can do about those things I cannot change. Help me to help myself. I trust you and rest in your strength and mercy, Amen.

Lord, help me to face those things which are unpleasant and difficult, not to turn away from them. No more going along to get along. Help me to take an active interest in my own life. I thank you that you created me and made me who I am. Help me to live in your will and be the person you created me to be. Amen.

Counseling Nines

Nines can be easygoing, pleasant, passive and agreeable. They may have difficulty making decisions and expressing their opinions. They may speak in long stories that are sometimes entertaining and sometimes boring; offering inessential details that sidetrack counseling. If relationship issues bring the Nine to therapy, he/she may appear distant and passive. They may have a diffused energy and be slow to respond. They may have difficulty identifying their own needs and feelings and focus on others, including the counselor. They may use indirect angry humor and exhibit passive-aggressive behavior. Substance abuse may develop as a way to numb feelings that might lead to conflict. It can also release suppressed feelings and thoughts that make them act combative and provocative, which is out of character for Nines.

At their best Nines connect with others in a way that allows everyone to feel valued. They do this without losing sight of their own contribution and significance.

When unhealthy, Nines merge with others and lose their sense of self. They feel angry at being overlooked but mask it by being agreeable. Their anger comes out in passive aggressive ways; by not following through, letting others down in a disengaged pleasant way. They fixate on finding peace and comfort, identifying with all points of view and avoiding conflict.

American culture rewards ambitious and competitive behavior. People who are articulate and clear about their interests are thought of as intelligent, strong and as leaders. Nines tend to seek consensus and are passive about their own goals. They can be seen as weak and devalued. Nine women on the other hand may merge with traditional female roles and be accepted by the culture.

Childhood Experiences

As children, Nines are innately clear about what matters to them while being sensitive to other people's feelings. But they often perceive their family environment as a place where they have to choose between being themselves and feeling connected with others. They feel that if their own desires differ from those of their parents it will lead to separation and loss. To compensate for this the child forgets his/her true self and pretends to want what others want. Though naturally empathetic Nines can lapse into defensive merging. They then distract themselves from their personal priorities and needs inducing in themselves a dazed, unfocused approach to life.

Some Nines only exist to mirror others. When recalling their family life, they may recount the life of another family member instead of their own. Nines can be the "no problem" child or the child whose troubles arise due to following a group. Nines who are unconscious of their sense of industry often achieve less in life than they have the potential for. The exception is when the Nine has merged with someone who is aggressive and highly motivated.

Nines ward off awareness of their lost self with the defense mechanism of narcotization, often referred to as numbing out. Depending on the individual, this defense can manifest as overeating, creating pointless busy work, watching TV excessively, daydreaming or getting lost in fantasy. Any activity that drains energy from a Nine can keep them from being present and awake to their own desires and needs.

Several books on the Enneagram refer to this as sloth, although the term is misleading because Nines can be very active and productive. They may still however be numb to what is important to them. Nines avoid consciousness because being aware of their own priorities could provoke conflict and rejection. They tend to get lost in activity as a way of escaping from reality.

Common Problems For Nines

Nines may seek help for relationship conflicts, depression, anxiety and angst about their life direction. Over time their tendency to sacrifice their own priorities generates anger, resentment and a deep sadness. Nines fear that getting angry will lead to separation and loss so they express their anger passive aggressively. They may make cruel jokes, sideways comments or just not listen. They may agree to do something and then not do it or become stubborn and not communicate. By passively refusing to take responsibility for their emotions Nines can stir them up in others. The Nine's partner could be overtly angry while the Nine appears amiable and a bit confused.

What To Avoid

Nines can deflect, deny or leave out important emotional content. They can play out this pattern in their relationships by allowing themselves to be overlooked, failing to communicate their thoughts and feelings or even recognize them. Later, they may suddenly awaken to feelings of resentment. They may act out this pattern with the counselor as well.

Previous attempts at counseling or therapy may have failed the Nine and they may feel that any counseling will also fail them. Ask them what has not worked in the past. This could help avoid repeating previous mistakes and it also helps Nines to hear their own story and observe their own problems.

Many Nines subconsciously believe they cannot have what they want, so they have a deep and potent fear of failing in counseling. A counselor could seem to stir up a lot of therapeutic insight. The Nine seems to be making a lot of progress in the sessions yet no action follows. Nines can banish therapeutic insights away from their consciousness especially if they threaten their core survival strategy. The counselor thinks he/she is getting to deep issues while the Nine subconsciously feels threatened. Counselors are confused and thwarted by this recurring mind set.

Nines are almost always pleasant people who are willing to explore a problem though. They are genuinely forgiving too, especially when someone makes a real effort to understand them, a gesture they may find therapeutic in itself.

Two things to avoid with Nines; 1.) not sufficiently challenging them to confront their anger and avoidance 2.) becoming too helpful.

The counseling session can become another place for the Nine to space out; being conscious but unconscious of what is going on, a kind of sleep. They need to take action rather than just waiting for their problems to just go away. Insight alone is not going to help. You can go over things in counseling until it just becomes ritualized, with no progress.

Nines need to be confronted, but at a slow pace. If rushed they tend to give up. They need to proceed at their own pace.

Counselors working with Nines should be mindful of any expectations they have that the Nine will change. They can offer a passive receptiveness that some counselors take as an invitation to offer solutions. Making suggestions while failing to uncover what the Nine really wants will ultimately lead to discouragement. Nines can appear interested and agreeable while just playing into what the counselor wants at the moment. The Nine seems to be trying but fails to change, leading to discouragement on the counselor's part. The Nine then feels bad about his or her self and begins to resent the counselor.

A counselor who fails to recognize this counter transference can easily begin setting goals for the Nine, which the Nine will subtly oppose. This leaves the counselor attached to an outcome and the Nine angry. The counseling just goes South after that.

Nines specialize in making people feel good, so good feelings may not indicate good work. To keep sessions moving forward, a counselor may need to honestly identify any counter transference and evaluate the reality of the Nine's good feelings. Counseling may seem to be helping but the counselor should ask if it is really working for the Nine.

Displacement is possible, where the Nine makes the counselor the problem. A counselor might suspect displacement if a subtle power struggle develops over time. The Nine may leave sessions increasingly discouraged and disgruntled yet never openly express it. For real progress to occur, Nines need to identify their own issues and take charge of their own problem solving, in effect creating and following their own treatment plan.

Nines are naturally compassionate and intuitive about the needs of others. In counseling, they can easily slip into taking care of the counselor's needs while avoiding their own work. They can be charming in a social conversational manner that can avoid their real pain. The Nine's childhood experience was that of not wanting to be a problem or call attention to their personal needs, this can carry over in counseling; they may present a sunny disposition and avoid being a problem. Nines will try to create a harmonious relationship with the therapist by merging with them. Making others comfortable is their defense and ironically is probably what brought them to counseling in the first place.

What Works For Nines

Nines who are caught in their unhealthy pattern tend to ruminate about their own problems from a passive observer's perspective while taking no corrective action. Encourage them, help set goals for counseling, provide suggestions for homework, but remain detached from any outcome.

One helpful technique is to get the Nine to look at the future from various possibilities. Have them imagine all possible outcomes of a given situation including what will happen if they do nothing. This technique takes advantage of the fact that Nines often know what they don't want. It shows them the negative outcome ahead if they stay on the path of least resistance. They may also have insights about negative past behaviors and their consequences as well as realizing their central role in shaping their destiny.

Another technique is having the counselee write a new story about themselves. We write stories about ourselves that match how we feel. We select memories that support our point of view. People who see themselves as having problems identify with stories that support that view. Help the counselee write a new story and find events in their past that support the story. By asking questions about their history you can unearth alternative stories that highlight the counselee's strengths. Find examples in their pasts that contradict their negative story lines. For example if their theme is they never get what they want, find examples in the past when they did get what they wanted. Ask how they did it, how it made them feel and what this says about them as a person.

You might ask about a time when they felt deeply alive, times of deep emotional feelings and richness. This highlights the difference between being comfortably numb versus being genuinely alive. Ask about what they are passionate about.

Journaling can be especially useful for Nines. Writing about their daily experiences helps them notice when and how they forget themselves. It also helps distinguish between their own feelings and those of others. It will help them discover how they avoid conflict. Journaling supports such self observation and can help it become a habit. Writing about their thoughts, feelings and experiences helps them get in touch with their sense of what matters to them. As Nines face the discomfort that comes with self awareness they often find the courage to speak their truth.

When Nines get in touch with what matters most it may stir up anxiety. They may be afraid that admitting what they want will cause conflict and loss. Reassure them that just noticing is enough; no action needs to be taken. As they become more congruent with their own desires and work through their fear, they will often spontaneously begin to take positive action on their own behalf.

Counselors can help Nines track their tendency to forget themselves back to its childhood origins. As children Nines often believed that other people's feelings were more important than their own. They tried to be good by hiding their pain or anger. Remembering their childhood may bring them in touch with the sadness and loss they felt. Meet their grief with understanding, empathy and patience.

Final Thoughts

By staying interested, compassionate and unattached, counselors can empower Nines to embrace what is most important to them. When Nines face their true selves they usually find all their personal feelings include anger. As they learn to accept the necessity for conflict they discover it actually improves relationships and leads to more authentic union with others – one of their primary motivations. Counseling Nines will often involve resolving grief over their loss of self. Nines ultimately learn they can use their empathic gift of understanding and caring for others while taking care of their own needs.

Dealing with unrecognized anger is another step Nines must take to become healthy. As Nines admit to being angry in specific instances they can begin to acknowledge the presence of anger more generally. Once they learn about and claim their anger, the next step is to work through their grief about having given up their own priorities. Working through their grief gives Nines the focus, clarity and initiative to act on what matters most to them. They awaken to the obligations that arise out of the responsibility of their being.

The Enneagram of Change

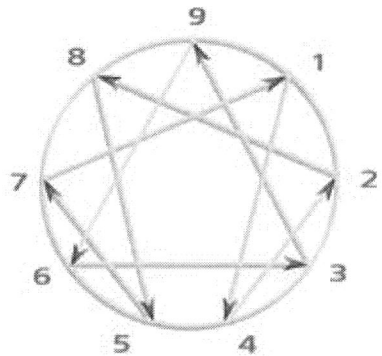

When I first wrote of **Create, Connect, Commit** in *"Change Anything"* I assigned two steps to each of the three concepts. When I reflected back on the entire process I had used to make permanent changes in my life, I realized that I had actually taken nine steps;

1. Determine your personality type. Study your personality types underlying fears, weaknesses and motivations
2.) Determine your preconceived notions and flawed premises. Write each flawed premise in the form of a statement.
3.) Challenge the premises and create new ones, based on logic and truth. (Reframe.)
4.) Create new boundaries.
5. Create a new self image.
6. Connect to what you want.
7. Connect to others.
8. Commit to change.
9. Commit to progress.

If the Enneagram is the model of completeness its proponents claim it is, then it can be applied to any concept, including the theory of change. For example, to run a successful business operation, one needs creative vision and confidence (<u>Eight</u>), the ability to bring people together and to listen to them (<u>Nine</u>), ethical standards and quality control that strives for perfection (<u>One</u>), the ability to serve people and anticipate their needs (<u>Two</u>), public relations, marketing and communication skills (<u>Three</u>), a well designed product and a sensitivity to its impact on people (Four), technical expertise, investigative skills and innovative ideas (Five), teamwork and the ability to troubleshoot (Six), and energy and optimism (Seven). Thus each type's unique characteristics are necessary components of the whole, and without each type represented the model would be incomplete.

Therefore if I had a complete system of change, each step would correspond with a different Ennegram type's characteristics.

1.) Find your personality type. (investigate) Type 5 The Investigator

2.) State the flawed premises your preconceived notions have formed; (troubleshoot) Type 6 The Troubleshooter

3.) Challenge the flawed premises and create new ones; (reform) Type 1 The Reformer

4.) Create new boundaries; (make peace with yourself) Type 9 The Peacemaker

5.) Create a new self image; (challenge your limitations) Type 8 The Challenger

6.) Connect to what you want; (design your future) Type 4 The Designer

7.) Connect to others; Type 2 The Helper

8.) Commit to change; (make new habits) Type 3 The Workaholic

9.) Commit to progress; (set new goals) Type 7 The Enthusiast

Create, Connect, Commit is a scientifically validated and complete system of change.

The Create, Connect, Commit Philosophy

Galatians 6:4

New Living Translation (©2007)

"Pay careful attention to your own work, for then you will get the satisfaction of a job well done, and you won't need to compare yourself to anyone else."

Kaizen

Kaizen(改善, Japanese for "improvement") is a Japanese word adopted into English referring to a philosophy focusing on making continuous improvements in manufacturing activities, business activities, and even life in general.

Kaizen was created in Japan following World War 11. The word Kaizen means "continuous improvement". It comes from the Japanese words kai which means to change or correct and zen which means good. Although considered a Japanese concept, it was an American who first brought the concept to Japan.

William Edwards Deming (October 14, 1900 – December 20, 1993) was an American statistician, professor, author, lecturer, and consultant. Deming is widely credited with improving production in the United States during the Cold War, although he is perhaps best known for his work in Japan. There, from 1950 onward he taught top management how to improve design, service, product quality, testing and sales through various methods, including the application of statistical methods.

Deming made a significant contribution to Japan's later reputation for innovative high-quality products and its economic power. He is regarded as having had more impact upon Japanese manufacturing and business than any other individual not of Japanese heritage.

Deming was the author of *Out of the Crisis* (1982–1986) and *The New Economics for Industry, Government, Education* (1993), which includes his System of Profound Knowledge and the 14 Points for Management.

In 1947, Deming was involved in early planning for the 1951 Japanese Census. The Allied powers were occupying Japan, and he was asked by the United States Department of the Army to assist with the census. While in Japan, Deming's expertise in quality control techniques, combined with his involvement in Japanese society, led to his receiving an invitation from the Japanese Union of Scientists and Engineers (JUSE). Deming trained hundreds of engineers, managers, and scholars in statistical process control (SPC) and concepts of quality. He also conducted at least one session for top management. Deming's message to Japan's chief executives: improving quality will reduce expenses while increasing productivity and market share. A number of Japanese manufacturers applied his techniques widely and experienced theretofore unheard of levels of quality and productivity. The improved quality combined with the lowered cost created new international demand for Japanese products.

In 1960, the Prime Minister of Japan (Nobusuke Kishi), acting on behalf of Emperor Hirohito, awarded Dr. Deming Japan's Order of the Sacred Treasure, Second Class. The citation on the medal recognizes Deming's contributions to Japan's industrial rebirth and its worldwide success. Among his many other honors, an exhibit memorializing Dr. Deming's contributions and his famous Red Bead Experiment is on display outside the board room of the American Society for Quality

Continuous Improvement Process (**CIP**, or **CI**) is an ongoing effort to improve products, services or processes. These efforts can seek "incremental" improvement over time or "breakthrough" improvement all at once. Customer valued processes are constantly evaluated and improved in the light of their efficiency, effectiveness and flexibility.

Deming saw CIP as part of the 'system' whereby feedback from the process and customer were evaluated against organizational goals. The fact that it can be called a management process does not mean that it needs to be executed by 'management' merely that it makes decisions about the implementation of the delivery process and the design of the delivery process itself.

The approach became known as **Kaizen**. This method was made famous through the book written by Masaaki Imai "Kaizen: The Key to Japan's Competitive Success."

Kaizen focuses on making **continuous small improvements** which keep a business at the top of its field. Many well known Japanese companies such as Canon use Kaizen, with a group approach which includes everyone from CEOs to janitors. This group approach has been adopted successfully in other regions of the world as well, but Japanese workers have refined it to an art form. Kaizen also suggests that everything constantly has room for refinement and improvement, and this value is contrary to the beliefs of some Westerners.

Kaizen is constant. Unlike many Western workplace improvement systems, it is not a problem based approach. Workers come up with new ideas and submit them all the time, and quality circles meet frequently. Any issue on the factory floor results in the meeting of a quality circle to talk about the issue and discuss changes to implement. As a result, Japanese companies are continuously becoming more efficient and streamlined, allowing them to effectively compete with other companies which also integrate the Kaizen philosophy into their daily practice.

Create, Connect, Commit incorporates Kaizen by taking large goals and breaking them down into smaller ones, and repeating this process until small incremental steps are left which can be taken each day. Our aim is to make sweeping, dramatic changes by setting goals large enough to inspire us, but reaching the goals by making small incremental changes that we can easily accomplish. **Create, Connect, Commit** further incorporates Kaizen by making a commitment to progress and constantly setting new goals. When

CCC to God is implemented churchwide, there must be a process in place whereby feedback from church members and visitors is evaluated against organizational goals. **Everyone must feel that they have a voice and take an active role in the process of creating Shalom in the church.**

The Six Stages of Change;

The Science Behind Create, Connect, Commit

Known as the **transtheoretical model** in health psychology, the 6 stages of change model assesses an individuals readiness to act on a new healthier behavior, and provides strategies, or processes of change to guide the individual through the stages of change to action and maintenance.

James O. Prochaska of the University of Rhode Island and colleagues developed the transtheoretical model beginning in 1977. It is based on an analysis of different theories of psychotherapy, hence the name "transtheoretical."

In the transtheoretical model as of 1997, change is a "process involving progress through a series of six stages"

- **Precontemplation** - "people are not intending to take action in the foreseeable future, usually measured as the next 6 months"
- **Contemplation** - "people are intending to change in the next 6 months"
- **Preparation** - "people are intending to take action in the immediate future, usually measured as the next month"
- **Action** - "people have made specific overt modifications in their life styles within the past 6 months"
- **Maintenance** - "people are working to prevent relapse," a stage which is estimated to last "from 6 months to about 5 years"
- **Termination** - "individuals have zero temptation and 100% self-efficacy... they are sure they will not return to their old unhealthy habit as a way of coping"

In addition, the researchers conceptualized "relapse" which is not a stage in itself but rather the "return from action or maintenance to an earlier stage

Precontemplation

Individuals in the precontemplation stage of change are not even thinking about changing their behavior. They may not see their problems, or they think that others who point out their problems are exaggerating. They are in **denial** about their problems.

There are many reasons to be in precontemplation, and they have been referred to as "the Four Rs" —reluctance, rebellion, resignation and rationalization:

- **Reluctant precontemplators** are those who through lack of knowledge or inertia do not want to consider change. The impact of the problem has not become fully conscious.
- **Rebellious precontemplators** have a heavy investment in their behavior and in making their own decisions. They are resistant to change and particularly resistant to being told what to do. Depressed rebellious precontemplators resists seeking professional help for their depression, thinking they can handle it on their own, or that it's not "that big" of a problem. The overweight rebellious precontemplator enjoys his/her food and lifestyle and refuses to change. The addicted rebellious precontemplator enjoys the effect of his/her drug of choice and refuses to give it up.
- **Resigned precontemplators** have given up hope about the possibility of change and seem overwhelmed by the problem. Many have made many failed attempts to quit or control their addiction, overcome their depression, lose weight or to control whatever the negative behavior may be.
- **Rationalizing precontemplators** have all the answers; they have plenty of reasons why their behavior is not a problem, for instance why drinking is a problem for others but not for them.

Contemplation

Individuals in this stage of change are willing to consider the possibility that they have a **problem, and the possibility opens the door** for change.

However, people who are in the contemplating stage are often fluctuating. They are on the fence. Contemplation is not a commitment; it is not a decision to change. People at this stage are considering the possibility of change and weighing the negative consequences of their behavior but still have not made the decision to change.

In the contemplation stage, often with the help of a treatment professional, people make a risk-reward analysis. They consider the pros and cons of their behavior, and the pros and cons of change. They think about the previous attempts they have made to change their behavior, and what has caused them to fail in the past. If a shift in mental frames takes place, they can move to the next stage.

Preparation: Commitment to Action

Deciding to stop the negative behavior is the hallmark of this stage of change. The contemplation, all the weighing of pros and cons and all the risk-reward analysis finally tip the scales in favor of change. Most individuals in this stage will make a serious attempt to stop the negative behavior in the near future. Individuals in this stage appear to be ready and committed to action. A shift in their mental frame has taken place.

This stage represents determination as much as preparation. The next step in this stage is to come up with a realistic plan. Commitment to change without the necessary skills can create a fragile and incomplete plan of action. When change is attempted without the benefit of profound knowledge, the attempts are counter productive. Often with the help of a treatment professional, individuals will make a realistic assessment of the level of difficulty involved in changing their behavior. They will begin to anticipate problems and pitfalls and come up with solutions that will become part of their ongoing plan for change. They will set goals and develop a realistic plan to reach those goals.

Action: Implementing the Plan

Individuals in this stage of change put their plan into action. This stage typically involves making some form of public commitment to change their behavior in order to get external confirmation of their plan. If they have not done so already, individuals in this stage may enter counseling or some form of outpatient treatment, start attending AA meetings, get baptized, make a public profession of faith or join a church in the case of religious change, start group therapy, tell their family members and friends about their decision—or some combination of the above. They make a commitment to change by connecting with others.

Making such public commitments not only helps people obtain the support they need to recover from alcoholism, addiction, depression or whatever the negative behavior is, it also creates external monitors. People often find it very helpful to know that others are watching and cheering them on. What about the others who may secretly, or not so secretly, hope they will fail? For people who change and maintain the change, one of their many newfound pleasures is to disprove the negative predictions of others.

Nothing motivates like success. A person who has implemented a good plan begins to see it work and experiences it working over time, making adjustments along the way. The many things that the negative behavior may have taken from the person begin to be restored, along with hope and self-confidence and continued determination to change. This is why we need to celebrate small success, and use it as a tool for further motivation.

Maintenance, Relapse and Recycling

The action stage lasts from 6 months to five years. Change requires building a new pattern of behavior over time. The real test of change is long-term sustained change over many years. This stage of successful change is called "maintenance." In this stage, the new lifestyle is becoming firmly established, and the threat of a return to old patterns of behavior becomes less intense and less frequent.

Because change is so difficult to maintain, the possibility of relapse is always present. Individuals may experience a strong temptation to regress and fail to cope with it successfully. Sometimes relaxing their **guard and** getting comfortable or "testing" themselves begins a slide back. People at this stage of change must be armed with a variety of relapse prevention skills. They must know where to get the support they need. This is why connecting and committing are so important. A proper support network consists of a reinforcing family and friends who can help the changed person to work through any major problems and in cases of depression or addiction a treatment professional who can help assure the person stays on the right track. A commitment to progress by constantly setting new goals helps to maintain the change, and keeps the individual motivated to move forward, preventing regression.

Alcoholics who relapse often learn from the relapse. The experience of relapsing and returning to sobriety often strengthens a person's determination to stay sober. We must learn to benefit from our failures and find the good in every experience.

Termination

The ultimate goal in the change process is termination. At this stage, people no longer find that their old behavior presents a temptation or threat; they have complete confidence in their ability to cope without fear of relapse and the process of change is complete. They have created a new life.

Create, Connect, Commit is a scientifically validated process which incorporates the 6 stages of change model, Kaizen, self analysis and personality typing to form a fail prove method of effecting enduring change in our lives. **Create, Connect, Commit** recognizes the psychological defenses which act as barriers to change **(Precontemplation),** calls for a shift in our mental frames **(Contemplation),** has us prepare for change by creating a new self image and setting goals **(Preparation),** follows up with the commitment to change by taking action to form new habits **(Action),** helps us maintain change by committing to progress and setting new goals **(Maintenance)** until our old behavior is no longer a threat, our changes are permanent and we have created a new life **(Termination).**

2 Corinthians 5:17, Psalm 51:10 and the Serenity Prayer

"Therefore, if anyone is in Christ, he is a new creation; the old has gone, the new has come!"

Create, Connect, Commit to God embraces the belief that followers of Christ are a new creation. It teaches us to create new mental frames, set new boundaries and change our belief systems. In order to become a New Creation one must first think and act like a New Creation.

"Create in me a pure heart, O God, and renew a steadfast spirit within me."

Psalm 51:10 is the dedication prayer of **Create, Connect, Commit to God**. We are taught to create new boundaries and create a new self image in concept one, Create. After we become a new creation, we must constantly be renewed, creating a steadfast spirit which never regresses and returns to our old ways. As a new creation, we must constantly study, learn, pray earnestly and set new goals for both our personal and spiritual development. We must avoid complacency and stagnation. Getting comfortable with where we are causes growth to cease and regression to set in.

The Serenity Prayer

God grant me the serenity
to accept the things I cannot change;
courage to change the things I can;
and wisdom to know the difference.

Living one day at a time;
Enjoying one moment at a time;
Accepting hardships as the pathway to peace;
Taking, as He did, this sinful world
as it is, not as I would have it;

**Trusting that He will make all things right
if I surrender to His Will;
That I may be reasonably happy in this life
and supremely happy with Him
Forever in the next.
Amen.**

--Reinhold Niebuhr

There are certain circumstances in our lives that are beyond our control. We have to accept that there are some things which we cannot change. Accepting the things that we cannot change is a step in the **Create, Connect, Commit** process. Accepting the things we cannot change does not mean that we have to accept the premise that there is nothing we can do about those things however. That premise is flawed. You will learn in Concept One that there are many things you can do about the things which you cannot change.

Concept One; Create

Preconceived Notions

"The most common of all follies is to believe passionately in the palpably not true. It is the chief occupation of mankind."

H. L. Mencken (1880 - 1956)

It may be hard to believe, but my journey to discover the process for change began with the search for a comfortable pair of shoes. After writing this chapter and the next I debated whether or not I should include them in the book. The illustration is so simple I felt that many readers would not take it seriously and the concept would be lost in the simplicity of the application.

After much deliberation, I decided to leave the account in the book. The concept is to examine our beliefs by applying logic and truth. It doesn't matter how simplistic or complex the belief may be, the process is the same.

This is the beginning of the process to create lasting change in your life.

Uncomfortable Shoes

All my life I have suffered from foot pain. My left foot was turned around backwards when I was born. The footprints on my birth certificate show the right foot facing forward and the left foot facing in the opposite direction. It's a strange sight. My left foot was put into a cast to straighten it so its growth was restricted the first year of my life. To this day my left foot is a size smaller than my right foot and has compensated for this by growing wider. It is widest at the metatarsals and the metatarsophalangeal joint (MTP). I broke my left leg water skiing in 1979 and broke some of the bones of the left foot in 1983. These injuries have contributed to the problem. The heel string is tight in that leg and my flexibility is limited in that foot.

My big toe on my right foot was broken one night on duty with the Police Department. I was chasing someone through a yard where the grass needed to be cut and I did not see a concrete stoop. My toe hit the stoop head on at full speed. It broke my toe and jammed it into the MTP joint. I now have arthritis in the MTP joint and limited movement in the big toe. The MTP joints form the ball of the foot; they swell and make my feet even wider. Pressure from my shoes on these joints is extremely painful. I also have a high instep which exacerbates the problem.

My son and I both wear size 12 shoes. I have been wearing size 12 shoes since Jr. High School. When my son started wearing a size 12, I would get his hand me downs. I would get a lot of wear out of the shoes that he would no longer wear. Sometimes in a hurry I would borrow his good shoes. He didn't care for this practice and expressed his disdain for it. He would politely ask me not to "Depot" his shoes. One day I had borrowed a pair of his good shoes to wear with my dress clothes. When I returned them, he told me to just keep the shoes because my feet were so wide that they stretched out his shoes and ruined them.

It had never occurred to me that my feet were unusually wide. I knew that I wore size 12 shoes. My mother had bought me size 12 shoes all through high school. I bought size 12 shoes after I graduated. My wife bought me size 12 shoes after we got married. I wore size 12 shoes to the Police Academy. I wore size 12 boots on duty. I wore size 12 dress shoes to Church and size 12 athletic shoes to the gym.

I wore size 12 shoes. They fit my right foot and were a little big on my left foot, but I wore size 12 shoes and had worn size 12 shoes for over 30 years.

Shoes hurt my feet, especially new shoes. I just accepted this as a fact of life. New shoes hurt my MTP joints and had to be worn and stretched out before the pain would ease up. Some shoes were just too small in the toe and never quit hurting. That's just the way it was. I had arthritis in my MTP joints and I had to live with the pain. There was nothing I could do about it.

A Revelation

In September of 2008 when I started the job at the warehouse I had been inactive for 9 months and weighed over 300lbs. My feet ached. Even standing still was painful. I loosened the strings in my shoes to where I could barely tie them to ease the pressure on my feet. I rubbed all kinds of liniments and warming gels on my feet. My MTP joints got so used to the feeling of heat that I often burned the skin with the capsaicin cream that I applied to them. Still, my feet hurt. With all the trouble I had learning a new job, being out of shape, sore and aching all over, I didn't need the added torture of foot pain slowing me down. I had to have some relief. I began to search for a comfortable pair shoes.

While I was shopping I thought about what my son had said about my feet being wide. That prompted me to do something that I had never done before; I asked the salesman for a pair of shoes in size 12 WIDE. I tried the shoes on when she brought them out to me and something amazing happened. They fit. They didn't hurt my feet. The sides and tops of the shoes didn't put pressure on my MTP joints and I could actually walk without pain. My ankles were still sore, but the relief on my feet was miraculous. It was a revelation. All along what I had needed were size 12 WIDE shoes.

The revelation that I had mistakenly believed that I needed size 12 shoes for over 30 years made me pause to examine my mistaken belief system and explore the origin of that belief. If I was wrong about my shoe size how many other things was I wrong about? How many other flaws were there in my belief system? How many of my preconceived notions were wrong?

How much needless pain and suffering had I endured due to a flawed belief system? Reflecting back on that incident led me to answer those questions and I began to examine all my beliefs by applying logical thinking and truth.

I wanted to know why people, including myself, persist in their self-destructive behavior while ignoring the fact that what they've been doing all their lives hasn't changed anything or solved any of their problems.

People seem to think that they need to repeat their self destructive cycles of behavior even more frequently or with more intensity as if they were doing the right thing but simply needed to work harder at it.

When alcoholics are miserable, they drink even more. When I was depressed I knew that I needed to become active, but I persisted in being even more inactive. As if lying in bed even longer would somehow make me feel better. I've seen people addicted to drugs desperately wanting to escape their derelict lives get saved, join the church and try to make sweeping changes only to return to their God forsaken lifestyles. Pentecostal churches frequently hold revivals. Believers flock to these revivals, requesting prayer and getting "refilled" with the spirit hoping to change their behavior or miraculously find the solution to all their problems. Still they return to the next revival needing more prayer, healing and refilling with the spirit. Has anything changed? We put criminals behind bars, and they come back out even worse criminals. They commit the same crimes again; so we put them back behind bars for even longer periods of time. Does this work? Does this change their behavior?

Even when we do manage to change, we seem to be unable to maintain that change. We eventually drift back into the same negative patterns of thought and our old habits return. We lose weight only to gain it back. We quit smoking only to start again. We make New Years resolutions and resolve to make sweeping changes in our lives. We start off with fervor and work hard to change but soon find ourselves back where we started. When we decide that we need to change again, we follow the same process we used in our previous attempts. We sincerely believe that if we only work harder and stay committed that somehow our failed system of change will miraculously work this time.

It's been said that the definition of insanity is doing the same thing over and over and expecting a different result. If that's the case, most of us are insane, at least when it comes to change. Why do people keep doing the same thing? Is it working?

Obviously not, but it seems to make sense to them. It seems to be the only thing to do. Why would I repeatedly buy shoes that did not fit? I had always bought size 12 shoes; to do anything else would seem stupid, ridiculous even. If someone had told me that size 12 shoes didn't fit my feet, I wouldn't have believed them. I would have told them they were crazy.

Plato uses the analogy of people living in a cave to illustrate a similar point in his work "Book VII of The Republic." Plato imagines a group of people who have lived chained in a cave all of their lives, facing a blank wall. The people watch shadows projected on the wall by people passing in front of a fire behind them, and begin to ascribe forms to these shadows. The prisoners can only watch the shadows cast by the men, not knowing they are shadows. There are also echoes off the wall from the noise produced from the walkway. According to Plato, the shadows are as close as the prisoners get to seeing reality. He then explains how the philosopher is like a prisoner who is freed from the cave and comes to understand that the shadows on the wall are not constitutive of reality at all, as he can perceive the true form of reality rather than the mere shadows seen by the prisoners.

"Suppose that a prisoner is freed and permitted to stand up. If someone were to show him the things that had cast the shadows, he would not recognize them for what they were and could not name them; he would believe the shadows on the wall to be more real than what he sees.

Suppose further, that the man was compelled to look at the fire: wouldn't he be struck blind and try to turn his gaze back toward the shadows, as toward what he can see clearly and hold to be real? What if someone forcibly dragged such a man upward, out of the cave: wouldn't the man be angry at the one doing this to him? And if dragged all the way out into the sunlight, wouldn't he be distressed and unable to see even one of the things now said to be true."

--| Plato's Cave |---

Change is a complicated process and **Create, Connect, Commit** involves opening yourself up to new ideas and new practices that may seem crazy to you until you've experienced them long enough to expand your boundaries and develop a new understanding.

I tried something different by accident. Noticing the difference and applying it to all areas of my life led to change. Instead of stumbling onto the truth by accident, why not apply the concepts of **Create, Connect, Commit** and make enduring changes in your own life?

Windows to the World

You may think I'm being overly simplistic using shoes for an example. It sounds too simple to be true. But the simple revelation that I had been wrong about my shoe size for over 30 years led me to the insight that changed my life. Examining the root of that belief led me to examine the root of all my flawed beliefs. I began to look at my life through the lens of logical thinking and truth. I read everything I could find about change, depression and psychology. I discovered 3 powerful concepts for creating change, and two steps for each concept. Then I put the concepts to work in my life.

Start Small

I started with my shoes. Never underestimate the power of thinking small. Change begins one small step at a time. If we can't make small changes, how can we ever make big changes? If I could figure out where I went wrong in developing the mistaken belief that I wore size 12 shoes, I could apply the same logic to every other flawed belief that I held. If I could break the cycle and change the behavior I had practiced for over 30 years, I could use the same process to change any behavior.

How long had I suffered needlessly simply because I had never asked for a pair of wide shoes? How much pain had I endured due to my ignorance? No one had ever told me that I needed wide shoes. All I knew was that I wore size 12 shoes.

I had 3 premises; that I wore size 12 shoes, that shoes hurt my feet and there was nothing I could do about it. The premises were partially true; I did wear size 12 shoes and they did hurt my feet. But I didn't have all the facts; what I really needed was a pair of wide shoes. My premises were flawed therefore my belief system was flawed. Even though it was true, it was wrong.

I broke the toe on my right foot in 1992 and it was now 2008. I had endured discomfort for at least 16 years on that side of my body. I just accepted the fact that shoes hurt my MTP joint and believed that there was nothing I could do about it.

Now I seemed to recall that new shoes had always hurt my left foot at the MTP joint. I used to pull my left shoe off during classes in High School to relieve the pressure. When I had worked for a wholesale company in the mid 80's I would pull my left shoe off during the long drives I made each day. My left foot was my "bad foot" and it gave me trouble. Shoes didn't fit it properly, they caused pain, and I believed that there was nothing I could do about this pain.

I had suffered needlessly for over 30 years simply because I had three preconceived notions which were flawed; 1.) I wore size 12 shoes. 2.) Shoes hurt my feet. 3.) There was nothing I could do about it.

I never questioned these beliefs. They had been programmed in my mind through years of experience and reinforcement. Change was out of the question because of my belief system. It never even occurred to me that I had the power to change the situation because it never occurred to me that my belief system was wrong. I believed that I wore size 12 shoes, that shoes hurt my feet and that there was nothing I could do about it. I would have fought anyone who tried to tell me otherwise. I had been programmed to accept these beliefs by authority figures, friends and family. Over the years the premise of these flawed beliefs laid the foundation for my belief system; a belief system that was distorted.

Reinforcing Our Beliefs

At some point in my life, my feet had grown from size 10 to size 11 to size 12. I had tried shoes on in the shoe department at a chain store and the salesman, an adult, an authority figure who knew what he was talking about told me that I needed a size 12. I believed him. What reason did I have to doubt him? Why would he lie? He was trying to help me. My parents had taken me to that store, they wouldn't entrust me to someone who wasn't looking out for my best interest. I tried the shoes on and they fit. The shoe salesman failed to tell me that I needed a wide shoe or that buying a wide shoe would prevent foot pain. Even though what he told me was true, it was wrong. I did need a size 12, but what I really needed was a size 12 wide. His failure to give me all the facts helped create my mindset. It paved the way to pour the foundation of my flawed belief system.

My mother reinforced the premise that I wore size 12 shoes and that my foot should hurt. She always bought size 12 shoes for me. She was concerned about my foot and always asked me if it hurt or if it was giving me trouble. I would tell her it didn't hurt, because I didn't want her to worry. But every time she asked about the foot she was reinforcing the belief that my foot should hurt, further pouring the foundation for my flawed belief system.

When we visited relatives, even after not seeing them for years, they remembered that I was born with my left foot facing backwards. They always asked me if my foot was giving me problems. Even though I always told them it was not and that I had done remarkably well despite the birth defect, they were reinforcing my belief that my foot should be causing me pain, pouring more layers into the foundation of my flawed belief system.

I accepted my preconceived notions as unquestionable, undeniable truth. I believed that I wore size 12 shoes, that shoes hurt my feet and that there was nothing I could do about it. That was my belief system. Buying wide shoes proved that my belief system was wrong; I actually needed size 12 wide shoes, they didn't hurt my feet, and I had done something about shoes hurting my feet.

Buying a wide pair of shoes did a lot more than ease my foot pain. It opened my eyes to the fact that our belief systems can be fundamentally wrong even when our beliefs are true. We are guided by our belief systems which consist of premises created with the influence of our preconceived notions. Finding the flaws in our belief systems opens the door to the possibility of change.

Forming a Belief System

A preconceived notion is a personal belief or judgment that is not founded on proof or certainty, but rather on experience. A premise is a statement that is assumed to be true and from which a conclusion can be drawn. A belief system is the framework of ideas and beliefs through which an individual interprets the world and interacts in it.

Our belief systems are formed in the following fashion; a preconceived notion is formed based on our perception of our experience– a premise is formed based on the preconceived notion – an action based on the premise is repeated, becoming habit – a belief system is formed out of habitually acting on the premise of that preconceived notion. To find the flaws in my belief system, I had to look at each individual premise I had formed. This was the process I used to make lasting changes in my life and beat depression.

A Flawed Premise

I was fascinated by the fact that even though I was wrong, there was some truth to what I believed.

Premise 1.)- I wore size 12 shoes.

This was absolutely true; I did wear size 12 shoes and had worn them for over 30 years. I was absolutely correct in my belief that I wore size 12 shoes. Still the belief was flawed; there was a critical piece of information missing from my premise. I was in denial about the fact that I needed wider shoes. Although my premise was true, it did not negate the fact that my actual foot size was 12 wide and that I actually needed 12 wide shoes.

The fact that our beliefs are true does not mean that our beliefs are correct. We can be absolutely correct about our beliefs but that won't change the fact that our beliefs are absolutely wrong. We can only see what our belief systems allow us to see. Our perception of reality is reality to us. If our perception is flawed, we can't recognize it because that perception is real to us and forms the basis of our belief system.

Windows to the World

Picture your mind as a home. It can be an elegant mansion overlooking a large estate or a dilapidated shack on an unkempt lot depending on your frame of mind. You observe the world through the windows in your home. Your vision is limited by the size of the frames around the windows. Your property is lined with barriers and bounded by corners. The boundaries determine the scope of your vision. **You only see as far as your boundaries allow you to see, through the frames of your windows.**

Your preconceived notions form the frames around the windows from which you see the world. These mental frames shape your perception and control the biased and limited way in which your brain processes information. The entire grounds make up the premises. The premises consist of all the property owned; that property, collectively, which is specified in the beginning of a legal document and which is conveyed, such as in a deed. A premise is also a proposition upon which an argument is based or from which a conclusion is drawn. Our premises are limited by our boundaries. The boundaries mark the property lines of our estates from corner to corner, and in our mental homes, determine what we let in and how we interpret the information that we do let in.

Anything that doesn't fit neatly into our boundaries is suspect. We take the information we are given and fit it neatly into the frames created by our preconceived notions. If the information doesn't fit, we question the source, question the facts and ultimately reject the information. This is what makes change so difficult. Learning the facts will not change the way we think, feel and act. The facts are filtered through our frames and we only perceive what our boundaries allow in.

You can provide the same facts to two people of opposing viewpoints and each one will interpret the facts in such a way as to support their own viewpoint. A defense attorney and a prosecutor will argue over the same evidence; the defense attorney argues that the evidence proves that his client is innocent while the prosecutor argues that the same evidence proves that the defendant is guilty. Your brain uses the same approach that the opposing attorneys use to scrutinize evidence when it processes the information given to it. It looks for the facts that support your case.

Schemata

Our preconceived notions form together to make up what psychologists refer to as schemata. A schema is a structured cluster of pre-conceived notions. Schemata (sometimes called schemas) are mental groups that our brains organize to condense loads of information about people, places and things into quickly identifiable matches and mismatches. For example we hear a bark and the brain quickly tells us it is a dog. If you own a dog, you picture a friendly companion. If you are afraid of dogs you quickly identify a threat. The same information is interpreted differently by individuals based on their schemata. Schemata are short cuts to identifying potential threats and contribute to our biases and prejudices. The more threatening a situation appears to be; the more likely we are to create a shortcut to identify future threats. Schemata form the mental frames that shape the way we see the world. We process information through the filter of these preconceived notions.

When Perception Meets Reality

"Facts are stubborn things; and whatever may be our wishes, our inclinations, or the dictates of our passion, they cannot alter the state of facts and evidence."

> **John Adams (1735 - 1826),** *'Argument in Defense of the Soldiers in the Boston Massacre Trials,' December 1770*

When we are overwhelmed by facts that do not support our case and information that does not fit into our boundaries, we feel hopeless and powerless. We respond by going into denial and becoming angry and defensive or by losing hope and sinking into depression. I discovered that the root of my depression was the fact that the reality of my life did not fit neatly into the boundaries my mind had created. There was a difference between what I believed and what I saw. Being unable to accept that difference drove me into depression. To beat depression I had to accept the fact that the boundaries that I had created in my mind were not consistent with reality. I had to examine my belief system logically and truthfully. I had to tear down the walls, build new premises and create new boundaries.

If you are going to change you are going to have to examine your long held beliefs and accept the fact that even though your beliefs may be true, they can still be wrong. You are going to have to let go of your preconceived notions and create a new belief system. This is Concept One – *Create* - **Create New Boundaries.**

New boundaries open the door to the possibility of change. To make that change a reality, you have to become who you want to be. You have to become the person you would be, without the limitations of your flawed belief systems and preconceived notions. You have to imagine yourself as you could be, and act as if you are that person. The more you play the part the easier it becomes. Eventually, it becomes habit. If you play the part long enough, you will become the person you want to be. This is the second part of Concept One - *Create* - **Create a New Self –Image**

Tearing Down the Premises

Premise 2.) - Shoes hurt my feet.

This too was true; shoes did indeed hurt my feet. Although this premise is true, it does not change the fact that wider shoes would not hurt my feet. My belief was true, but it was flawed. The truth was that shoes that fit properly would not hurt my feet. Why was it so difficult to believe that I could actually find shoes that did not hurt my feet? Why did I so easily accept the premise that shoes hurt my feet? Why did I accept this belief as a fact and never challenge the belief?

Because I could only see my options through the boundaries I had created based on the premise of my preconceived notion that I wore size 12 shoes.

"Only as you do know yourself can your brain serve you as a sharp and efficient tool. Know your own failings, passions, and prejudices so you can separate them from what you see."

Bernard M. Baruch (1870 - 1965)

To change the situation, I had to change the boundaries. I had to challenge the preconceived notion that I had held for over 30 years. If you are going to change, you will have to challenge the boundaries that your brain has built over the course of your lifetime. You will have to change the way you see the world. The existence of mental frames is a widely accepted concept in the field of psychology. It's where we get the term "frame of mind." I developed the concept of boundaries out of my own experience however.

Reframing my boundaries started by accident. When my son told me that my feet were wide, I opened up to a new concept. I accepted the idea because it came from someone I loved and respected. My guard was down. No one had ever told me that I had wide feet. Everyone, including myself had always been too distracted from seeing the width because we were busy looking at the size difference. My boundaries told me that my feet were unusual; that they were deformed and shoes hurt my feet, but never that my feet were wide. The idea that I had wide feet was a totally new concept. The simple suggestion from my son began to change my boundaries.

To change your life, you have to change your boundaries. Open your mind to the possibility that things can change. Shoes had always hurt my feet and I had just accepted that premise as a fact. I challenged that premise when I decided to shop for comfortable shoes.

You have to make up your mind what it is that you want. I wanted shoes that didn't hurt my feet. I made the connection between wanting comfortable shoes and what my son had said about my feet being wide. Now I knew exactly what I wanted; I wanted wide shoes. Decide what you want and begin to frame your thoughts in such a way as to compel you toward that end. Your desires have to be strong enough to motivate you to take action. Decide what you want to see out of your windows and begin to reframe your thoughts until you see that image. Know what you want and create a step by step plan to get what you want. Have clearly defined goals and objectives. This is Concept Two; *Connect*. **Connect With What You Want.**

The suggestion that my feet were wide came from my son. I never would have asked for wide shoes if he had not made the comment about my feet. It's often the other people in our lives who motivate us most to change. You need the influence of other people in your life to help you change; people who encourage you, people who criticize you, and people who relate to you.

We need all the encouragement we can get when we're depressed, but constructive criticism can be a powerful motivator when we act on the criticism and make positive changes. My son telling me that I had stretched his shoes out and ruined them was a form of criticism. I had worn his shoes in the past and he had not said anything, he didn't want to offend me. When he finally told me the truth, it opened the door for the process of change to begin. When I was slipping back into depression it was my wife's criticism that prompted me to make changes. The influence of those two people led to the creation of this book. You need someone who is not afraid to tell you the truth. Find someone who will be open and honest with you, and not just tell you what you want to hear.

Socialize. Find people you want to emulate and spend time with them. Over time, we adopt the boundaries of the people we spend time with. They influence our perceptions. Read the stories of people you admire. Talk to people you respect. Don't be afraid to ask questions, people naturally love to talk about themselves. If you seem interested in them, you won't have to do much talking, just listen and ask questions. Dale Carnegie said that the way to be successful is to become genuinely interested in other people.

You also need people you can relate to. Read the stories of people who have suffered through problems like yours. I read blogs and forums about depression on the internet. There I connect with other people who have shared my battle, and at the same time remain anonymous.

I tell very few people about my struggle with depression. I have a few close friends that I can talk to about it. Group therapy has its benefits and may work for you, but it was something that I was not interested in and did not work for me. Being a Youth Minister and Preacher for so many years, I was used to speaking to crowds from a position of authority. Telling my problems to a group of people that I couldn't relate to just didn't work for me. Still, I had to find someone I could talk to about my problems. I confided in a few special friends. Find someone who you can tell your problems to and in turn, listen to theirs.

I have one special friend I communicate with through e-mail and occasional phone calls. I can e-mail her anytime I feel the need. I can tell her anything and not be embarrassed. I see a psychiatrist every three months. In between visits, I send her letters to update her on how I am doing. I tell her everything and hold nothing back. I can communicate much better in writing than I can express my feelings verbally. I have a close friendship with someone who has suffered a nervous breakdown in the past. We e-mail each other, chat on Facebook, share our stories and confide in each other. Even though we rarely see each other, we enjoy a special connection and closeness. My sister-in-law became a confidant when my wife left me. She accompanied me to the first hospital I went to when I became so depressed. She has remained a close friend, my wife and I socialize with her and her husband and we share e-mails and chat on Facebook. I have another friend I communicate with exclusively through e-mail. These people and a few others form my support network. Each one has no idea about the others; indeed most of them don't even know each other. But together they have acted as a form of Group Therapy for me.

Even though I was a Youth Minister, preacher, public speaker and very effective communicator, my messages were always written out on paper beforehand. I knew exactly what I was going to say before I ever started speaking. I'm an introvert. I compensated for this by speaking to crowds and avoiding one on one conversation with people I was uncomfortable with. I have become more introverted since suffering from depression. I compensate for this by communicating in writing. Writing about my problems in the course of writing this book was a way to connect with the people who would eventually read it. It was a form of therapy for me. I had to find a way to make connections with other people in spite of my tendency to be a loner. These connections are vital.

This is the second part of Concept Two; **Connect With Others**. To effect lasting change in our lives, we must connect with other people. Programs that are successful in bringing about change all use the power of socialization; Weight Watchers, 12 Steps, AA, and various religious organizations all utilize the power of connecting. We are more likely to do something if we know that other people are doing it too. We want to read bestsellers. We want to see the #1 movie in the country. We want to drive the bestselling cars. We buy the bestselling brands and wear the bestselling clothes. We want to do what other people are doing. We have a tendency to follow the crowd, even if we don't always recognize it. This is not a bad thing. If you are going to change, you are going to need people to help you along the way.

Self Limiting Beliefs

Premise 3.) – There was nothing I could do about it.

This was the most limiting belief of all. There are situations which we are powerless to change and the best solution is to just accept the situation. Even in those cases, we are doing something; we are choosing not to worry about what we have no power to control. This was not the case in my situation. Clearly there was something I could do. I could buy wide shoes. Before we throw up our hands and say "There is nothing I can do" we need to exhaust all other options. There is something we can do about every situation, even if it is only accepting the situation and choosing not to worry about it. "There is nothing I can do about it" was attached to the end of many of my flawed premises.

It's true that we must accept what we cannot change, but we still have to take action to change everything we can. We have to work around our limitations. I cannot jog and long brisk walks hurt my feet, but I need to do aerobic exercise. So I get my aerobic exercise by doing a kettlebell workout. I work around having arthritis in my feet. I still manage to walk about the buildings I protect at work, climb stairs and even run if I have to. No one knows that I have problems with my feet. I work around my limitations.

Instead of saying "I have arthritis in my feet so I can't exercise" I say "Certain exercises hurt my feet. I have to work around those exercises and substitute exercises that I can do comfortably." My goal is to be in shape. Since I can't use jogging as a tool to accomplish that goal, I simply use another tool.

There is always *something* you can do. Once you have decided what you want to change and formulated a plan for achieving that change you have to take the next step and take action to carry out that plan. Thought, action, habit is the way the process works. Decide what you want and form a plan. Take action and follow the plan. Repeat the action until it becomes a habit. Keep up the habit and you'll get what you want.

Notice that buying wide shoes did not eliminate my problem. I still have arthritis in my feet. My feet still hurt after long walks. But buying wide shoes helped tremendously. Buying wide shoes was an action. I repeated that action until it became a habit. Every time I buy a pair of shoes now I get size 12 wide. I've made a commitment to always get wide shoes, and to always shop for the most comfortable ones.

The commitment to buying wide shoes was not the only one I had to make. It was simple and easy to maintain unlike the many other commitments I had to make which were difficult and trying. I had recovered from depression before, only to slip back into it again. I began to see that after I made changes, I typically got comfortable and slowly regressed into my old familiar way of thinking and acting. Our habitual patterns of behavior are the ones we're most likely to follow, even after we've made changes and seen the results. That's why changes are not only difficult to make, they're difficult to maintain.

Having lost over 40 pounds at least nine times in my life, and then repeatedly gaining the weight back, you would think that I would have learned not to repeat the behavior that caused me to gain the weight in the first place. The same is true for depression, having broke the cycle and came out of depression, you would think that I would have learned to watch for the signs and not let depression take hold of me again. But our habits are so deeply ingrained and our mental frames so well established that the subconscious draws us back to the familiar without us even realizing it, even if the familiar is bad.

It was only when I discovered the 3 Concepts of Change and applied all 3 that I was able to make lasting changes, keep the unwanted weight off and put my depression on hold permanently. **Create, Connect, Commit** and you will change too.

Get Motivated

Start by making small changes. Repeat the changes until they become routine. Following a routine will allow you to make progress. Seeing progress will motivate you to sustain the change and make more changes. Progress is the best motivator. You think you have to get motivated, and then take action, but this premise is flawed. Take action even when you don't feel like it. Do something then say "Look what I did". You'll feel better once you've done something, not before. Keep doing something until you see progress. Once you see progress, you'll be motivated to make more progress. Celebrate small success. Give yourself credit for taking action and reward those actions. *Do something.* Something is always better than nothing. This is step three - **Commit**.

Commit to changing what you can. Commit means taking action. Commit to keep taking that action until you see progress. Commit to continue making progress until you reach your goal. *Commit to setting a new goal every time you reach one.* This is the key to making lasting change in your life. You must never allow yourself to get comfortable and drift back into old patterns of behavior. You must commit; *commit* to changing your life forever.

This is Concept Three 3; **Commit. Commit to Change. Commit to Progress.**

Create, Connect, Commit is the process for changing anything. I developed this process out of a need for something that worked. Use this process and I guarantee that you can change anything. Now take the process and apply it to your own situation and you'll soon see improvement in your depressive symptoms and positive changes taking place in your life.

Do not let this opportunity go to waste. Even if you are skeptical, do yourself a favor and *believe* that this process will work for you. Believe in it because *it will work*. It is the only system of self help that has ever worked for me, and believe me I've tried them all. I not only tried self help, I tried professional help, but nothing worked until I learned this process and committed to living it everyday. **Create, Connect, Commit** is a life changing experience and I believe in it so much that I am dedicating my life to getting it into the hands of everyone who needs it. I desperately needed something that would work and this process works so well I want to make sure it is available to everyone who suffers from depression, anxiety, codependency, the fear of failure, addiction, low self esteem, obesity or just wants to change. All these issues have at least one thing in common; **the inability to change.**

This is not the first time that someone has *asked* you to change, but it is the first time that someone has *told* you **how to change.** No one has ever given you step by step instructions to show you exactly what to do in order to effect enduring change in your life. Follow the instructions laid out in the rest of this book and you will change your life forever.

Why Can't People Change?

Denial

I have guard that works for me named Betty. Betty is a fifty year old white female with a decent work ethic. Betty is overweight and out of shape and she is one the employees who were already working at the company when I took over.

The first thing I did when I took over was to impose physical standards on the Guards. We work in a 5 story building, so they should be able to climb the stairs and reach the 5th floor in a reasonable amount of time in the event the elevator is not working, They should also be able to traverse the perimeter of the campus in a reasonable amount of time. These are "Essential Functions" of the job. We hired a consulting agency to determine what exactly a "reasonable amount of time" was. The consulting agency made the standard ridiculously easy, but for liability reasons my employer accepted it.

Betty was able to pass the physical test and keep her job. She had an extremely difficult time catching her breath after climbing the stairs and I sensed something more was wrong with Betty other than simply being out of shape. 3 months later, Betty was hospitalized with chest pain. She had angioplasty the next day and a stent was put in to open a blocked artery.

Betty's doctor told her to make lifestyle changes including losing weight, exercising and eating a healthy diet. Betty has not made those changes, and soon she will need to have another stent put in to open another blocked artery. Why would someone fail to make simple changes knowing that failing to do so would lead to intrusive surgery and could even result in death? Betty is not alone. Studies show that after surgery 90% of heart patients fail to make the necessary lifestyle changes to prevent future surgery. Even the possibility of death is not enough to make people change.

If you attend church, you have probably heard your share of Hellfire and brimstone sermons. Often in revivals the Hellfire sermons of zealous evangelists inspire vivid images of the unimaginable suffering one would endure in Hell. The prospect of losing one's soul and being condemned forever to eternal torment often results in religious conversions which entail drastic lifestyle changes. But more often than not, such conversions are short lived. Lifestyle changes based solely on fear rarely endure.

Such converts routinely resort back to their habitual lifestyles and repeat the cycles of behavior they had hoped to break by making the religious conversion. Even the fear of Hell is not a compelling enough reason to make someone change. They simply block it out of their minds and choose not to think about it.

When we find ourselves faced with information that conflicts with our mental frames and threatens our self esteem we have automatic psychological defense mechanisms which help us to cope with the stress brought on by reality. We protect ourselves from the threatening ego destroying facts and stay within our boundaries. Heart patients avoid thinking about how their disease threatens to kill them. Alcoholics do the same. Smokers deny the damage they are doing to their bodies. Overweight people deny that their weight problem is the result of their eating habits. They choose not to think about it. Domestic violence victims put the abuse out of their minds. They banish the reality that they are in an abusive relationship from their conscious awareness. They believe that their abusers will change and they repeat the cycle of abuse over and over again.

The power of denial is awesome and overwhelming. Denial is your number one enemy in your battle to change. Most denial takes place at the subconscious level, and we are not even aware of it.

One of Sigmund Freud's theories was that the ego constructed coping mechanisms to protect the individual when anxiety levels became too high. He called these coping mechanisms "ego defenses" and they are often referred to as "defense mechanisms". Defense mechanisms are unconscious psychological strategies brought into play by various entities to cope with reality and to maintain self-image.

Freud believed there were three structures of the psyche or personality:

- **Id**: a selfish, primitive, childish, pleasure-oriented part of the personality with no ability to delay gratification. "The Child".
- **Superego**: internalized societal and parental standards of "good" and "bad", "right" and "wrong" behavior. "The Parent".
- **Ego**: the moderator between the id and superego which seeks compromises to pacify both. It can be viewed as our "Sense of Self." "The Adult".

According to his theory, id impulses are based on the **pleasure principle**: instant gratification of one's own desires and needs. Freud believed that the id represents biological instinctual impulses within ourselves, such as aggression and sexuality. For example, when the id impulses (e.g. desire to have adulterous sexual relations) conflict with the superego (e.g. belief in societal conventions of fidelity and faithfulness), unsatisfied feelings of anxiousness or feelings of anxiety come to the surface. To reduce these negative feelings, the ego employs defense mechanisms (conscious or unconscious blocking of the id impulses).

When anxiety becomes too overwhelming, it is then the place of the ego to employ defense mechanisms to protect the individual. Feelings of guilt, embarrassment and shame often accompany the feeling of anxiety.

Denial is defined as refusal to accept external reality because it is too threatening; arguing against an anxiety-provoking stimulus by stating it doesn't really exist; resolution of emotional conflict and reduction of anxiety by refusing to perceive or consciously acknowledge the more unpleasant aspects of external reality. In other words, just flat out refusing to believe something that causes us anxiety; a subconscious denial of the facts which cause us discomfort and anxiety, or a conscious denial of a truth that is too difficult to accept.

The religious convert who finds the lure of sin too tempting to resist and denies that Hell exists, or chooses to believe that a loving God would never condemn him/her to such a place is practicing a form of denial. Unending torment for eternity is not something they want to think about, so they just choose not to.

The heart patient who refuses to exercise, quit smoking and make changes in his/her diet, the alcoholic who denies his/her illness, and the victims of domestic violence who deny the violent tendencies of their partners and believe that their relationships will actually get better in time are all living in denial.

In 1936, Freud's daughter Anna wrote a book entitled The Ego and the Mechanisms of Defense which cataloged the defense mechanisms. There are over 40 different known mechanisms of defense. Methods other than denial by which we shield ourselves from unacceptable truths include blaming others for our problems and coming up with excuses to explain away the real motives behind our behavior.

In his groundbreaking book "Change Or Die" Alan Deutschman asserts that ego defenses are one of the principle reasons why people cannot change. Deutschman says much of Freud's thinking hasn't withstood the test of time, but on ego defenses, he has been proven absolutely right. Deutschman's Change or Die theory relies on the notion of ego defenses as the primary impediment to change.

To some extent, denial is actually good for us. We all need some degree of denial to maintain our peace of mind. For instance we all know that we will die someday, we are mortal and our days on earth are limited. But what kind of life would we live if we were fixated on the reality that every moment that passes by is taking us one step closer to death's door?

Natural disasters, acts of terrorism, pandemic spread of deadly viruses and even the threat of nuclear war are eventualities with which we live everyday. There's little any of us can do about any of these threats. If we spent our time worrying about such things, we'd have little energy to do anything else.

Even though some level of denial is useful, this same coping mechanism masks our shortcomings, blinds us to reality and prevents us from changing.

Mental Frames

"Change your thoughts and you change your world."

Norman Vincent Peale (1898 - 1993)

We've already seen how the brain uses schemas (mental groups that our brains organize) to condense loads of information about people, places and things into quickly identifiable matches and mismatches. Schemas are short cuts our brains use to quickly identify people, places and things, scents, sounds and sights and to quickly recall things like routes and potential threats. How often do you use landmarks to guide you when you travel? Do you prepare yourself to take evasive action when you hear a siren? Do you get aroused when you smell a certain perfume or cologne? Does the smell of food make you hungry?

As we interact with the daily events of our lives, we interpret it through a mental frame of our own making. These mental frames either result in positive or negative feelings about events that occur. The concept of a **mental frame** may refer to a person's personal perception of their own world; a type of mental processing composed of a series of psychological transformations by which an individual can acquire code, store, recall, and decode information about the relative locations and attributes of phenomena in their everyday or metaphorical spatial environment. Put more simply, mental frames are a method we use to construct and accumulate spatial knowledge, allowing the "mind's eye" to visualize images in order to reduce cognitive load, enhance recall and learn new information.

An example of how we can use this to our advantage is using spatial locations to remember things. The oldest known formal method of using spatial locations to remember is the "method of loci". This method was originally used by students of rhetoric in ancient Rome when memorizing speeches. To use it you memorize the appearance of a spatial location (for example, the sequence of rooms in a building). When a list of words needs to be memorized, the learner visualizes an object representing that word in one of the pre-memorized locations. To recall the list, the learner mentally "walks through" the memorized locations, noticing the objects placed there during the memorization phase.

Another example would be putting a name with a face. I have a terrible time remembering names, but if I can think of something to associate with the name, then I can recall it. For example I recently met a woman named Sherry Mott. She was quite attractive, so I remembered her name by thinking "Sherry Mott is very hot." Now when I see her, this phrase comes to mind and I can remember her name. This process is referred to as mental mapping. Her image acts as a shortcut that triggers the memory of the familiar phrase, thus I remember her name.

Mental frames work the same way, and we can be biased and narrow minded without even realizing it. We may be more persuaded by the argument of a person we find attractive. We may prejudge a person based on their appearance. Our mental frames account for the prejudiced and limited way in which we perceive and understand information. Because the human brain is inherently prejudiced and narrowly focused, we are always in some mental frame. That frame determines how we relate to and understand reality. As far as we can tell, **that frame is reality**. This is why our mood can determine our outlook. The world seems better when we are happy and worse when we are sad. Mental frames ultimately determine not only our perceptions, but our whole mindset about what is valuable, practical, or dangerous, and what behaviors are responsible and acceptable. The good news is that we can switch mental frames. Your mood and other factors can help determine your outlook.

Many influences can shift your frame, such as reading books, watching a movie, listening to an audio book or exercising, but one of the most powerful influences is other people. Have you ever had an idea you were excited about, but when you shared it with someone else, they somehow ridiculed, doubted, or otherwise criticized it? Did that make you feel a little less excited, more doubtful, or even somewhat embarrassed about the idea? If so, you've started to enter their frame -- their reality is becoming your reality. If you want to create an environment of change where you can nurture your dreams, connect with people who share your enthusiasm and whose frame is compatible with your dreams.

But it's not always easy to find such people. Where do we find positive, happy, successful people who we can spend time with? In books, movies, audio books, novels, biographies, autobiographies, how to books, self help and self development books. Even fictional characters can be inspirational. Find role models and learn all you can about them. Watch movies and read books about people who made extraordinary achievements, overcame great odds, or who simply inspire you for whatever reason. Open your mind to the power of possibility. If someone else has done it, then you can do it to. Our faith easily embraces what our eyes have seen. Seeing is believing and if we can believe it, we can achieve it.

We tend to synchronize frames with our friends, family, co-workers, and even people we watch in movies and on television or read books about. It's often the other people in our lives who motivate us most to change. We have to connect with other people in order to be successful at changing and maintaining those changes once we've made them.

Stairway to Heaven

A dramatic demonstration of the power of mental frames can be seen on YouTube's website at www.youtube.com/watch?v=0bG7EFhMw8w. If you're going to watch the demonstration, do so before you read any further. The effect will be ruined once you read the following phrase.

In one of Simon Singh's lectures on the Big Bang Theory, he plays a portion of Led Zeppelin's Stairway to Heaven backwards. He then asks the audience if anyone heard the word "Satan" in the backward lyrics. A few audience members indicate that they did, as laughter breaks out through the auditorium. He then asks if anyone heard the phrase *"It's my sweet Satan; the one whose little path would make me sad whose power is Satan. Oh he will give you 666. There was a little tool shed where he made us suffer, sad Satan."* Laughter erupts in the audience.

He then explains to the audience that he is going to play the backwards excerpt again, and he promises them that this time they will all hear the phrase which he has displayed on a screen at the front of the auditorium. He assures the audience that he has not cheated, that the backwards segment they are about to hear is the exact same one he has already played for them. He feels he must explain this because the audience is going to be so shocked by what they hear, they will assume he has cheated or manipulated the backward segment in some way.

As the backwards music begins to play the individual words of the phrase are highlighted on the screen and that is exactly what you hear. Every single word of the phrase *"It's my sweet Satan; the one whose little path would make me sad whose power is Satan. Oh he will give you 666. There was a little tool shed where he made us suffer, sad Satan"* suddenly become remarkably clear and discernable. Applause breaks out after the demonstration and Singh asks how many people heard the words that time.

Everyone indicates that they heard the phrase. The presentation leaves no doubt that the phrase exists in the backward lyrics. Go to YouTube and watch the demonstration and I promise that you will hear this exact phrase word for word. Having watched the demonstration, I can now hear the words just by listening to the backwards segment without looking at the words.

There's only one problem. There is no backwards message. All the audience members and I are really hearing is the same garbled gibberish we heard the first time Singh played it.

The second time the segment was played Singh had suggested that the words were there. He promised us that we would hear the words, and created an expectation. He compelled us to hear the words then he put them on a screen where we could see them. He implanted the words in our minds without us even realizing it.

The brain desperately tries to make sense of the information which it is given. When information is missing it fills in the gap and makes the best use of whatever it is given to work with. We may not hear all the conversation on a bad cell phone connection or in a crowded room; we have to fill in the gaps and make sense of what we heard. We do it all the time. If you give the brain flawed or biased data, it fills in the gap and you end up hearing something that really isn't there.

Sometimes we develop vivid memories that are flawed because our brain didn't have all the information it needed to recall an event and it filled in the gaps creating a memory of something that didn't really happen the way we remember it. Witnesses to crime sometimes confidently pick a person out of a photo line up who wasn't even at the scene of the crime. Their memories of the events can easily be influenced by the power of suggestion.

Cold Reading

The desire to make sense out of an experience can open the door for us to be easily deceived, by ourselves and others. Con artists and professional manipulators employ a set of techniques to get us to behave in a certain way or to think that the con artist has some sort of special ability that allows him to "mysteriously" know things about us. Sometimes referred to as "Cold Reading" this technique goes beyond the usual tools of manipulation: suggestion and flattery. In cold reading, salespersons, hypnotists, advertising pros, faith healers, con men, and even some therapists bank on our inclination to find more meaning in a situation than is actually there. We have a natural inclination to disregard and quickly forget all the things they get wrong while we key in on and remember the amazing things they seem to get right.

"In the course of a successful reading, the psychic may provide most of the words, but it is the client that provides most of the meaning and all of the significance." --Ian Rowland

A few of the churches I have attended invited "Prophets" to speak who came and told the congregation amazing things about themselves and the future God had in mind for them. I'm not so sure that the same phenomenon was not occurring when these "Prophets" spoke a "Word of Knowledge" to believers who saw truth and found comfort in their words.

Unrealistic Expectations

One of the areas in which mental frames were contributing to my depression was in my marriage. My preconceived notions about my marriage had to be reframed through the lens of logic and truth. I had to be realistic about the relationship my wife and I shared and reframe some of my long held beliefs. I had to create new mental frames for my marriage.

My wife and I had been together for over 20 years. In our youth, we had been the metaphorical good girl, bad boy couple from the classic Tom Petty song "Free Falling" and in my mental frame she was still my "good girl." My 'good girl" could never have left me or exhibited the behavior I was now observing in my wife. Seeing my wife change so much had driven me into the deepest levels of depression. The image of her drinking and partying did not fit neatly into the boundaries I had established for her. I longed for the Sunday school teacher, doting mother, Suzy Homemaker image that she had been to me for so long. I wanted my "good girl" back. What was going on in reality was in direct contrast to my mental frame, and being unable to accept the difference nearly drove me insane.

The premise that my wife was still a "good girl" was flawed. She was not the 15 year old girl that I had fallen in love with. She was now 40 years old, she had changed and I had to accept those facts. I was still holding her to the unattainable standard of perfection I had imposed on us during our time in ministry. She needed friends and socializing with those friends filled the need she had for being loved and appreciated. She had always stifled her own emotions and needs and took care of everyone else. Now it was her turn to unwind, have a good time and take care of her own needs. She lost her inhibitions, threw caution to the wind and another side of her personality came out. In order to be happy and overcome my depression, I had to accept the new person that she had become.

Even though I longed for the relationship we had once known in our youth and often feared that we were headed for a divorce; when I examined our marriage through the lens of logical thinking and truth, I found cause to be positive.

We had started dating when she was only 15 years old and I was 20. We were married 2 years later. On August 23rd 1986 she became a 17 year old bride. On August 6th 1987 she became an 18 year old mother. Statistics now support the claims that couples can lower their odds of eventually being divorced by waiting to get married until they have earned their college degrees and they are at least 25 years old. Neither of us went to college, and we were married at the youthful ages of 22 and 17.

America's divorce rate began climbing in the late 1960s and skyrocketed during the '70s and early '80s. The rate peaked at 5.3 divorces per 1,000 people in 1981, just 5 years before we married. The divorce rate has gone down since but why? The number of couples who live together without marrying has increased tenfold since 1960; the marriage rate has dropped by nearly 30 percent in the past 25 years; and Americans are waiting about five years longer to marry than they did in 1970.

In light of these facts, the truth that we had managed to stay married for over 23 years was cause to be positive and believe that there was some reason that we had stayed together. Reframing helped me belief that there was hope for our future as a couple. Tearing down my old premises and building a new mental frame was the first step in creating new boundaries for my marriage.

When she left again, I had just finished my second book and got my website online. An IT company wanted $1100 a year to design and maintain the website. I did it for $21 and had no idea what I was doing when I started. I went to church the day after finishing my website and when I got home from church, she left me. I was devastated again. To keep from getting depressed I had to put CCC into action. (Another breakthrough followed by a huge setback. This is the normal pattern in my life and I have now come to expect it.)

I reframed. I had to be confident that I could make it on my own. Understanding my personality type was the key to reframing. Being a Type 6, I had tried to hang on to the relationship at all costs. She was my sense of security and the trusted person I checked with before making decisions. I reframed my beliefs about her, she couldn't control her feelings and I couldn't change them, no matter what I did. Being a type 2, she had grown bitter toward me. She had spent her life catering to me and taking care of my needs. Over time resentment had built up. She no longer had romantic feelings for me. This was not her fault or mine, it was just a fact. Fixing the blame would not fix the problem.

I reframed my beliefs about myself; I had written 2 books and built a website with no input from her. She told me that she felt writing was just another phase I was going through and that I would never finish my first book. When I told her I had finished two books, she thought I had lost it. She said there was no way I could have done it in the matter of weeks it took.

I now felt I could accomplish anything I set my mind to. I made a decision to move on, but to remain friends with her no matter the outcome of our separation. I decided to live my life to the fullest no matter what hardships life threw at me. I knew that **CCC** worked and I had to get my books published and teach **CCC** to others.

I turned to God and my friends in my "support network" to help me through. When I had difficult times at work, I took long walks along the perimeter of the campus on foot patrol, talking to trusted friends on my cell phone as I walked. This proved to be a very effective therapy. The power of exercise to improve mood and the power of connecting worked together to get me through the difficult times.

I **created** new mental frames, **connected** with God and with others, and **committed** to reaching my goals no matter what obstacles were placed in my way or what setbacks I suffered. **CCC** worked, just like it had in the past. Statistically speaking, our marriage should have failed long before it did. The fact that we were married for 23 years should be seen as an accomplishment, not a failure.

Create New Boundaries

Psalms 51:10

New International Version (©1984)
"Create in me a pure heart, O God, and renew a steadfast spirit within me."

Resocialization refers to the process of discarding one's traditional behavior patterns and accepting new ones as part of a transition in one's life. This occurs throughout the human life cycle and can be an intense experience, with the individual experiencing a sharp break with their past and needing to learn and be exposed to a radically different environment or system of values. An example might be the experience of a young man leaving home to join the military, the shock of boot camp and the dramatic lifestyle changes he must quickly make to adapt to that environment. Another example would be the experience of a religious convert internalizing the beliefs and rituals of a new faith. **Our goal is to create new patterns of behavior and avoid regressing back into the old ones.**

Reframe

In Victor Frankl's classic book "Man's Search for Meaning" he describes how even a trifling thing can cause the greatest of joys. Frankl was a prisoner in concentration camps during World War 2. He and his fellow prisoners were on a transport train leaving Auschwitz. They feared there destination was the death camp at Mauthausen. They became more and more tense as they approached a certain bridge over the Danube which the train would have to cross to reach Mauthasen. "Those who have never seen anything similar cannot possibly imagine the dance of joy performed in the carriage by the prisoners when they saw that our transport was not crossing the bridge and instead was heading "only" for Dachau" writes Frankl.

"And again what happened on our arrival in the camp, after a journey lasting 2 days and 3 nights? There had not been enough room to crouch on the floor of the carriage at the same time. The majority of us had to stand all the way while a few took turns at squatting on the scanty straw which was soaked with human urine. When we arrived the first important news that we heard from older prisoners was that this comparatively small camp had no "oven", no crematorium, no gas!" This meant that those chosen for termination could not be taken to the gas chamber, but would have to wait until a sick convoy had been arranged to return to Auschwitz. "This joyful surprise put us all in a good mood. ….We laughed and cracked jokes in spite of and during all we had to go through in the next few hours."

"When we new arrivals were counted, one of us was missing. So we had to wait outside in the rain and cold wind until the missing man was found. He was at last discovered in a hut, where he had fallen asleep from exhaustion. Then the roll call was turned into a punishment parade. All through the night we had to stand outside, frozen and soaked to the skin after the strain of our long journey. And yet we were all very pleased! There was no chimney in this camp and Auschwitz was a long way off"

Learning that they were not going to the death camp at Mauthausen and the fact that Dachau had no "oven" caused a shift in frame for the prisoners. They were able to be happy despite their unimaginably terrible circumstance.

The Warehouse

During the time I worked in the warehouse, my self esteem and self confidence were at an all time low. I was paranoid. I was troubled by a constant fear that someone in management would suddenly realize that I was incompetent; too old, out of shape and mentally unprepared to do my job. I covered for it the best I could, and just did whatever I had to do to make it through the day.

One night after working a long shift, my wife and I went over to another couple's house and had a few drinks. I didn't have much to eat that day and was worn out from working long hours and having little time off. It didn't take but a few drinks before the alcohol took effect.

When we got home, my wife and I got into an argument. I slammed a door and busted the mirror that was hung on the back of the door. My wife packed some clothes and left. She would not tell me where she was going. The next morning I called her on her cell phone but she still wouldn't tell me where she was and she didn't know when or if she was coming back.

This was a situation I was not prepared to deal with at all. I was having a hard enough time just functioning at work. Losing my wife would mean losing the sense of security I so desperately needed. I could hardly think of anything else other than seeing to it that she came back home. I knew I had to put it out of my mind and go to work though. I had to try to function and just get through the day without revealing what a nervous wreck I was under the surface.

When I arrived at work, the warehouse manager wasn't there. He had called in sick, and I was expected to take his place. I had no choice but to step into his role and get the job done, it was sink or swim. I couldn't just go through the motions, do the physical labor and avoid any real responsibility as was my usual M.O. I was responsible for seeing that the orders got pulled in sequence, organized by route and properly loaded on the trailers. I had to see that reloads, add ons and special orders were taken care of and the trucks left on time. I also had to find out what had been shorted or missed the day before, pull those orders myself and find a driver to rerun those routes. I had to do my job as well; no one was there to fill in for me.

I ran around like a chicken with its head cut off making sure every detail was taken care of. I was so busy I didn't have time to worry about failing or think about my wife. All I could focus on was getting the job done, no matter what it took. At the end of the day, everything was taken care of; all the trucks left on time and the entire operation had run smoothly. The operations manager thanked me for a job well done.

I left work with a sense of pride, accomplishment and self confidence. I called my wife and with my newfound enthusiasm convinced her to come back home. A day filled with events that could have easily pushed me over the edge had turned out to be one of the best days of my life.

I returned to work the next day and performed my job with such enthusiasm it is difficult to describe. Where I had once felt inept and insecure, I now had the sincere belief that I could master any task no matter how difficult if I only tried. Making it through that one day shifted my mental frame. I had new boundaries about my abilities and limitations.

I learned to drive every type of forklift and reach-lift we had. I learned to drive the tractor trailer rigs and back trailers to the door. I learned to do every job in the warehouse. The order selectors had to pull flour at the end of each route they pulled. They had to get a stocker to move the 2500lb loads of flour stacked on a pallet with a reach lift then add or pull off 50 lb bags of flour until they had the required number for all the stops on their route. It was an arduous task, but they fought over who would do it because they were paid by volume and they wanted the points. I started pulling the flour for all of them, and dividing the points between them evenly. 8 times a day, I was stacking 50 lb. bags of flour. I was getting in shape and increasing production at the same time.

In 4 months I went from an order selector who knew nothing about the job to warehouse manager. It's amazing what a shift in frames can do for you.

"You only lose energy when life becomes dull in your mind. Your mind gets bored and therefore tired of doing nothing. Get interested in something! Get absolutely enthralled in something! Get out of yourself! Be somebody! Do something! The more you lose yourself in something bigger than yourself, the more energy you will have."

Norman Vincent Peale Pastor, Speaker and Author

Shift Your Frames

Imagine that you are late for work, and you're stopped at a red light behind another vehicle. The light changes but the vehicle in front of you goes nowhere. The driver is talking on a cell phone, not paying attention to the light. You can't go around him due to traffic. Moments are ticking by and you are getting later for work. You lay on the horn, but the light changes to red again. You get out of your vehicle and approach the distracted driver, intending to give him a piece of your mind. When you walk up to the window of his car, you see tears rolling down his cheeks. "I'm sorry. I just got a call, my son was killed in Afghanistan" he says, staring at the cell phone in his hand.

How would you react? How would your mental frame have shifted? Would you suddenly go from anger to sympathy? You certainly wouldn't give him the piece of your mind you intended to. We can control our mental frames and we must learn to do so. Putting things in the proper perspective, we can keep our spirits high even in the worst of circumstance. We can control our tempers, our moods and even manage to be happy when everything around us is falling apart. This is one of the most powerful weapons in the battle against depression and you must learn to use it.

Accept What You Cannot Change

"The truth that many people never understand, until it is too late, is that the more you try to avoid suffering the more you suffer because smaller and more insignificant things begin to torture you in proportion to your fear of being hurt."

Thomas Merton (1915 - 1968)

Depression, at least in my case, was partially the result of trying to control the uncontrollable. If someone had wanted to shoot into my house, could I really have stopped that? If my wife decided to leave me again, was there anything I could have done to stop it? Was worrying about it going to prevent it? Would worry prevent me from being laid off or losing my job? My happiness was based on events that I couldn't control. Knowing I had no control over the future made me feel anxious, helpless, insecure, worried and depressed. This is typical of type sixes.

Victor Frankl made a decision not to try to avoid the inevitable while he was a prisoner in World War 2 concentration camps. He found that those who tried most to cheat death often brought it upon themselves by the very means they deployed to prevent it. The plight of his fellow prisoners often reminded him of the story of Death in Teheran;

A mighty Persian king went walking in his pleasure gardens one day and heard a great cry; he was immediately set upon by a panicked servant.

"Mighty king," said the servant, "I have need of your aid! I was working in the garden and came upon Death here, who threatened me. I managed to escape from him, but I fear now for my life. Give me your fastest horse and I know I can make it to the city of Teheran by nightfall, and there I will get away from him."

The king considered for a moment, weighing the good servant's years of loyal help, and assented, providing him with the horse and silver. The king continued to walk in his gardens, and amid the sound of the horse and servant riding off together, the king himself came upon Death.

"Why have you threatened my servant?" the king asked.

Death shook his head. "A thousand apologies, sir, but I did not threaten the man. I merely expressed my surprise at finding him here in your gardens today."

"And why should my servant's presence here be a surprise to you?" the king asked.

And Death replied with a smile, "I was surprised to find him here, good king, because I know that we have an appointment to meet tonight in Teheran."

Make peace even with death. Enjoy each day as one more precious gift from God to be enjoyed to the fullest. Use every minute of it. Don't waste time worrying.

I made it through my worst fears and survived. Few of the terrible things I was certain were going to happen to me actually did. I worried myself into a state of physical and mental illness for no reason.

Even when it comes to the circumstances and events which you have no control over, never say there's nothing you can do about it. You can do something; you can accept it and choose not to worry about it.

"Character cannot be developed in ease and quiet. Only through experience of trial and suffering can the soul be strengthened, ambition inspired, and success achieved." Helen Keller (1880 - 1968)

How to Stop Worrying

"If you can solve your problem, then what is the need of worrying? If you cannot solve it, then what is the use of worrying?"

    Shantideva

The way to stop worrying about the uncertainty of any situation or circumstance, even the future is to determine what the worst possible outcome of the situation could be. Determine the worst case scenario imaginable. Now prepare yourself mentally to deal with that outcome as if it were reality. What steps would you take? Busy your mind attending to the details. The worst case scenario rarely happens. Once you have prepared yourself to handle the worst, you can easily handle anything less.

"Worry a little bit every day and in a lifetime you will lose a couple of years. If something is wrong, fix it if you can. But train yourself not to worry. Worry never fixes anything."

Mary Hemingway

Accept Responsibility

You are the owner of your life. Like it or not, you are where you are today as a direct result of decisions you have made. There have been tragedies and events out of your control, but it is your responsibility to take what life gives you and make the best of it. Take responsibility for where you are. Blaming others, making excuses and feeling sorry for yourself are all forms of denial, ego defenses. They may make you feel better temporarily, but they will do nothing to change your situation. Take full responsibility for where you are.

Realizing that you are ultimately responsible for where you are will give you some sense of control. There are some things that are within your power to change, and knowledge of this fact will help you overcome the feelings of helplessness that accompany depression.

Fix the Problem, Not the Blame. Stop living in denial. Don't blame others or make excuses.

The worst thing that happens to you may be the best thing that happens to you. Look for good in every experience.

"We all have big changes in our lives that are more or less a second chance." Harrison Ford (1942 -), *quoted by Garry Jenkins in 'Harrison Ford: Imperfect Hero'*

Some of the worst things that have happened to me have also been the best things that have happened to me. My wife leaving me led me to get help for depression. My depression at its worst was one of the reasons she left but later prompted her to stay with me and not give up. Losing my career in law enforcement eventually resulted in a better job with less stress and better pay. Getting laid off at the warehouse led to me to that job. Coming down with atypical depression led me to write this book. Getting a divorce seemed devastating, but led to growth, self development and reaching my dreams. Some of our worst problems lead to our best outcomes.

"Emergencies have always been necessary to progress. It was darkness which produced the lamp. It was fog that produced the compass. It was hunger that drove us to exploration. And it took a depression to teach us the real value of a job." Victor Hugo (1802 - 1885)

The 4 Cornerstones

A boundary is something that indicates or fixes a limit or extent. On property lines, boundaries are indicated by corners. The corners are usually iron pipes driven into the ground, and may be marked externally with columns, stones or fence corners. A lot can have many corners, having one at each point where the property lines take a turn. But the ideal lot in a perfect world would have four. By creating new boundaries, we are preparing to build the mental home in which we will live for the rest of our lives. We are going to drive four corners to create the new boundaries on our perfect lot.

Creating New Boundaries is the first step of Concept One, and it's a drastic change. Dramatic, sweeping changes are difficult to make all at once, and even more difficult to maintain. Having 4 cornerstones breaks the process down into doable steps. As in everything else we do, we are going to take big steps and break them down into smaller ones.

> **1.) Reframe**
> **2.) Accept What You Cannot Change**
> **3.) Accept Responsibility**
> **4.) Look For Good In Every Experience**

What Do You Want To Change?

Plan; Ask yourself what it is that you want to change. Why haven't you been able to change? What are the preconceived notions that have prevented you from changing? Ask yourself, "What is the sin in my life? What would I like to change in my relationships? What would I like to change about my job? What would I like to change about myself? Do I need to lose weight?

Do I need to exercise more? Do I need to read the Bible more often? What do I need to change in my relationship with God? What are my weaknesses?" What are the underlying fears of my personality type? Knowing your personality type and your direction of growth (integration) will help you in this process.

If you don't know what to change, then ask yourself what your problems are. Another powerful question you can ask yourself is *"What am I trying to control?"* Attempting to control those things which we have no control over is often the root of our problems. Evaluate your problems and determine what it is that you need to change in order to eliminate the problems. Examine your problems and your inability to change through the lens of logical thinking, truth and scripture. Determine the preconceived notions that have held you back. Determine the premises you've created based on those preconceived notions. **Ask yourself, "What are the premises which my flawed belief system is based on?"** Write each of the flawed premises in the form of a statement. Then challenge those premises and create new ones based on logic and truth. Doing so should reveal the solutions to your problems.

Work the solutions to your problems into goals, and then break those goals down into small, easily attainable goals. Take some type of action each day toward your goals, baby steps if you will.

Do: Small goals don't have the power to motivate like big goals do. But big goals often lead to disappointment and failure, because they seem so distant and hard to reach. We need a combination of the two to provide long term motivation knowing that we are making drastic, compelling changes in our lives; but that we are doing so using a process of small, easily accomplished changes which we can be successful at (*Kaizen*). It is crucial that we be successful, and that we celebrate that success and reward ourselves for making progress toward our goals. We must stay motivated.

These small steps repeated over and over become habits. Practicing these habits brings progress and progress is the greatest motivator of all. So change must be drastic enough to motivate you into action, but gradual enough that you can do it in small steps. Attempting to make drastic changes all at once will overwhelm you, leading to frustration, a sense of failure and actually making your depression worse. We'll go into more detail on goal setting in Chapter 13.

When I started this process my main problems were depression and inactivity. To eliminate theses problems, I needed to become active, however, I had no motivation to become active. I wanted to be active, I knew it would make me feel better but I just couldn't do it. I would mentally picture each of the steps involved in any task and how difficult each of those steps was going to be. I turned molehills into mountains in my mind. I didn't feel like being active because I was depressed. I was depressed because I was inactive. I was caught in a cycle of behavior that exacerbated my problems and there didn't seem to be anything I could do about it.

As I discussed in Chapter 8, "There's nothing I can do about it" is one of the most self-limiting beliefs of all. **You have to start by knowing that there is something you can do.** Even in the instances where there are situations we face which we have no control over, we've already demonstrated that there is *something* we can do. We can choose to accept what we cannot change and not waste time worrying about it.

Corner One; Reframe

My first step was to decide that there was something I could do about my problems. Just like depression itself, the cure starts in the mind. I had to reframe my belief system from believing that depression was out of my control and there was nothing I could do about it to believing that I could do something about it and that it could be controlled if the right steps were taken. My first step was mental. I read as much as I could about depression and learned that I was now suffering from a type of depression known as atypical depression.

Atypical Depression

Atypical depression is a type of depression that can be difficult to treat and has symptoms that include weight gain, sleeping too much, and feeling anxious. What distinguishes it from clinical depression is mood reactivity; the person with atypical depression may see his or her mood improve if something positive happens. In clinical, or melancholic, depression, positive changes will not bring about changes in mood.

In general, people with atypical depression don't have as many of the symptoms that people with clinical depression have. They also tend to have first experienced depression at an early age, during their teenage years. The ***Diagnostic and Statistical Manual of Mental Disorders*** (DSM-IV) mandates at least two of the following symptoms for atypical depression: increase in appetite or weight gain (as opposed to the reduced appetite or weight loss of "typical" depression); excessive sleeping (as opposed to insomnia); leaden paralysis; and sensitivity to rejection.

I was going to work at 1:00pm, Monday through Friday and did little else. I often slept until time to get ready for work. I felt as though I weighed a ton, my limbs seemed heavy and cumbersome. I would try to be active and had to prepare myself mentally to do even the simplest of tasks. I simply could not find the motivation. The thought of doing anything seemed to wear me out. I would imagine each of the steps I was going to have to go through in whatever the activity might be, and how difficult and tiresome each of these steps would be. I was particularly sensitive to criticism and had a deep sense of rejection. I had all the symptoms of atypical depression.

Despite its name, atypical depression is rather common. Many doctors believe that it is under diagnosed. It is actually the most common subtype of depression in outpatients, according to Andrew Nierenberg MD, Associate Director of the Depression and Clinical Research Program at Massachusetts General Hospital, affecting anywhere from 25 to 42 percent of the depressed population. Researchers are considering whether or not atypical depression might be a type of dysthymia -- a low-level depression that has lingered for at least two years. Researchers are also investigating the idea that atypical depression may be a milder form of bipolar disorder called cyclothymia. People with cyclothymia typically have less extreme switches in mood than others with bipolar disorder.

There Is Always Something You Can Do

Study; Reading various blogs, researching about depression and studying the treatment options available, I became interested in Adderall. I was particularly interested in it because Adderall is widely reported to increase alertness, concentration and overall cognitive performance while decreasing user fatigue. I was constantly fatigued and felt heaviness in my limbs. I couldn't concentrate on anything for very long. I spent a great deal of time getting my paperwork done at work, and constantly rechecking it for mistakes. I would work on it in shifts, taking breaks because I found it hard to concentrate for long periods of time. I performed poorly at basic tasks like simple construction and general upkeep around the house.

While some may criticize my decision to resort to medicine to fight depression, I felt it was part of a comprehensive plan. My plan was to attack depression from every possible angle, and this included taking medication if necessary. I felt that my depression was at such a level again that I needed to take drastic action to prevent it from becoming worse. As I discussed in *"Change Anything"*, I made a decision to ask my psychiatrist about Adderall and she prescribed it to me.

Clearly Adderall has been effective for me. But one of the reasons it has been so effective is because I *believed* it would work. I reframed my beliefs about medicine and depression, choosing to believe that the right combination of medicine did exist for my particular symptoms, and that Adderall was right for me. My best friend's nine year old son was taking Adderall at a dosage stronger than what was prescribed to me, so I wasn't afraid to try it. It improved my ability to focus and was instrumental in my becoming an author. It improved my performance at work and made me a more well rounded individual.

Act; I reframed other beliefs as well. I decided that medicine alone could not cure my depression but would be an important component of a comprehensive treatment plan. This plan would include spiritual, mental, social and physical changes as well. I learned about how diet and exercise play a vital role in fighting depression, and made necessary lifestyle changes. I learned about personality types and how my personality traits contributed to my depression. I learned to ignore my fear of failure and pursue my dreams. I reframed deeply ingrained fears, inward motivations, and instincts and became a better person. I became aware that I was responsible for my sense of security and stopped looking to outside sources to provide it. These fears, motivations and instincts were revealed through my Enneagram personality type descriptions. This invaluable self analysis tool paved the way for my transformation by helping me discover what areas of my thinking needed to be reframed.

I reframed my long held notions about my wife and our relationship. I learned about her personality type and our codependent relationship. I broke my dependence on her and learned to be more independent, self confident and self reliant. Eventually we separated, and CCC enabled me to get through that process without falling into depression. CCC was the key to getting through my divorce and going on with life.

I reframed my spiritual beliefs. I had become bitter toward those who had hurt me, and I had to truly forgive. I realized that my faith had been an integral part of who I was, and that I could not abandon it. I came to terms with my beliefs and was no longer concerned with what anyone else thought about them. I learned to live by my convictions and no one else's.

I reframed the way I felt toward my job. It provided me with a steady income, good benefits and a respectable position. Without my job, I wouldn't have the time or money to pursue my newfound passion; writing. I stopped taking it for granted and decided to make the most of it. I gave 110% to every aspect.

Romans 12:2

New Living Translation (©2007)
"Don't copy the behavior and customs of this world, *but let God transform you into a new person by changing the way you think*. Then you will learn to know God's will for you, which is good and pleasing and perfect."

Psalms 51:10

New International Version (©1984)
"Create in me a pure heart, O God, and renew a steadfast spirit within me."

Corner Two; Accept What You Cannot Change

There are certain circumstances in our lives that are beyond our control. We have to accept that there are some things which we cannot change. Accepting the things that we cannot change does not mean that we have to accept the premise that there is nothing we can do about those things however. That premise is flawed.

Examining my premises which were based on my preconceived notions was one of most vital steps I took to conquer my depression and create lasting change. Here are a few examples of my flawed premises;

Premise; "I will always have problems with depression and there is nothing I can do about it." This premise is flawed. The correct premise is *"I will always have problems with depression, but there are many things I can do about it."* I can exercise, make changes in my diet, talk to my friends, take supplements, take antidepressants, meet with my psychiatrist every three months and more often if problems arise, write her letters, write books, blog about my feelings, stay active, educate myself and take an active role in my treatment.

Premise; There is nothing I can do about what happened in the past. This premise is flawed, there is something I can do, I can choose not to worry about it and go on with my life. I can learn from the past and try not the make the same mistakes again. I can use my experience to help others. The correct premise is *"I cannot change what happened in the past."*

Premise; One day I will die and there's nothing I can do about it. This premise is flawed. I have no control over death, but there are plenty of things I can do about it. I can accept the fact that I will die someday and choose not to worry about it. I can make peace with my faith and live by my religious convictions. I can take steps to remain healthy and live as long as possible and as well as possible. I can be thankful for everyday I'm given, make the most of each day and realize that everyday above ground is a good one. The correct premise is; *I have no control over death.*

Premise; I could lose my job tomorrow. My employer could lay me off and there's nothing I can do about it. This premise is flawed. The first thing I can do is perform my job well enough that my employer realizes how valuable I am. This will ensure that I get good references in the event that I am laid off. I can acquire as many skills as possible which I could use at another job. I can educate myself and find alternate means of supporting myself. I can choose not to worry about things which I have no control over. The correct premise is; *I have no control over the future.*

Accept that there are things which you have no control over. Don't base your happiness on the ability to control the uncontrollable. Choose to accept the things you cannot change, and live at peace with those things.

**"God grant me the serenity
to accept the things I cannot change;
courage to change the things I can;
and wisdom to know the difference."**

Corner Three; Accept Responsibility

I had to accept the fact that I was ultimately responsible for where I was in life. You will have to accept responsibility for where you are as well. Yes, I had suffered injustice, had some misfortunes and had been through a terrible time with depression. But I was where I was in life due to the decisions I had made. Blaming others, blaming my illness or making excuses was not going to help anything. I just had to accept it, start where I was and go forward.

Romans 3:23

<u>New Living Translation (©2007)</u>
For everyone has sinned; we all fall short of God's glorious standard.

Corner Four; Look For Good in Every Experience

"Happiness is always a by-product. It is probably a matter of temperament, and for anything I know it may be glandular. But it is not something that can be demanded from life, and if you are not happy you

had better stop worrying about it and see what treasures you can pluck from your own brand of unhappiness."

    Robertson Davies

The worst thing that happens may also be the best thing that happens. Look for good in every experience. Learn from your mistakes and benefit in some way from everything that happens to you. What may seem tragic at the time may actually work to your benefit in the future. Losing my career at the Sheriff's Department seemed like the end of my life. In the long run it led to a less stressful job with higher pay. Going through a divorce seems like the worst possible thing that could happen to me. It was my lifelong goal not to be divorced, and I did everything I could to save my marriage. I have to believe that in the long run, it will end up being one of the best things that has ever happened to me. CCC is helping me stay focused on my goals in spite of the circumstances.

Romans 8:28

<u>**New Living Translation (©2007)**</u>
"And we know that God causes everything to work together for the good of those who love God and are called according to his purpose for them.

Create a New Self Image

"Any transition serious enough to alter your definition of self will require not just small adjustments in your way of living and thinking but a full-on metamorphosis."

Martha Beck, *O Magazine, Growing Wings, January 2004*

In Steve Chandler's book "100 Ways to Motivate Yourself" Chandler describes meeting Arnold Schwarzenegger. "Arnold Schwarzenegger was not famous yet in 1976 when he and I had lunch together at the Doubletree Inn in Tucson, Arizona. Not one person in the restaurant recognized him.

He was in town publicizing the movie Stay Hungry, a box office disappointment he had just made with Jeff Bridges and Sally Field. I was a sports columnist for the Tucson Citizen at the time, and my assignment was to spend a full day, one on one with Arnold and write a feature story about him for our newspaper's Sunday magazine.

I too, had no idea who he was or who he was going to become. I agreed to spend the day with him because I had to – it was an assignment. And although I took to it with an uninspired attitude, it was one I'd never forget.

Perhaps the most memorable part of that day with Schwarzenegger occurred when we took an hour for lunch. I had my reporter's notebook out and was asking questions for the story while we ate. At one point I casually asked him, "Now that you have retired from bodybuilding what are you going to do next?"

And with a voice as calm as if he were telling me about some mundane travel plans, he said, "I'm going to be the number one box office star in all of Hollywood."

Mind you, this was not the slim, aerobic Arnold we know today. This man was pumped up and huge. And so for my own physical sense of well being, I tried to appear to find his goal reasonable.

I tried not to show my shock and amusement at his plan. After all, his first attempt at movies didn't promise much. And his Austrian accent and awkward, monstrous build didn't suggest instant acceptance by movie audiences. I finally managed to match his calm demeanor, and I asked him *just how* he planned to become Hollywood's top star.

"It's the same process I used in bodybuilding" he explained. "What you do is *create a vision* of who you want to be, and then live into that picture as if it were already true."

It sounded ridiculously simple. Too simple to mean anything. But I wrote it down. And I never forgot it.

I'll never forget the moment when some entertainment TV show was saying that box office receipts from his second Terminator movie had made him the most popular box office draw in the world. Was he psychic? Or was there something to his formula?"

To create a new self image, you have to create a vision and act "as if" it were already true. When I went on my diet as I began the **Create, Connect, Commit** process, I bought new clothes and had them professionally cleaned and starched. I grew a go-tee. Go-tees make the face look longer, creating the appearance that the face is thinner. I told people I was on a diet, and they began to comment on how much weight I had lost almost immediately. Their comments bolstered my self confidence, and motivated me to stay on my diet.

It just so happened that my transformation was taking place about the time I needed a new vehicle. I bought a new truck, and felt like a new person coming to work in it, dressed in new clothes and sporting new facial hair. I created a vision of who I wanted to be and began playing that part.

In my vision I was confident, successful, disciplined, fit, trim and strong. My depression was under control. I was the author of several books and had a website where my books were available and the **Create, Connect, Commit** philosophy was taught. I was traveling, doing book promotions, giving interviews and lectures and promoting the **Create, Connect, Commit** lifestyle. Therapists were using **Create, Connect, Commit** to help their patients and thousands of people were changing their lives after reading my books. **Create, Connect, Commit** was helping people stop smoking, lose weight, overcome depression, break addictions, get out of dysfunctional relationships and even to commit to their religious beliefs and make the lifestyle changes that had been so difficult for them in the past.

I created a vision of the person I wanted to be; accomplishing my goals and reaching the potential that lied within me. I knew I was setting the bar high, and at times I was uneasy and nervous, wondering if I had set the bar too high. But I just kept believing in that image I had of myself being successful and depression free. I stepped into that image and played the part until I became that person. **Plan – Do – Study – Act. Plan -** create a vision of who you want to be. **Do-** act "as if" it was already true. **Study** – where are you making progress by acting "as if" and where are you falling short? **Act** – make corrections and act "as if" until you fully become the person in your vision. **Plan – Do – Study – Act.**

Isaiah 40:31

New Living Translation (©2007)
"But those who trust in the LORD will find new strength. They will soar high on wings like eagles. They will run and not grow weary. They will walk and not faint."

Concept Two; Connect

"There is a time when we must firmly chose the course we will follow, or the relentless drift of events will make the decision" – Herbert V. Prochnow

Type Six personalities tend to fear making important decisions, although at the same time, they resist having anyone else make decisions for them. Sixes have been described as being like a ping-pong ball, constantly shuttling back and forth between whatever influence is hitting the hardest in any given moment. They have difficulty making decisions which leads to avoidance of responsibility and procrastination. As I've told you, the Enneagram type description of myself was incredibly accurate. The description was eerily similar to my own experience.

When I graduated from high school I had no idea what I wanted to do. I drifted from one job to the next. I seemed to have no control over the course my life would take. I was like a pinball. A pinball sits in a hole with the other pinballs, bored to death. They can hear the bells and see the flashes of light from the pinball machines and they can't wait for their chance to get into the game. Then it's time. They leave the hole and are thrust full speed into the lights, bumpers, noise and confusion for which they are totally unprepared. Confused and frightened, they try their best to get back into the hole, back to the familiar, but the flippers keep knocking them back into the action. When they finally make it back to the hole, they realize they liked it there. Things weren't so bad in there. They were with other pinballs just like them. They knew what was expected of them. They knew how things worked in there. There were very few surprises. So, they settle in and get comfortable and happy. Just when things get back to normal, someone else comes along and puts another quarter in. Then the whole process starts over again.

When it came to my career I had no idea what I wanted. In contrast, when it came to my training routine, I knew exactly what I wanted. I set a goal to lose 40 lbs. in 3 months. I came up with a routine designed to accomplish that. I didn't let anything deter me. I had a goal. I had a clear picture in my mind of what I would look like when I reached the goal. I worked toward the goal until I reached it. This is the first step in connecting. Know what it is that you hope to achieve. *Know what you want.*

KNOW WHERE YOU'RE GOING

"If you don't know where you are going, you might end up somewhere else" Yogi Berra

Looking back, what has limited me more than anything else in my life is not knowing what I wanted to do. When I reflect back on it now I ask myself, **"Who starts a journey with no destination in mind?"** Who just sets out, and starts going with no preparation and no set destination? When you plan a trip, you plan on getting somewhere. Once you've chosen a destination, you refer to a map or a GPS device to get directions on how to get there. Follow the directions, and you'll reach points along the way until you finally arrive at your destination.

Life works the same way. I didn't know where I wanted to go. I didn't have anyone to give me directions. When I did think I knew where I wanted to go, I couldn't find a map to show me the way. I looked for short cuts. I got lost. I kept turning around, going in circles and starting over. No wonder it took me so long to get my life in order! Can you imagine a trip like that?

That's the trip most people take in life. When I worked with young people I tried to impress upon them the importance of finding what they would like to do as early as possible. Most people have no idea what they want to do when they graduate from High School. Others think they know what they want, yet have no idea what's involved in attaining their desired career. **It is the rare individual who decides early on what he/she wants to accomplish in life and works diligently with single minded purpose to fulfill that desire.** People who do just that are the people about whom books are written and movies are made. They are among the most successful and most accomplished individuals in the world, because they know what they want and they go after it until they get it. They don't let setbacks, obstacles or difficulties stop them and they reach their goals. When they reach their goals, they set new ones. They always stay hungry.

To become a new creation and make the changes in your life permanent, you must commit to progress. God accepts us as we are, but He refuses to let us stay that way. Never accept the status quo. You should always have something to look forward to. Constantly striving to achieve a new goal is the key to happiness, fulfillment and purpose in life. You are what you do, and having something to do will give you what everyone inwardly strives for in life; meaning.

When I worked for a surveyor, one of my responsibilities was cutting out property lines. Sometimes we cleared out the actual lines, sometimes we just had to make our way through the brush to set points that would be used to triangulate and determine where the boundaries lay. One person would use a transit and looking through it, he would tell you where to put a point. Looking back at the transit and this point would put you "on line". Two points make a line. The person with the transit is able to see the line looking forward. If you're cutting it out, however, the only way to see the line is to look behind you, at the points that have already been set.

The person at the transit would put you on line, but they would have to help cut too. They couldn't just stand behind the transit all day and constantly tell you where you should be cutting. So it was difficult to stay on line and be clearing in the right place. If you got off line, you wasted time and energy cutting through brush that didn't have to be cut.

I learned to look back at the points on line, lining my bush axe up like a rifle, then turn my head 180 degrees without moving the bush axe, and see what the other end of the bush axe was pointing at. I would pick a large tree or some other focal point in the distance that the bush axe was aimed at and cut toward it. Once I had an object to focus on, I could stay on line easily. Occasionally, I would look back and line the points up to make sure I was still on line and make slight adjustments.

You have to do the same thing in life. **Pick something in the distance to focus on, keeps your eyes on it and work toward it.** Look behind you occasionally to make sure you're on the right path and make adjustments as needed. This is how you reach your goals. Once you reach one goal immediately set another one. Life is too short to rest on your laurels.

"We always do what we MOST WANT to do, whether or not we like what we are doing at each instant of our lives. Wanting and liking many times are not the same thing. Many people have done what they say they didn't want to do at a particular moment. And that may be true until one looks deeper into the motivation behind the doing. What they are really saying is the price they will have to pay or the consequences they will have to endure, for not doing that something may be too high or onerous for them not to do it. Such as going to work. Many people say they don't want to go to work and yet they go. Which means they don't want to risk losing their jobs and the negative hurting emotions associated with not having a job. It has been estimated about 90% to

95% of all people work at jobs which are unfulfilling and which they dislike and would leave in a minute if they only knew what they really wanted to do."

Sidney Madwed

Setting Goals

Goal Setting is a useful technique at any time but is especially beneficial to those who have been suffering from depression. It can be used in conjunction with problem solving, an effective strategy for fighting depression. It promotes the process of breaking down problems into small attainable goals. It causes us to examine whether or not our goals are realistic. Having impossible goals can increase a sense of anger, frustration or helplessness resulting in further depression. Some depressed individuals make the achievement of only one or two specific goals a prerequisite for personal happiness. This unrealistic approach to goal setting has been named Conditional Goal Setting (CGS). Findings suggest that CGS is significantly related to depression. Make sure your goals are realistic and attainable; don't set yourself up for failure and more depression. Set time frames for your goals, and then break them down into smaller goals. Have yearly, monthly, weekly and daily goals.

Set aside some time each night to plan the next day and set goals for the day. Tonight for instance, you should be setting a goal to exercise in some form or fashion for 30 minutes tomorrow. Make a list of the things you want to get done, and then tomorrow check those things off as you do them. Making the list will get your mind off your problems tonight and checking off that list will give you a sense of control, accomplishment and self empowerment tomorrow.

Setting goals shifts our focus away from our problems, and promotes a focus on the future. Noted author and self help guru Zig Ziglar once said that he has never seen a depressed person with goals. Why is it that you cannot be a diligent goal setter and still be depressed? The answer, says Ziglar, is that your mind can only hold one thought at a time. That thought will either be positive or negative. Therefore, it is reasonable to assume that if you are focused on your goal, which is purely positive, then you cannot simultaneously be focusing on the negative thought that is causing your depression.

When you have a good day and reach the goals you have set for yourself that day, reward yourself. Celebrate small success. This is the opposite of what most people do. Most people, when they are depressed about not reaching their goals decide to do something to make themselves feel better. In effect they are rewarding negative behavior. You wouldn't reward your child for inappropriate behavior, so you shouldn't do it for yourself either. Reward yourself for good behavior instead. Decide what the reward should be, and reinforce positive behavior with positive rewards.

As soon as you feel yourself turning negative, remind yourself of your goals. Remember to focus on what you do want, and not on what you don't want. You will be drawn toward whatever you focus on. Behavior begins in the mind and Thought, Action, Habit is the way the process works. By setting aside a few minutes each night to plan the next day's activity and set small goals, you'll be focusing on something positive. This will help you feel better and be a positive step toward accomplishing your major goals and beating depression.

What if I Don't Know What I Want?

The first thing you can do is decide to be successful where you are. You will never be a success somewhere else unless you are first a success where you are. **What are the problems at your job**? If you're married, what are the problems in that relationship? What are your goals for exercise and diet? You may not know everything you want just yet, but there are plenty of areas in your life that you know could be improved upon. Start by setting goals to make these improvements. **Start where you are. Start with your job.**

Before sin ever entered the world, God created work to be a part of our experience. Genesis tells us, "The LORD God took the man and put him in the Garden of Eden *to work it and take care of it*" (Gen. 2:15). Adam had a job. He took care of the garden and named the animals as well. The goal of his work was to bring order to things. The Hebrew word for this idea is *shalom*. **Shalom** (שָׁלוֹם) (Sephardic Hebrew/Israeli Hebrew: Shalom; Ashkenazi Hebrew/Yiddish: Sholem or Shulem) is a Hebrew word meaning *peace*, *completeness*, and *welfare* and can be used idiomatically to mean both *hello* and *goodbye*. As it does in English, it can refer to either peace between two entities (especially between man and God or between two countries), or to *the well-being, welfare or safety of an individual or a group of individuals*

Shalom means "peace," but it's more than just a state of being. *Shalom* implies a state of peace because all things are in their proper order, and peace between man and God. Our goal is to move into a state of Shalom. We want Shalom for ourselves and our church. The goal of implementing **Create, Connect, Commit** churchwide, is to bring Shalom to your church. To bring a sense of purpose and order, peace among members and peace between members and God.

Finding Your Passion

God never told David ***"Stop writing Psalms, you love it too much."*** **God has given each of us unique gifts to use for His purpose, His kingdom, and His pleasure. He is the Giver of all gifts, and our success depends on His work being done through us.** ***"Lord, You will grant us peace, for all we have accomplished is really from You"*** **(Isaiah 26:12, NLT).**

I was an effective Youth Minister and popular preacher because I was good at what I did. I was good at what I did because I was passionate about it. I cared about the young people who had been entrusted to me. I opened my home to them and they became part of my family. Some of them still spend time with me and I have watched them grow up as if they were my own children.

When I preached I saw it as my way of serving. Preachers need time off just like everyone else. By filling in for them, I was providing a service that they desperately needed. By opening up their pulpits to me they were conveying the message that that they trusted me to stand in their place and lead their people. It was an obligation that I didn't take lightly. I considered it an honor to be given such a significant responsibility. I didn't want to let anyone down. I put everything I had into preparing those sermons and delivering them with enthusiasm. There was always a sense of expectation and excitement in my audiences when I stood before them. I fed off that enthusiasm. There was a sense that if I was speaking, they were going to hear something special, something worthy of their attention. I always strived to meet their expectations.

While the concern I had for the Youth and the importance which I placed on preaching were contributing factors to my success, there was another factor at work here; I had a passion for reading and learning, then sharing what I had learned with other people. The most effective way for me to learn is to prepare material to teach to other people. Preparing lessons for the Youth Group and doing research for my sermons filled the need that I had to be constantly learning something new. Teaching and preaching filled the need that I had to share what I had learned.

Being out of ministry left a void in my life. I needed to be learning and teaching. I searched for a degree program that I could complete on-line. I was interested in psychology, but I had to be realistic. A PhD was necessary to put a degree in psychology to good use. By the time I earned a PhD, I would be nearing retirement and would have accumulated more debt than I could hope to repay in the process.

So I looked at other fields. Nursing was the field with the most demand in the future. With a projected need of 1,001,000 RNs over a 10 year period and a projected growth rate of 18 – 26%, nursing was a solid career choice. There was a College in my community that had a highly acclaimed nursing program. I was even eligible for a scholarship program that would pay my tuition. There was only one problem; I didn't want to be a nurse.

I wanted to fill the need I had to learn and teach. I wanted to study subjects that interested me, and then share what I learned with other people. I wanted to help people who had been through what I had been through.

Nine Steps to Setting Goals

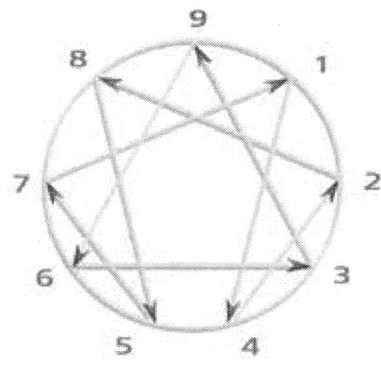

1.) *I found something I was passionate about*

"Unprovided with original learning, unformed in the habits of thinking, unskilled in the arts of composition, I resolved to write a book."

Edward Gibbon (1737 - 1794)

I decided to write a book. I didn't know how to write a book, I just knew that I wanted to do it. So I set a goal. I found a publishing company that would accept manuscripts for review online (company A). If they thought the manuscript was good enough, they would do all the marketing. They would publish your book as a hard copy, an e-book and an audio book. That was what I wanted. I wanted my book on audio. I love audio books; my ipod is full of them. I set out to write a book that was good enough to be published by company A. That was my goal. I gave myself 5 years to reach that goal. I finished my first book in only months and submitted it to company A. While I was awaiting their decision, I started another book. In 2 weeks, I had an unedited manuscript which I also submitted. I now had the concepts in mind for my next five books. I bought the domain name createconnectcommit.com and began to put my ideas to work.

Writing was something I was passionate about. It was my way of connecting with what I wanted, and connecting with other people. Even if I never got a book published, I was spending time doing something that I wanted to do. Writing filled the need I had to learn and teach. I studied and wrote about what I was interested in. Someday others would read what I had written and it would help them. Writing was a form of therapy for me. I was analyzing what had happened to me in the past, applying logic and truth, and then plotting a course for my future.

God has gifted each of us with unique talents to use for His purpose. Mine are studying and teaching. Although I do quite well with public speaking, this is not a gift. It is something I have to work diligently at. I have a fear of public speaking, but have learned to compensate for my weaknesses and overcome my fear. In order to use my gifts (studying and teaching) I have to practice something that I'm not gifted at (public speaking.)

I'm not good at witnessing to people, public prayer nor most forms of outreach. I have had times in my life when I have lived a carnal lifestyle and set a terrible example. I suffered from depression to the point that I thought I would never recover, and the idea of ever speaking publicly again was unfathomable; I couldn't even express myself long enough to carry on a normal conversation. Through the grace of God I overcame depression and I'm now able to serve Him by focusing on what He has gifted me at and compensating for my weaknesses.

Find something you have a passion for. You have a unique quality about yourself which no one else has. Find your gift and put it to use.

2.) *I put my goal in writing and set a deadline. I wrote the goal "as if" I had already accomplished it. I was realistic about what I could accomplish.* **(PLAN.)**

When I wrote the introduction to my first book, I wrote it as if it was five years in the future. I wrote the goals I set for myself as if they had already happened. I had to go back and change the introduction because I finished the book much sooner than I expected. I wrote the table of contents and used it to frame the book. Seeing the table of contents written out gave me a mental image of what the book would look like when it was finished. It was a way of writing my goal as if I had already accomplished it.

Writing your goals as if you've already accomplished them programs your subconscious mind for success. Your faith easily accepts what your eyes have seen. Writing your goals this way will give you a mental picture of what you want to achieve.

The goal has to be big enough to have the power to inspire you, but realistic enough to believe. Your subconscious will not accept the impossible. You have to set a goal that you have faith in yourself to achieve. It is better to set a big goal and accomplish part of it, than to set a small goal and accomplish none of it.

3.) *I broke my goal down into small, measurable steps and took action.* Once I had set the date for accomplishing my goal, I just back stepped and set the points along the way. I told myself that books are written one word at a time. I wrote words until I had a sentence, sentences until I had a paragraph, paragraphs until I had a page and pages until I had a chapter. Each time I finished a chapter, I celebrated a small victory. Setting a goal and having the faith that you can achieve it is powerful, but taking action and actually making progress toward that goal is much more powerful. There is nothing like progress to motivate you. **(DO.)**

4.) *I celebrated small success.* Having small projects ensures that you will have small success and small failures. Small failures are easy to overcome. If you take on big projects all at once, you fail big. Start small, fail small. Celebrate small victories, learn from small failures.

5.) *I developed a workable plan of action for future success. (Be flexible).* I had an outline, but I wrote as I was inspired, not in sequence. Whatever I was passionate about at the time is what I wrote about. I had the book laid out as to what would go where, but filled in sections as I was so inspired. This allowed my melancholic temperament to have a sense of freedom to be creative and uninhibited while allowing my choleric temperament to have a sense of order. My goal was carved in stone, my plan was written in sand.

I read over and edited each chapter until it was perfect, one chapter at a time. Before I finished the book, I set goals for writing other books. Once I finished one project, I wanted to immediately have another project to start working on. You have to commit to progress, never kick back, get comfortable and rest on your laurels. **(STUDY)**

I wanted a manuscript good enough to be accepted by the publishing company I had picked (company A) but what if they didn't like it?

6.) *I had a back up plan.* I found another publishing company where I could pay to have my book published (company B). If I was rejected by company A, I would have my book published by company B. I was going to write a book and I was going to have it published one way or another. I knew there was an audience for my book. I knew that there were people like me who wanted something different and something that worked. I knew that **Create, Connect, Commit** worked and I had to get it into the hands of the people that desperately needed it.

Once my book was published, I was going to write another book and submit it to company A. If they rejected it, I would have it published by company B and I would keep writing manuscripts and submitting them to company A until I got it right and they agreed to publish one of my books. I was going to be the author of a bestselling audio book, even if it took the rest of my life to do it.

7.) *I never gave up* (**ACT**)

8.) *I had balance* – Finishing my book was my #1 objective. I knew that I was on to something with **Create, Connect, Commit** and it was difficult to control my enthusiasm. I could sit at the computer for hours working on my book, and then wonder where the time went. There just didn't seem to be enough time available to work on my book, and anything else I had to do was an inconvenience. I was skipping workouts, putting things off and was almost late to work a couple of times because I spent so much time working on my book. I was like a kid with a new toy. I had to put things into perspective and prioritize. I didn't need problems with my wife from neglecting my responsibilities and I sure didn't need any problems at work.

I was developing Van Gogh Syndrome. Van Gogh Syndrome is not the unexplainable desire to cut off one's own ear; it is a lack of balance. It is the extreme concentration of all effort on one aspect of life at the exclusion of everything else. It can be defined as having such an intense focus on one objective that it leads to the unhealthy neglect of all other goals and responsibilities.

PRIORITIZE

"Taking first things first often reduces the most complex human problem to a manageable proportion." – Dwight Eisenhower

I had to put my priorities in order. It goes without saying God should be at the top of your list. He's at the top of mine now. At the time I wrote this list, I was doing some soul searching. When I organized my priorities in order of importance, they looked like this;

1.) Work

2.) Exercise and Diet

3.) Projects

4.) Relationships

5.) Writing.

1.) Work. I know I will be criticized for putting work first, and I don't necessarily recommend that you do this. For most of my life I had put work first at the exclusion of the more important things in life. I had been a workaholic. A stereotypical Type 6, I gained my sense of security from an undying allegiance to an authority outside myself which I could obey. Work provided the sense of security I so desperately needed. When I went into law enforcement, the law became the trusted authority I could obey.

Then, the 10 years I was in ministry, I put ministry first. God became my trusted authority to be obeyed. When you prioritize, I highly recommend putting spiritual issues first on your list. Drawing strength from a higher power plays a crucial role in overcoming depression. I did not put spiritual issues first in my priorities on this particular list because I was not addressing them at that time. Like everything else in my life, I had preconceived notions and erroneous premises about religion. I had to examine my beliefs through the lens of logical thinking and truth, reframe, develop correct premises and create new boundaries for my spiritual life. I applied **Create, Connect, Commit** to my spiritual life and that process will be the subject of another book.

Some will feel family should come first, or second after spiritual needs. I agree. But in my case, by putting work first I was taking care of my family. My job provided the income and stability necessary to support our lifestyle. I had to take my job seriously and do it well enough to get noticed. The company I worked for could go out of business, and I had to develop a new track record in private security and prove that I could turn an incompetent security department into a team of well trained professionals. I had to prove myself as an innovative and effective manager. If something did happen to the company I worked for, I would need references to find another job. By having a proven track record at my current job, I was laying the foundation for future success. You must first be successful where you are before you can be successful somewhere else. My job also made it possible for me to pursue my love, writing. By not having to be at work until 1:00pm, my mornings were free to work on my book. If I should lose my job, I would become preoccupied with the search for another one, and possibly have to take one with less pay and more hours, making it difficult to find time for writing. It was crucial that I do my job well, so putting it first on my list of priorities was the right choice for me.

2.) Exercise and Diet. We'll learn in the last two chapters what an important role diet and exercise play in fighting depression. I had to commit to getting some exercise everyday for the psychological benefits. I also desperately wanted to get back in shape; to look and feel good.

Being fit, trim, healthy and looking good were vital to my self esteem and self confidence.

I often preferred to spend my time writing rather than exercising. I had to overcome this desire, and keep my priorities in order. Putting exercise and diet second was crucial to my relationship with my wife as well. I was less depressed when I was in shape. I was self confident and more outgoing. I felt better and was more fun to be around. I made the commitment to exercise for 30 minutes 3 times a week and slowly worked my way up to 5 times a week. I eliminated unhealthy foods and continued to lose weight. I committed to following a healthy diet for life.

3.) Projects. I had to get things done around the house. There were many repairs and basic upkeep that had to be done. I couldn't spend all my time sitting at the computer writing. There were simply too many other things that had to be done.

4.) **Relationships.** I had to socialize. I had to connect with others I wanted to be like. I had to find people who offered constructive criticism, as well as people who empathized with me. I had to get involved in church again and connect with other Christians. I could not be a hermit and stay at home writing all the time. Writing did help me connect with others, but I couldn't just use writing as a substitute for genuine socialization.

When my wife left I really needed the relationships with people in my support group. I had to connect with them to stay positive and get the support I needed to make it through. I also felt it was important to maintain a friendship with my wife. She could not help her feelings, and blaming her was not going to fix the problem. Whatever the outcome of our separation, I was determined to remain friends. We worked through the terms of our divorce in a fair and amiable manner and became even better friends.

5.) **Writing**. This was the most difficult choice to make but I had to do it. Writing has become my favorite pastime. I actually have to force myself to stop working on my books. There are times when I have to finish a project and writing comes first, but that can't be all the time. There must be balance.

9.) **Create, Connect, Commit.** Once you've chosen your goals, reframe your preconceived notions about your ability to change. Develop new premises and create new boundaries that include your goals. Commit to reaching your goals and then setting new ones. **Plan –Do – Study – Act.**

9 Steps to Success

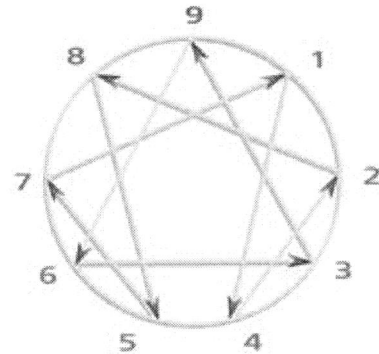

My passions were all gathered together like fingers that made a fist. Drive is considered aggression today; I knew it then as purpose.

    Bette Davis (1908 - 1989), *The Lonely Life, 1962*

In my exercise plan, I had followed the same 9 steps. These steps are crucial to making any goal a reality.

Step One; I found something I was passionate about.

 Lifting weights had shaped me and made me who I was. Working out had always been the high point of my day. Seeing how much I could lift and how far I could push myself was more play than work. I enjoyed every minute of it. I was passionate about lifting weights.

 Through depression and inactivity, I lost that passion. Starting over was not easy. Not being able to use the weight I was accustomed to and gasping for air after each set was humiliating. Lifting weights was no longer fun, it was work. I had to be passionate about it to make it work, so I focused on two things that I was passionate about;

1.) I wanted results. Lifting weights was a means to an end and I could bear the discomfort and humility if it meant I would achieve the results I wanted in the end. **I was passionate about looking better.**

2.) Lifting weights made me feel better. I had to exercise for the mental benefit that it gave me, and not just to get physical results. I began to see exercise as a type of medicine. I prescribed myself a set number of workouts a week for a set amount of time each session. I would never think about missing a dose of my prescribed medicine; I developed the same mindset for exercise.

Finishing a workout and marking it off on my calendar gave me a sense of accomplishment. I got instant gratification knowing that I had taken another step toward reaching my goal. Taking positive action to prevent my depression from coming back made me feel that I was more in control. Instead of feeling helpless and having a victim mentality, I felt that there was something I could do. This sense of control made me feel better. **I was passionate about feeling better.** I knew that looking better and feeling better would help me beat depression, and that was something I was passionate about.

Step Two; I put my goal in writing and set a deadline. I wrote the goal "as if" I had already accomplished it. I was realistic about what I could accomplish.

Writing your goals as though you have already achieved them is a powerful motivational tool. I can't stress this enough. It was the first of December and I was going to Las Vegas in 6 months. I wanted to look my best for that trip, then stay trim and fit for the coming summer. By writing down what my weight would be at the first of May, I programmed myself to take action to make that goal a reality. Writing your goals in the present tense, as though you've already accomplished them triggers your subconscious mind to beginning telling you to change your behavior. Your subconscious mind accepts the information as fact (if it is within reason) and sets out to make that fact a reality.

I got a calendar book and wrote what my weight would be at the beginning of each month for the coming year. I set a goal each month for how many workouts I would do per week. I was realistic about how much weight I could lose, and how many workouts I would actually do. I started with 3 – 30 minute workouts a week. I gradually increased to 4 – 30 minute workouts and then to 5 – 30 minute workouts. These were realistic expectations for the amount of time I would dedicate to exercise. You have to be realistic when you set goals. If you set goals that are unrealistic, you are just setting yourself up for failure. Making commitments for yourself that you will not be able to keep will just make you feel a sense of failure and cause you to give up. Be sure and set goals that are attainable.

Step Three; I broke my goal down into small measurable steps and took action.

I had a certain amount of weight to lose each month. I had a certain amount of workouts to do each week. I had a certain amount of food I could eat each day. Everything has to be broken down in steps. Big goals have to be broken down into smaller, reachable goals. Projects have to be broken down into small measurable steps. The key to success is simplicity. Think small and get the little things done. Actions repeated become habits. Habits create progress. Progress creates motivation.

Step Four; I celebrated small success.

Every workout was a small victory. I had a place in my calendar book where I could write down which muscle groups I worked on what particular day. Finishing my workout and recording it in my calendar book was the highlight of my day. Looking at that calendar at the end of the month, I could see how much work I had done toward reaching my goal.

I weighed myself and took measurements at the first of each month. I could see how much weight I had lost and how many inches I had lost off my waist. Seeing progress motivated me to work even harder. Progress is the best motivator.

Step Five; I developed a workable plan of action for future success.

Once I got back in shape, I was determined not to get out of shape again. I set goals for maintenance and made plans to steadily increase the intensity of my weightlifting workouts and the frequency of my aerobic workouts. I was committed to making progress and would set new goals once I reached my previous ones. *This is critical.* Never accept the status quo. Don't get comfortable after you've made some progress and fall back into your old habits. This is one of the reasons why changes don't last, we become comfortable with the progress we've made, relax our standards and drift back into the same self defeating behavior that caused us to have to make changes in the first place. We constantly shift between momentum and inertia.

I have lost over 40 lbs in a 3 to 4 month period at least 9 times in my life. I was doing this about every 3 to 4 years on average. When I got the weight off this time, I had a plan in place for keeping it off. You have to set new goals to stay motivated and make a commitment to continue making progress. Once the ball is rolling in the right direction, you have to keep it rolling. Learn to recognize the signs. When you see yourself losing momentum, make adjustments, change scenery, set new goals, do whatever it takes to keep making progress. Progress creates motivation, motivation creates more progress. Remember, an object at rest tends to stay at rest and an object in motion tends to stay in motion. Stay in motion. *Commit to progress.*

Step Six; I had a back up plan.

I planned to be at the Gym at 5:30 every morning. If I didn't make it to the gym, I would workout at home. If I missed a workout altogether, I would just workout the next day. As long as I met the minimum requirement for number of workouts, it didn't matter what day I did them on. This plan was rigid enough to be effective, but flexible enough to be practical. My goal was carved in stone but my plan was written in sand.

Step Seven; I never gave up.

If I ate something I wasn't supposed to eat, I compensated for it by eating less the rest of the day. If I missed a workout, I made up for it. If I didn't feel like working out, I went through the motions anyway. I wanted to have something to write down. I had to do at least enough to be able to write down my workout in my calendar book. I kept chipping away, step by step, making exercise a regular part of my life and celebrating small victories. I mastered small success. Small success led to big success, and I reached my goals.

Step Eight; I had balance; I prioritized.

Exercise couldn't come first in my life, but it did take a high priority. I had to decide what was important to me, set my priorities and spend my time accordingly. Don't focus on one aspect of your life at the expense of others. Decide which elements of your life have the highest priority. Prioritize and then develop a plan to live according to those priorities.

Step Nine; Create, Connect, Commit. This will cement your goals into reality and ensure that the changes you make are permanent. Evaluate your progress and set new goals. **Plan – Do – Study – Act.**

Connect With Others

Socialization

We are the product of heredity and environment. Scientific research provides strong evidence that people are shaped by both social influences *and* their hard-wired biological makeup. Genetic studies have shown that a person's environment (socialization) interacts with their genotype (heredity) to influence behavioral outcomes.

Socialization is a continuing process whereby an individual acquires a personal identity and learns the norms, values, behavior, and social skills appropriate to his or her environment.

Socialization is important in the process of personality formation. While much of our personality is the result of our genes, the socialization process can mold it in particular directions by encouraging specific beliefs and selectively providing experiences. Our boundaries are shaped by the people we interact with. Their beliefs become our beliefs. Their prejudices and preconceived notions influence and shape our own.

Our heredity determines our potential. Our environment determines how much of that potential we reach. We cannot change our heredity, but we can change our environment. We can connect with people we want to emulate. We can socialize with people who we want to be like, people who are positive, happy and successful. People who have done the things that we hope to do. We can read about such people, listen to audio books and watch movies about them. Such people can help us shape new boundaries.

"It is not a bad idea to get in the habit of writing down one's thoughts. It saves one having to bother anyone else with them."

    Isabel Colegate

Writing became a way of connecting for me. Eventually people would read what I was writing, so it seemed as though I was talking to people about my problems, sharing what I had been through and how I had changed. Writing was a crucial step in my recovery and remains an important part of my strategy to fight depression. Communicating with my psychiatrist through letters, e-mailing those I confide in and writing books are all effective forms of connecting with other people for me.

Prayer is also a powerful form of connecting. Telling your problems to God helps to get the burden off of you. He is always available.

Socialization and Therapy

In his book *Change or Die* Alan Deutschman writes about finding a book first published in 1961 called *Persuasion and Healing* by Jerome D. Frank MD, who had been a professor of psychiatry at Johns Hopkins University.

Franks ran the psychiatric outpatient clinic at the university's hospital in the 1950's and he wanted to know what really worked in psychological therapy. He decided to compare three forms of therapy; the classic approach where the patient meets with the therapist in intense private sessions, group therapy, and minimal therapy, with the patient meeting with a doctor for sessions lasting 30 minutes repeated every 2 weeks.

The results of the study astonished Franks. It turned out that all three kinds of therapy worked just as well even though they were so different from one another. In the following decades the psychology profession continued to compare the effectiveness of different types of therapy, studying and comparing over 400 different types of psychotherapy and the results were still the same. Every kind of psychotherapy was helpful to patients, but no particular kind was significantly more helpful than others.

Different types of therapy work because of what they have in common; they all have the same active ingredient that makes them effective. What is the common denominator that makes all types of therapy equally effective? Going to therapy inspires a new sense of hope, the belief and expectation that one will overcome his/her problems. This hope is inspired by the connection of the patient to the therapist or the group, not the theories or techniques that differentiate the different types of therapy.

Frank applied these ideas to religious and shamanic healing as well as western medicine and psychiatry. He called the religious practices psychotherapies from different cultures. The same principles applied in those traditions. A preacher speaking to a congregation, a shaman speaking to a group of tribesmen, a therapist listening to a patient and a group of people meeting to discuss their problems are all examples of the power of connecting and could equally inspire a distressed person. What works in therapy is the power of connecting. Connecting inspires hope, belief and faith.

Connecting is the key to maintaining healthy relationships and feeling well deserved and part of someone's life. For most individuals with a healthy social support network, major stressors in life can be more easily managed. A proper support network consists of a reinforcing family and friends who can help you to work through any major problems, such as the death of a family member, loss of a job, major injury, or any of a number of other stressors that can contribute to depression. For individuals with an undeveloped social network, or those with a negatively reinforcing social network, these major life events can cause greater harm because of a lack of the support that healthy individuals have. An underdeveloped social network cannot handle the pressure of an individual looking for support, and a negatively framed social network can actually reinforce thoughts of hopelessness, failure, and being worthless. Without a support network, it is more likely for an individual to develop symptoms of depression (Wade & Kendler, 2000). We need the emotional support of other people in our lives.

Connect with God

Connecting with God is our ultimate aim. **Create, Connect, Commit to God** will move us into a closer relationship with God, reveals our responsibilities and move us to meet those responsibilities through goal setting, and keeps us committed to growing in our spiritual walk by committing to progress. **Create, Connect, Commit to God** prevents us from becoming stagnant, regressing and falling away. As we move into *Shalom*, we experience the most dynamic relationship with God we've ever known.

Connecting with God can be a powerful tool in overcoming depression as well. A study published in the November-December 2002 issue of *Psychosomatics* concluded that;

"Prayer may heal depression. Moderate levels of prayer and other types of religious coping may help combat depression."

It seems prayer really does have the power to heal. Moderate levels of prayer and other types of religious coping may help combat depression among spouses of people with lung cancer, says the study.

The study involved 156 spouses of people with various stages of lung cancer. The spouses were 26 to 85 years old (mean age 63.9 years), and 78 percent of them were women.

Researchers assessed the spouses' levels of religious coping and depression, along with their sense of control over events and level of social support.

The researchers define religious coping as a person's use of religious beliefs or practices to manage stressful life events.

Religious coping includes prayer, drawing comfort from faith, and having support from church members.

The study found that spouses who used moderate levels of religious coping were less depressed than spouses who used lower or higher levels of religious coping.

The connection between depression and high levels of religious coping may reflect an over-reliance on less adaptive religious coping strategies and neglect of other important coping strategies, the researchers say. However it may be that those who are using higher levels of religious coping have turned to religion out of desperation.

Researchers say that spouses who feel the most desperate may be more likely to turn to religion for comfort. That means those people may already be depressed before they begin using religious coping.

The following prayer paints a picture of the struggle I've been through in my battle to overcome depression and come full circle with my faith.

May we discover through pain and torment,
the strength to live with grace and humor.
May we discover through doubt and anguish,
the strength to live with dignity and holiness.
May we discover through suffering and fear,
the strength to move toward healing.
May it come to pass that we be restored to health and to vigor.
May Life grant us wellness of body, spirit, and mind.
And if this cannot be so, may we find in this transformation and passage
moments of meaning, opportunities for love
and the deep and gracious calm that comes
when we allow ourselves to move on.

- **Rabbi Rami M. Shapiro**

Source: SoultoSpirit.com

Concept Three Commit

Commit to Change

Exodus 35:2

New International Version (©1984)
"For six days, work is to be done, but the seventh day shall be your holy day, a Sabbath of rest to the LORD. Whoever does any work on it must be put to death."

We take the second part of this command seriously, but what about the first part? *For six days, work is to be done.* This is a call to action. You must put action behind your faith; *faith without works is dead.* You must also put action behind your decision to change. Without action, all the mental preparation and goal setting will have been in vain.

You've learned how to create new boundaries and create a new self image. You've learned how to connect with what you want and connect with other people. You have changed your way of thinking. Now you must commit to that change by taking action. Thought, Action, Habit is the way the process works.

"Blessed is the person who is too busy to worry in the daytime and too sleepy to worry at night." – Unkown

All the mental preparation you've done so far will be useless unless you take action to put it into effect in your life. If you are serious about changing, you must commit to change by taking action. Faith without works is dead.

Saying "I am a Doctor" over and over again will not make you a Doctor. You have to take action, go to school for many years, do an internship, get a license and go through many other steps before you become a Doctor.

I have nothing against positive thinking, affirmations, prayer and meditation but the thought must become an action to be of any real value. It is action that creates results.

"Speech is conveniently located midway between thought and action, where it often substitutes for both."

John Andrew Holmes, *"Wisdom in Small Doses"*

Saying "I feel good" over and over again will not keep you from being depressed. Getting up and taking a walk will do more to relieve your symptoms than repeating affirmations will. Saying "I feel good" over and over while you are walking will actually work. In this way, you will be putting action behind your thoughts.

Our goals start in our minds, but it is action towards those goals that makes us feel better, gives us a sense of control and purpose and inspires us on to reach our goals. Thought, action, habit is the way the process works. An action repeated becomes a habit. Habits create progress. Progress creates motivation. Motivation creates results.

The same is true of study and prayer. You can pray all you want, but if you never put action behind those prayers, you'll rarely see any results. Noah had faith in God to save him from the flood, but he had to take action and build the ark.

"We should be taught not to wait for inspiration to start a thing. Action always generates inspiration. Inspiration seldom generates action."

Frank Tibolt

We have been conditioned to believe that we must first get motivated before we can change. We have to get over that believe. Those of us who've been depressed know that depression creates a cycle of inactivity and more depression. We're inactive because we're depressed; we're depressed because we're inactive.

The hardest thing to do when you are depressed is to get motivated. Making yourself start doing something is the most difficult task. If you can just start, you will feel better. To get started, you have to do something that you don't feel like doing. You have to be active even when you don't want to. The same applies for anyone who has been inactive. Getting started is the hardest part.

If you are starting an exercise program, your first goal should be to feel better. Don't worry about seeing physical results at first, look at exercise as a type of medicine. You have to take the medicine before it starts working. You have to exercise; then you will feel better.

It's the same for any action. You are not going to feel like doing it before you start. You have to start; then you will feel like doing more. Don't wait to get motivated; go ahead and start, and then you will get motivated. It won't always be easy, but nothing worth doing ever is.

Commit to Progress

"People have a hard time letting go of their suffering. Out of a fear of the unknown, they prefer suffering that is familiar."

Thich Nhat Hanh

2 Peter 2:22

<u>New International Version (©1984)</u>
Of them the proverbs are true: "A dog returns to its vomit," and, "A sow that is washed goes back to her wallowing in the mud."

Once you've made changes in your life, you must work diligently to maintain those changes. You must never become satisfied with the progress you've made and decide to kick back and take it easy. Doing so will result in a gradual regression to your old ways of thinking and old habits. You'll be back where you started before you know it. Much of this regression takes place at the subconscious level.

Our subconscious mind strives to maintain the status quo. Even if the norm is bad, the subconscious knows we can handle it. The subconscious seeks comfort, and encourages indulgent behavior. Change is a threat. The inner child (Id) tells us that we want to eat what we shouldn't, we want to feel sorry for ourselves, we want to stay in the bed a little longer, and we want to stay with the familiar. The Id wants to go back where it's been. It takes effort to maintain change, and if you don't make the effort you will lose all the ground you've worked so hard to gain.

Inertia and Momentum

A body at rest tends to stay at rest and a body in motion tends to stay in motion. Anything that is at rest stays at rest unless something else gives it a push. Then it is a moving body. And when in motion, it tends to keep moving in a straight line unless some force pushes or pulls to stop it or make it turn. So inertia simply means that something tends to keep on doing whatever it is doing. When something is moving it has momentum. The heavier it is and the faster it is moving, the harder it is to stop. So momentum is a kind of measurement of how hard it is to stop something in motion. In everyday life there is always some resistance to movement, which we call friction. Friction is like a drag or a pull against the direction of motion. This always works to slow down something in motion and make it come to rest again.

The longer you stay inactive the harder it is to become active. Inertia is difficult to overcome. It takes a push from an outside force to get you moving. For me it was realizing the seriousness of my situation and making a change in my medication. That was the push I needed. What will it take to get you moving? Once something starts moving, it tends to keep moving. Once you get the ball rolling, habits form and change takes place. But the friction created by preconceived notions, flawed premises, self doubt, depression, inactivity, denial, projection and excuse making drag against your direction of motion; they threaten to stop you and make you come to rest again. It is friction that causes regression.

Regression is a defense mechanism leading to the temporary reversion of the ego to an earlier stage of development rather than handling unacceptable impulses in a more adult way. The defense mechanism of regression, in psychoanalytic theory, occurs when thoughts are temporarily pushed back out of our consciousness and into our unconscious. A person may revert to an old behavior to ventilate feelings of frustration. Regression is also defined as a relapse to a less perfect or developed state. Regression is what you want to avoid. You don't want to go back where you've already been.

You have to keep the ball rolling, at all times, at all costs. You must avoid your comfort zone; this is the worst place you can be. Once you've made some progress and seen the positive effects of **Create, Connect, Commit** you cannot allow yourself to get comfortable, sit back and just be satisfied with that progress. You must stay hungry. You must **commit to progress**. Failure to do so is why most changes that people make, even dramatic ones are short lived. Alcoholics and addicts regularly complete rehab programs and come out as totally new people, having changed and beaten their habits. But if they don't stay in a follow up program, more often than not they regress into their old habits. They sometimes end up worse than they were to begin with and frequently have to go to another rehab program, repeating the cycle of improvement and regression. Only lifelong programs or programs that get participants to commit to a Higher Power are effective at creating lasting change. There has to be a continuing commitment to combat regression.

People who lose weight routinely gain it back. I have fought this cycle of weight gain in my own life for nearly 30 years. Only when I made a commitment to progress by constantly setting new goals was I able to keep the weight off permanently. I went on a diet for life, never got comfortable with the progress I made and constantly set higher standards for my fitness goals.

The same is true for depression. Once I got my depression in check, I made a commitment to keep it in check. I see my psychiatrist every three months. My goal is to impress her each visit with how well I'm doing and how much I've accomplished since my last visit. **(Plan)** I constantly research and educate myself about the causes, prevention and treatment of depression. I take supplements and eat a diet designed to combat it**. (Do)** I set goals for every area of my life, starting a new project each time I finish the last**. (Study)** Having something to focus on keeps me motivated, driven and happy. It keeps me from drifting back into old negative patterns of thought and cycles of behavior. Once you've reached one goal, you must always quickly set another. It is only this never ending commitment to progress that will make the changes in your life permanent and prevent regression. **(Act)**

PLAN – DO – STUDY – ACT is the key to continuous progress. It is the component of Create, Connect, Commit that keeps us from regressing and makes our changes permanent. It is evident throughout the CCC process. To Commit to Progress you must PLAN – DO – STUDY – ACT.

The Serenity Prayer

**God grant me the serenity
to accept the things I cannot change;
courage to change the things I can;
and wisdom to know the difference.**

**Living one day at a time;
Enjoying one moment at a time;
Accepting hardships as the pathway to peace;
Taking, as He did, this sinful world
as it is, not as I would have it;
Trusting that He will make all things right
if I surrender to His Will;
That I may be reasonably happy in this life
and supremely happy with Him
Forever in the next.
Amen.**

--Reinhold Niebuhr

This book is dedicated to all who have been affected by depression in any way. My hope is to spread the message that Create, Connect, Commit can help you beat depression and create a new life. Live each day with purpose and never look back! You have been given the tools to change your life now go out and use them! You are a New Creation and you'll never be the same!

Coming soon; Upcoming books will be available at **createconnectcommit.com,** *Change Anything; How I Beat Depression and the Process I used to Create a New Life* is currently available at https://www.createspace.com/3431622 Coming soon;

Create, Connect, Commit; The Complete Guide to Change and Personal Growth

Visit blog.createconnectcommit.com

To arrange speaking engagements, seminars, or to implement CCC to God as a Growth Group or study in your church visit createconnectcommit.com or e-mail rt@createconnectcommit.com.

PLAN – DO – STUDY – ACT

Shalom!

My Vision

I had a vision in church one day, as I went to the altar and knelt to pray,

A mighty judge sat in my sight, accusers on my left, a screen on my right,

The judge was solemn, clothed in white; His face was a blinding light.

I always heard that when I died, my life would flash before my eyes,

But now I watched as every scene

Of my life was played on a giant screen,

My accusers shouted "Look at what this man has done!"

And I begged. "Please don't show that one!"

Every idle word I had ever said,

Every evil thought that was in my head,

Every single thing I ever did,

All was revealed, nothing was hid.

My accusers shouted, "He deserves to die!"

"Men like this we should crucify."

As the judge opened His book, I held my breath.

He read aloud, "The wages of sin is death."

Then a man stood up, I couldn't see His face.

He approached the judge and said "I will take his place."

Soldiers came and they beat him with their fists,

Then they tied him to a post and beat him with a whip.

Then they held him down and they nailed him to a tree,

I began to cry, he was there because of me.

He hung on the cross until he had died,

Then a soldier took a spear and pierced his side.

Blood gushed out and some fell on me,

The screen went blank, the judge said, "You are Free!"

I yelled to the judge, "Who was this great one?"

"I must tell everyone what He has done!"

The judge looked down and began to cry,

"He is my only Son and I sent Him to die."

Bibliography

Psychological Types (Collected Works of C.G. Jung Vol.6) by C. G. Jung, Gerhard Adler, and R. F.C. Hull (Paperback - Oct. 1, 1976)

http://www.slideshare.net/daverudd/church-dropouts-how-many-leave-church-and-why

http://www.intothyword.org/apps/articles/default.asp?articleid=36557&columnid=3958

The Enneagram: Understanding Yourself and the Others In Your Life by **Helen Palmer (Paperback - Apr. 12, 1991)**

An Introduction to the Enneagram: Personality Styles and Where You Fit by **Ph.D. Jerome Wagner, Helen Palmer, and Thomas Condon**

The Wisdom of the Enneagram: The Complete Guide to Psychological and Spiritual Growth for the Nine Personality Types by **Don Richard Riso** and **Russ Hudson (Paperback - June 15, 1999)**

THE ENNEAGRAM THE DEFINITIVE GUIDE TO THE ANCIENT SYSTEM FOR UNDERSTANDING YOURSELF AND THE OTHERS IN YOUR LIFE by **HELEN PALMER**

Neurosis and Human Growth: The Struggle Towards Self-Realization by Karen Horney (Paperback - May 17, 1991)

Yes!: 50 Scientifically Proven Ways to Be Persuasive by Noah J. Goldstein, Steve J. Martin, and Robert B. Cialdini (Paperback - Dec 29, 2009)

Man's Search for Meaning by Viktor E. Frankl (Mass Market Paperback - Jun 14, 2006)

Brewer, W. F., & Treyens, J. C. (1981). Role of schemata in memory for places. Cognitive Psychology, 13, pp207-230

Bartlett, F.C. (1932). *Remembering: A Study in Experimental and Social Psychology.* Cambridge, England: Cambridge University Press

^ Freud, A. (1937). *The Ego and the Mechanisms of Defense.* London: Hogarth Press and Institute of Psycho-Analysis.

The 7 Habits of Highly Effective People by Stephen R. Covey (Paperback - Nov 9, 2004)

Change or Die by Alan Deutschman (Hardcover - Jan 1, 2007)

Stumbling on Happiness by Daniel Gilbert (Paperback - Mar 20, 2007)

How To Win Friends & Influence People by Dale Carnegie (Hardcover - Jan 1, 1936)

100 Ways To Motivate Yourself: Change Your Life Forever by Steve Chandler (Paperback - Sep 2004)

^ Dusheck, Jennie, The Interpretation of Genes. *Natural History*, October 2002.

^ Carlson, N. R. *et al.*. (2005) Psychology: the science of behaviour (3rd Canadian ed) Pearson Ed. ISBN 0-205-45769-X

^ Ridley, M. (2003) Nature Via Nurture: Genes, Experience, and What Makes us Human. Harper Collins. ISBN 0-00-200663-4

^ Carlson, N. R. *et al.*. (2005) Psychology: the science of behaviour (3rd Canadian ed) Pearson Ed. ISBN 0-205-45769-X

^ Westen, D. (2002) Psychology: Brain, Behavior & Culture. Wiley & Sons. ISBN 0-471-38754-1

The Wisdom of the Enneagram (Bantam, 1999)

^ Ouspensky, P. D. (1977). *In Search of the Miraculous*. pp. 312-313. ISBN 0156445085. "Schools of the fourth way exist for the needs of the work... But no matter what the fundamental aim of the work is... When the work is done the schools close."

^ De Penafieu, Bruno (1997). Needleman, Jacob; Baker, George. eds. *Gurdjieff*. Continuum International Publishing Group. p. 214. ISBN 0826410498. http://books.google.com/books?id=3R9vGrR5IEUC&pg=PA214&dq=Gurdjieff+the+work#v=onepage&q=Gurdjieff%20the%20work&f=false. "If I were to cease working... all these worlds would perish."

^ Gurdjieff International Review

^ P. D. Ouspensky (1949). In Search of the Miraculous

^ Meissner & Kuper, 2008.

The Enneagram Field Guide by Carolyn Bartlett Nine Gates Publishing 9780979012649

^ Paranoid personality disorder - International Statistical Classification of Diseases and Related Health Problems 10th Revision (ICD-10)

^ Millon, Theodore, Personality Disorders in Modern Life, 2004

^ Millon, Theodore - Personality Subtypes

^ a b c Internet Mental Health - paranoid personality disorder

^ a b "eMedicine - Personality Disorders : Article by David Bienenfeld".

http://www.emedicine.com/med/topic3472.htm. Retrieved 2008-02-13.

^ Kendler KS, Czajkowski N, Tambs K, *et al.* (2006). "Dimensional representations of DSM-IV cluster A personality disorders in a population-based sample of Norwegian twins: a multivariate study". *Psychological medicine* **36** (11): 1583–91. doi:10.1017/S0033291706008609. PMID 16893481.

^ ""Paranoid Personality Disorder" at Cleveland Clinic". http://www.clevelandclinic.org/health/health-info/docs/3700/3796.asp?index=9784. Retrieved 2008-02-13.

Myers, Isabel Briggs with Peter B. Myers (1980, 1995). *Gifts Differing: Understanding Personality Type*. Mountain View, CA: Davies-Black Publishing. ISBN 0-89106-074-X.

^ Jung, Carl Gustav (August 1, 1971). "Psychological Types". *Collected Works of C.G. Jung, Volume 6*. Princeton University Press. ISBN 0-691-09774.

The Wisdom of the Enneagram: The Complete Guide to Psychological and Spiritual Growth for the Nine Personality Types by Don Richard Riso and Russ Hudson (Paperback - Jun 15, 1999)

^ Riso, *Wisdom of the Enneagram*, p.24

http://www.mcmanweb.com/atypical_depression.html

^ Tolman E.C. (July 1948). "Cognitive maps in rats and men". *Psychological Review* **55** (4): 189–208. doi:10.1037/h0061626. PMID 18870876.

^ Kitchin RM (1994). "Cognitive Maps: What Are They and Why Study Them?". *Journal of Environmental Psychology* **14**: 1–19. doi:10.1016/S0272-4944(05)80194-X.

^ Downs, Roger; Stea, David (1973). *Image and Environment: Cognitive Mapping and Spatial Behavior*. Edward Arnold. ISBN 978-0202307664. OCLC 7690182.

The Enneagram in Love and Work: Understanding Your Intimate and Business Relationships by Helen Palmer (Paperback - Dec 15, 1995)

Personality Types: Using the Enneagram for Self-Discovery by Russ Hudson and Don Richard Riso (Paperback - Oct 29, 1996)

Personality Types by Don Richard Riso; Houghton Milton Company Boston Copyright 1987, 1990

^ Robert Bolton, Person, Soul and Identity. A Neoplatonic Account of the Principle of Personality.

^ *Mubabinge Bilolo: *Fondements Thébains de la Philosophie de Plotin l'Égyptien* (Academy of African Thought & African Institute for Future Studies, Sect. I, vol. 9), Kinshasa-Munich-Paris, 2007. ISBN 978-3-931169-00-5

^ Neoplatonism and Gnosticism Negative theology in Neoplatonism and Gnosticism by Curtis L Hancock pg 177
http://books.google.com/books?id=WSbrLPup7wYC&pg=PA173&dq=plotinus+energeia&sig=_pNuhvtMY4HEJWulC7-WTIWGDTA

John 3:16

Printed in Great Britain
by Amazon